Why

So Different?

Why Are We So Different?

Your Guide
to the 16 Personality Types

JAROSLAW JANKOWSKI
M.Ed., EMBA

This is a book which can help you exploit your potential more fully, build healthy relationships with other people and make the right decisions about your education and career. However, it should not be considered to be a substitute for expert physiological or psychiatric consultation. Neither the author nor the publisher accept any responsibility whatsoever for any detrimental effects which may result from the inappropriate use of this book.

ID16™© is an independent typology developed by Polish educator and manager Jaroslaw Jankowski and grounded in Carl Gustav Jung's theory. It should not be confused with the personality typologies and tests proposed by other authors or offered by other institutions.

Original title: Czy wiesz, kim jesteś? Przewodnik po 16 typach osobowości ID16™©

Translated from the Polish by Caryl Swift

Proof reading: Lacrosse | experts in translation

Layout editing by Zbigniew Szalbot

Published by LOGOS MEDIA

Paperback: ISBN 978-83-7981-099-4

EPUB: ISBN 978-83-7981-100-7

MOBI: ISBN 978-83-7981-101-4

DEDICATION

To my wife Iwona and my son Maciej, with love

Putting the Reader first.

An Author Campaign Facilitated by ALLi.

Contents

Preface   9

ID16™© and Jungian Personality Typology   11

The ID16™© Personality Test   15

The Administrator (ESTJ)   30

The Advocate (ESFJ)   49

The Animator (ESTP)   70

The Artist (ISFP)   90

The Counsellor (ENFJ)   110

The Director (ENTJ)   130

The Enthusiast (ENFP)   151

The Idealist (INFP)   173

The Innovator (ENTP)   192

The Inspector (ISTJ)   216

The Logician (INTP)   235

The Mentor (INFJ)   255

The Practitioner (ISTP)   273

The Presenter (ESFP)   293

The Protector (ISFJ)   316

The Strategist (INTJ)   336

Additional information   356

Bibliography   360

About the Author   363

Preface

It was with the dawn of history that thinkers, philosophers and common-or-garden observers of life first became interested in the phenomenon of the human personality. What intrigued them was the way that some people display a marked similarity in their behaviour and attitudes despite their very different life stories and often disparate upbringings.

Observing this, the thoughts of many turned to reflections upon types of personality. One of the fruits of these musings which remains popular to this day is the typology devised by Hippocrates. That remarkable doctor and thinker of ancient times distinguished four fundamental temperaments; the sanguine, the choleric, the phlegmatic and the melancholic. History has seen many another, equally interesting endeavour to identify and describe recurring personality types. Although some of those attempts may seem oversimplified when viewed from a contemporary perspective, they played an extraordinarily important role in their time, paving the way for subsequent, more extensive cogitations on the human personality.

The theory developed by Carl Gustav Jung (1875-1961), a Swiss psychiatrist and psychologist, came as a breakthrough in the field. It was instrumental in popularising the notion of personality types and, as of the twentieth century, it became the foundation both for the formulation of what is now known as Jungian typology and for creating personality tests grounded in that typology, the ID16™© test being a case in point[1].

Nowadays, personality typologies drawing on Jung's theory are widely used in teaching, training, coaching and human resource management, as well as in career and relationship counselling. They also form a basis for numerous programmes geared towards supporting personal development and improving interpersonal relationships. The majority of global businesses employ Jungian personality tests as a standard tool in their recruitment and vocational development processes. This practice was initially applied primarily in corporations of American origin; however, in recent years, it has been enjoying a steadily growing popularity in Europe as well.

Every year, thanks to Jungian personality tests, millions of people around the world are able to obtain a more profound knowledge of themselves and of others and, as a result, their lives and their relationships are changed for the better.

We sincerely hope that your exploration of personality types, with our ID16™© tools as your compass, will lead to positive transformations of exactly that kind.

---

[1] More information on this topic can be found in the ID16™© and Jungian Personality Typology section.

ID16™© and Jungian Personality Typology

ID16™© numbers among what are referred to as Jungian personality typologies, which draw on the theories developed by Carl Gustav Jung (1875-19161), a Swiss psychiatrist and psychologist and a pioneer of the 'depth psychology' approach.

On the basis of many years of research and observation, Jung came to the conclusion that the differences in people's attitudes and preferences are far from random. He developed a concept which is highly familiar to us today: the division of people into extroverts and introverts. In addition, he distinguished four personality functions, which form two opposing pairs: sensing-intuition and thinking-feeling. He also established that one function is dominant in each pair. He became convinced that each and every person's dominant functions are fixed and independent of external conditions and that, together, what they form is a personality type.

In 1938, two American psychiatrists, Horace Gray and Joseph Wheelwright, created the first personality test based on Jung's theories. It was designed to make it possible to determine the dominant functions within the three dimensions described by Jung, namely, **extraversion-introversion**, **sensing-intuition** and **thinking-feeling**. That first test became the inspiration for other researchers. In 1942, again in America, Isabel Briggs Myers and Katherine Briggs began using their own personality test, broadening Gray's and Wheelwright's classic, three-dimensional model to include a fourth: **judging-perceiving**. The majority of subsequent personality typologies and tests drawing on Jung's theories also take that fourth dimension into account. They include the American typology published by David W. Keirsey in 1978 and the personality test developed in the nineteen seventies by Aušra Augustinavičiūtė, a Lithuanian psychologist. Over the following decades, other European researchers followed in their footsteps, creating more four-dimensional personality typologies and tests for use in personal coaching and career counselling.

ID16™© figures among that group. An independent typology developed by Polish educator and manager Jaroslaw Jankowski, it was published in the first decade of the twenty-first century. ID16™© is based on Carl Jung's classic theory and, like other contemporary Jungian typologies, it follows a four-dimensional path, terming those dimensions the **four natural inclinations**. These inclinations are dichotomous in nature and the picture they provide gives us information regarding a person's personality type. Analysis of the first inclination is intended to determine the dominant **source of life energy**, this being either the exterior or the interior world. Analysis of the second inclination defines the dominant **mode of assimilating information**, which occurs via the senses or via intuition. Analysis of the third inclination supplies a description of the **decision-making mode**, where either mind or heart is dominant, while analysis of the fourth inclination produces a definition of the dominant **lifestyle** as either organised or spontaneous. The combination of all these natural inclinations results in **sixteen possible personality types**.

One remarkable feature of the ID16™© typology is its practical dimension. It describes the individual personality types in action – at work, in daily life and in interpersonal relations. It neither concentrates on the internal dynamics of personality nor does it undertake any theoretical attempts at explaining or commenting on invisible, interior processes. The focus is turned more toward the ways in which a given personality type manifests itself externally and how it affects the surrounding world. This emphasis on the social aspect of personality places ID16™© somewhat closer to the previously mentioned typology developed by Aušra Augustinavičiūtė.

Each of the ID16™© personality types is the result of a given person's natural inclinations. There is nothing evaluative or judgemental about ascribing a person to a given type, though. No particular personality type is 'better' or 'worse' than any other. Each type is quite simply different and each has its own potential strengths and weaknesses. ID16™© makes it possible to identify and describe those differences. It helps us to understand ourselves and discover our place in the world.

Familiarity with our personality profile enables us to make full use of our potential and work on the areas which might cause us trouble. It is an invaluable aid in everyday life, in solving problems, in building healthy relationships with other people and in making decisions relating to our education and careers.

Determining personality is a process which is neither arbitrary nor mechanical in nature. As the 'owner and user' of our personality, each and every one of us is fully capable of defining which type we belong to. The individual's role is thus pivotal. This self-identification can be achieved either by analysing the descriptions of the ID16™© personality types and steadily narrowing down the fields of choice or by taking the short cut provided by the ID16™© personality test (see next chapter). The role played by each 'personality user' is equally crucial when it comes to the test, given that the outcome depends entirely on the answers they provide.

Identifying personality types helps us to know both ourselves and others. Nonetheless, it should not be treated as some kind of future-determining oracle. No personality type can ever justify our weaknesses or poor interpersonal relationships. It might, however, help us to understand their causes!

ID16™© treats personality type not as a static, genetic, pre-determined condition, but as a product of innate and acquired characteristics. As such, it is a concept which neither diminishes free will nor engages in pigeonholing people. What it does is open up new perspectives for us, encouraging us to work on ourselves and indicating the areas where that work is most needed.

The ID16™© Personality Test

The ID16™© Personality Test is a set of eighty-four questions concerning your reactions and behaviour in normal, everyday situations. The answers make it possible to determine your personality type.

Essential information!

- The test consists of three parts. Each part contains twenty-eight questions about your personal preferences or behaviour patterns. The questions take the form of sentences which you need to complete by choosing one of two options.

- The test is designed to determine your personality type and NOT your intelligence, knowledge or skills. The results are not in the least a value judgement! There are no 'good' or 'bad' answers and no 'right' or 'wrong' ones. So please don't try to work out which answer is 'the proper one' and choose that. Each of the ID16™© personality types

15

is different, but they all have the same worth. No particular personality type is 'better' or 'worse' than any other.

- Select each of the answers in line with the way *you behave* in the situation being described and NOT in the way *you would like* to behave or in the way that, in your opinion, *one ought* to behave. If you have never been in a given situation, then give some thought to what your natural reaction would be if you did find yourself in those circumstances. When a question concerns preferences, choose the answer which reflects your real inclinations and NOT the one which seems to be 'correct' or 'desirable'.

- You will need to answer *all the questions*. In the event that you can't fully identify with either of the available choices, select the one which is closer to the way you think you would react or behave.

- There is no time limit, so you don't need to rush. On the other hand, don't spend too long pondering your answers, either.

- Each of the answers is followed by a letter in brackets: E, I, S, N, T, F, J or P. As you do the test, make a note of the letter which follows the answer you've chosen. When you've answered all the questions, count how many times you chose each of the letters. As an example, your results might look like this:
  - o E: 18;
  - o I: 3;
  - o S: 7;
  - o N: 14;
  - o T: 4;
  - o F: 17;
  - o J: 0;
  - o P: 21.

- You'll find the rest of the instructions at the end of the test.

Part 1 of 3

1. I often wonder about the meaning of life:
    a. yes. [I]
    b. no. [E]
2. The solutions that appeal to me more are:
    a. tried and tested. [S]
    b. innovative and creative. [N]
3. I like working:
    a. as part of a team. [E]
    b. on my own. [I]
4. I more often:
    a. take the advice of others. [P]
    b. advise others myself. [J]
5. In order to maintain good relations with people, I often make concessions to others, even when it doesn't suit me to do so:
    a. yes. [F]
    b. no. [T]
6. I relax best when:
    a. I'm on my own or in a small group, in a quiet and peaceful spot. [I]
    b. I'm in a crowd, in a spot where something's always going on. [E]
7. I often finish a job before the deadline or do more than is strictly necessary:
    a. yes. [J]
    b. no. [P]
8. The following description fits me better:
    a. I like to have my day planned out and I'm not very keen on sudden and unexpected changes of plan. [J]
    b. I dislike rigidly planned days and view sudden changes as variety. [P]
9. When I'm in company, I normally say:
    a. more than the other people. [E]
    b. less than the other people. [I]

10. I prefer authors who:
    a. make use of interesting comparisons and invoke innovative ideas and concepts. [N]
    b. write in a sober style and focus on facts. [S]

11. When I'm solving a problem, I try, above all:
    a. to remain objective, even at the cost of being liked by people. [T]
    b. to preserve people's liking for me, even at the cost of my objectivity. [F]

12. I would rather be involved with:
    a. tasks similar to ones I've carried out before. [S]
    b. new tasks that I've never encountered before. [N]

13. When I want to sort something out and put it behind me, I often make decisions prematurely:
    a. yes. [J]
    b. no. [P]

14. The following description fits me better:
    a. I'm capable of concentrating on one thing for a long time. [I]
    b. I'm easily distracted and often break off what I'm doing. [E]

15. I'm more irritated by:
    a. dreamers who mainly think about the future. [S]
    b. realists who are interested in the here and now. [N]

16. I'd rather attend classes or training sessions given by lecturers or instructors who are:
    a. cold and sometimes discourteous, but highly logical, conveying their knowledge in an orderly fashion. [T]
    b. vague, with a rather chaotic teaching style, but really likeable and warm-hearted. [F]

17. When I have to do something within a fixed time limit, I usually:
    a. try to get the job done as fast as I can, so that I can turn to more pleasant things. [J]
    b. deal with more pleasant things first and only get down to the job when the deadline is looming. [P]

18. I believe that:
    a. objective and warranted criticism is desirable in the majority of situations and that it helps people to perceive their oversights and errors. [T]
    b. criticism, even when it's objective and warranted, often does more harm than good, since it damages interpersonal relations. [F]

19. I like to make a note of the dates and times of future meetings and get-togethers, trips and matters that need sorting out:
    a. yes. [J]
    b. no. [P]

20. I often wonder whether what people say contains hidden allusions or comments directed at me:
    a. yes. [F]
    b. no. [T]

21. If I were investing my savings, I'd prefer:
    a. a higher profit earned over a longer period of time. [N]
    b. a lower but faster profit. [S]

22. I'd rather:
    a. learn new things. [N]
    b. improve my current skills. [S]

23. I'm more irritated by people who:
    a. are poor organisers and lack any predilection for order. [J]
    b. are too inflexible and can't adapt readily to new circumstances. [P]

24. I believe that it's worse to:
    a.   treat people unjustly. [T]
    b.   lack understanding for people who find themselves in a difficult situation. [F]
25. I more often regret:
    a.   saying too much. [E]
    b.   saying too little. [I]
26. When I'm carrying out a task, I usually:
    a.   split it into smaller parts and work on them steadily, systematically pressing on with the job. [S]
    b.   I have moments when the ideas flow and moments of intensive work and thanks to that I move ahead with the job. [N]
27. I often wonder why people:
    a.   don't think about others. [F]
    b.   behave illogically. [T]
28. I find it hard to put up with:
    a.   hubbub, confusion and the presence of large numbers of people. [I]
    b.   quietness, boredom and solitariness. [E]

Part 2 of 3

1.   I feel more comfortable psychologically when:
    a.   I still haven't made a final decision and have room to manoeuvre. [P]
    b.   I've made a final decision and the matter is closed. [J]
2.   I'm normally one of the first to phone and comfort someone who's in a difficult situation:
    a.   yes. [F]
    b.   no. [T]
3.   I'm often moved when I see reports about people who have met with misfortune:
    a.   yes. [F]
    b.   no. [T]

4. When I'm beginning a job:
   a. I often prepare a plan of action or list what needs to be done. [J]
   b. I don't usually waste time on drawing up a plan of action, but get to work straight away. [P]

5. When I want to learn how to use a new device, I usually:
   a. read the instructions carefully first and only then try starting it up. [S]
   b. have a look at it and then start it up, only having a look at the instructions if there's a problem. [N]

6. Once I've completed a task, I get more satisfaction from:
   a. my own awareness that I've done a good job. [T]
   b. praise and recognition from other people. [F]

7. I often tell others about my experiences:
   a. yes. [E]
   b. no. [I]

8. I usually act:
   a. impulsively. [P]
   b. after deliberation. [J]

9. When I'm working in a group of people, I prefer it if:
   a. minor disagreements and conflicts occur within the group, just as long as there are clear and transparent rules in place. [T]
   b. there are no clear and transparent rules within the group, just as long as a good, friendly atmosphere prevails. [F]

10. I'd rather do a job which demands:
    a. imagination and the ability to predict. [N]
    b. adherence to a number of detailed procedures. [S]

11. I often wonder what the future will bring:
    a. yes. [N]
    b. no. [S]
12. I prefer tasks which:
    a. require me to work by myself. [I]
    b. require contact with people. [E]
13. I like watching programmes:
    a. which present original theories and stimulate the imagination. [N]
    b. are of the 'how-to' ilk and proffer instructions which can be put into practice. [S]
14. I often interrupt people while they're speaking:
    a. yes. [E]
    b. no. [I]
15. I prefer people whose decision-making is guided by:
    a. internal conviction and fellow-feeling or compassion for others. [F]
    b. logic and an objective analysis of the situation. [T]
16. I like:
    a. playing a major role. [E]
    b. operating in the background. [I]
17. I more often:
    a. listen to the opinions and viewpoints of other people. [P]
    b. present my viewpoints and opinions to others. [J]
18. I believe that it is worse:
    a. to be overly critical. [F]
    b. to be overly lenient. [T]
19. I often make a note of the things I have to do during a given day:
    a. yes. [J]
    b. no. [P]

20. When I'm given a larger task to perform, I'd rather:
   a. receive concrete instructions explaining how I should do it. [S]
   b. have the opportunity of doing it in line with my own ideas. [N]

21. When I'm discussing a problem that needs solving with others, I usually:
   a. start by considering the issue in question and only enter the discussion once I have an idea. [I]
   b. enter the discussion spontaneously, with new ideas coming into my mind as we talk. [E]

22. Conflict resolution depends first and foremost on:
   a. calming the situation down and achieving a compromise. [F]
   b. clarifying who was in the right and who was in the wrong. [T]

23. When I'm asked about something, I usually:
   a. reply at once. [E]
   b. need a moment to think. [I]

24. When I'm solving a problem, I'm capable of:
   a. seeing the wider context of the issue in question and predicting its consequences. [N]
   b. focusing on all the details concerning the issue in question. [S]

25. When I have a task to do, I usually:
   a. put off finishing it, so as to have the chance to make any changes which might be needed. [P]
   b. try to finish it as quickly as possible, so that it's over and done with. [J]

26. I'd rather work with people who are:
   a. practical, precise and meticulous. [S]
   b. creative, inventive and resourceful. [N]

27. My mood and emotional state are usually:
    a. difficult to discern. [I]
    b. easy to discern. [E]
28. Some people would judge me to be:
    a. disorganised. [P]
    b. too inflexible. [J]

Part 3 of 3

1. I prefer people who:
    a. are capable of thinking logically. [T]
    b. are able to empathise with other people's situations. [F]
2. I like:
    a. a life full of changes and surprises. [P]
    b. a well-ordered life where everything happens according to plan. [J]
3. When I'm in a large group, I usually:
    a. talk to a handful of people, mainly those I already know. [I]
    b. talk to a lot of people, including those I don't know. [E]
4. I'd be more bored meeting someone who:
    a. proffers huge amounts of detailed information and asks a great many practical questions. [N]
    b. floats a sweeping vision of new solutions, but one devoid of details. [S]
5. A decision is worse when:
    a. it's illogical. [T]
    b. it brings harm to a large number of people. [F]
6. Others would judge me to be reserved and say that I rarely show my emotions:
    a. yes. [I]
    b. no. [E]

7. When I'm on holiday, I often plan what I'm going to do the next day in advance:
    a. yes. [J]
    b. no. [P]
8. I'd rather be praised because:
    a. it's pleasant spending time with me. [F]
    b. I'm capable of making the right decisions. [T]
9. I prefer:
    a. solitary walks. [I]
    b. meeting new people. [E]
10. Others would judge me to be someone who:
    a. acts as previously planned. [J]
    b. acts spontaneously. [P]
11. If I'm looking for a job, my main focus is on:
    a. the terms and conditions of employment on offer. [S]
    b. the future potential of the position in question. [N]
12. The following description fits me better:
    a. I frequently fail to be prepared in time and get myself out of trouble by improvising. [P]
    b. I'm normally well-prepared and I don't need to improvise. [J]
13. Being amongst people normally:
    a. drains me. [I]
    b. gives me an added boost. [E]
14. I feel uneasy when I'm the centre of attention:
    a. yes. [I]
    b. no. [E]
15. The following description fits me better:
    a. I'm often late when I've arranged to meet someone. [P]
    b. when I've arranged to meet someone, I generally arrive punctually or early. [J]

16. If I'm searching for someone to collaborate with, my main focus is on:
    a. whether our personalities are suited and we'll be able to work together harmoniously. [F]
    b. if a given person has the necessary qualifications and abilities for the tasks in question. [T]
17. Others would say that I'm:
    a. practical. [S]
    b. ingenious. [N]
18. When I'm listening to other people's problems:
    a. I often wonder what their objective cause was and whether the person concerned wasn't responsible for the current state of affairs. [T]
    b. I usually feel a heartfelt sympathy for them and wonder how I can help them. [F]
19. I'm more interested in:
    a. people's actual behaviour and real events. [S]
    b. the general principles driving people's behaviour and events. [N]
20. When criticising other people, the most crucial thing is:
    a. to remain objective. [T]
    b. to take care not to hurt their feelings. [F]
21. A pleasant weekend is one spent:
    a. relaxing at home with a good book or film. [I]
    b. meeting friends, talking or enjoying ourselves together. [E]
22. I get more joy from:
    a. finishing work on a task. [J]
    b. beginning work on a new task. [P]

23. Established procedures, instructions and guidelines:
    a. are usually a practical aid and make the job easier. [S]
    b. often restrict creative ideas and make the job more difficult. [N]

24. I often put off making a decision, wanting to gather more and more information or think things over:
    a. yes. [P]
    b. no. [J]

25. When I hear about an unusual venture, I'm usually:
    a. fascinated by the idea or concept itself. [N]
    b. interested in the way it was or is being accomplished. [S]

26. The following description fits me better:
    a. I'm reluctant to make adverse comments to others and, if I have to, then I do it tactfully. [F]
    b. I'm direct; if I don't like something, then I'll say so. [T]

27. I'd rather work:
    a. by myself or with two close colleagues. [I]
    b. in a new, ten-person team. [E]

28. Once I've completed a form or questionnaire, then I usually go back and check that I've filled in all the details or answers properly:
    a. yes. [S]
    b. no. [N]

And that's it … the end of the test! Now it's time to interpret the results.

Step 1

Check how often you've selected answers followed by each of the letters: E, I, S, N, T, F, J or P.

As an example, your results might look like this:

- E: 18;
- I: 3;
- S: 7;
- N: 14;
- T: 4;
- F: 17;
- J: 0;
- P: 21.

Step 2

Below, you'll find the letters arranged as four sets of pairs. For each pair, select the letter you chose more often and make a note of it:

Pair 1: **E** or **I**;

Pair 2: **S** or **N**;

Pair 3: **T** or **F**;

Pair 4: **J** or **P**.

Your result will now take the form of a four-letter 'code'; in our example, it's **ENFP**.

The higher number in each of the pairs stands for the dominant inclination in the respective dimension of the personality:

- Source of life energy: E, the exterior world or I, the interior world;
- Mode of assimilating information: S, via the senses or N, via intuition;

- Decision-making mode: T, with the mind or F, with the heart;
- Lifestyle: J, which is organised or P, which is spontaneous.

Step 3

Now find your four-letter 'code' on the list below and check out your personality type!

- ENFJ: the Counsellor (see p. 110)
- ENFP: the Enthusiast (see p. 151)
- ENTJ: the Director (see p. 130)
- ENTP: the Innovator (see p. 192)
- ESFJ: the Advocate (see p. 49)
- ESFP: the Presenter (see p. 293)
- ESTJ: the Administrator (see p. 30)
- ESTP: the Animator (see p. 70)
- INFJ: the Mentor (see p. 255)
- INFP: the Idealist (see p. 173)
- INTJ: the Strategist (see p. 336)
- INTP: the Logician (see p. 235)
- ISFJ: the Protector (see p. 316)
- ISFP: the Artist (see p. 90)
- ISTJ: the Inspector (see p. 216)
- ISTP: the Practitioner (see p. 273)

The Administrator (ESTJ)

THE ID16™© PERSONALITY TYPOLOGY

The Personality in a Nutshell

Life motto: We'll get the job done!

In brief, *administrators* ...

are hard-working, responsible and extremely loyal. Energetic and decisive, they value order, stability, security and clear rules. They are matter-of-fact and businesslike, logical, rational and practical and possess the capability to assimilate large amounts of detailed information.

Superb organisers, they are intolerant of ineffectuality, wastefulness and slothfulness. True to their convictions and direct in their contact with others, they present their point of view decisively and openly express critical opinions, sometimes hurting other people as a result.

The *administrator's* four natural inclinations:

- source of life energy: the exterior world
- mode of assimilating information: via the senses
- decision-making mode: the mind
- lifestyle: organised

Similar personality types:

- the Animator
- the Inspector
- the Practitioner

Statistical data:

- *administrators* constitute between ten and thirteen per cent of the global community
- men predominate among *administrators* (60 per cent)
- the United States is an example of a nation corresponding to the *administrator's* profile[2]

The Four-Letter Code

In terms of Jungian personality typology, the universal four-letter code for the *administrator* is ESTJ.

General character traits

Administrators are decisive, self-confident and brimming with energy. They are extraordinarily true to their convictions and have a common-sense attitude to life. They do not concern themselves with abstract theories,

---

[2] What this means is not that all the residents of the USA fall within this personality type, but that American society as a whole possesses a great many of the character traits typical of the *administrator*.

conjectures and digressions. What interests them is the nitty-gritty: facts, figures and evidence.

Perception and thinking

Administrators unceasingly monitor the world around them, seeking out manifestations of ineffectiveness and wastefulness. An awareness of any potential for improvement spurs them into action. It is normally difficult to involve them in an activity which produces anything other than concrete solutions to tangible problems. They generally have a sceptical attitude towards new concepts and speculations on matters of potential possibilities or theories which have no practical application. They have no fondness for experiments, preferring tried and tested methods of action. If they have to make a decision about the future, they most often do so on the basis of either their own previous experience or that of others.

When preparing to get involved in something, they usually begin by studying the situation thoroughly and devote considerable time to gathering the relevant data. They work to obtain as much information as possible in order to select the best option.

Administrators express their opinions openly. If they dislike something, they will say so. As a rule, they are convinced that they are in the right. Because they assume that what other people have to offer them is negligible, they set little store by their opinions and viewpoints.

As others see them

Other people perceive *administrators* as industrious, hard-working and responsible. However, their directness, self-assurance and condescending manner often intimidate or irritate others. They are frequently considered to be people who 'always know best'. Some also give the impression of being rather inflexible, overly formal, inordinately organised and 'too fussy by half'.

In turn, what irritates *administrators* in others is incompetence, carelessness, thoughtlessness and recklessness. They are incapable of understanding people who are notoriously unpunctual, fail to keep their word, spend money rashly or have no respect for time, be it their own or other people's. They have no liking for those who flout widely recognised principles, take short cuts or think only of themselves. People who, despite their lack of experience, believe themselves to be outstanding experts are another source of annoyance to them.

Life compass

Administrators value tradition, widely accepted standards and time-honoured rules of behaviour. They are extraordinarily true to their convictions and behave in accordance with the principles they hold dear. In general, they have an enormous respect for authority and are good citizens, being responsible and dutiful. They wish to make a practical contribution to the proper functioning of state and local community alike. They value stability, security and predictability and have zero tolerance for behaviour which disrupts the harmony of the social order and represents a threat to it. Radicalism and extremism affront them.

They also dislike outlandishness and any kind of deviation from the widely accepted norms of behaviour. Their attitude towards changes, new concepts and experiments is cautious. While not opposed to them, they do want to be certain that the results will be practical and beneficial, for instance by giving rise to increased productivity or greater economisation. They adhere to the 'if it ain't broke, don't fix it' philosophy and thus dislike the 'change for change's sake' approach.

Organisational modes

Administrators need structures. They cannot abide muddle, chaos and improvisation. They like things to be orderly and well-organised and are incapable of functioning in an environment which lacks rules and norms. When they can see the potential for streamlining a system, improving its effectiveness and efficiency or putting a stop to waste, they feel stirred to take action. They readily take on the responsibility of solving an existing problem and are natural leaders.

With their ability to create plans of action and determine procedures and their competence in organising the work of others, they are outstanding administrators ... hence the name for this personality type. They like to have control over a situation. To some people, this appears to spring from a desire for power or authority; however, in that, they are mistaken. In fact, it follows from the *administrator's* conviction that a task will only be done properly if he or she supervises everything in person. In general, *administrators* are extremely demanding, of themselves just as much as of others, as well as being highly critical. They hold no brief for laziness, unreliability and neglect of responsibilities and duties. Incapable of standing passively by and observing injustices in the making or idly watching as the rules they believe in are broken, they are ever ready to voice their opposition, even though it may cost them dear.

By nature responsible, practical and punctual, they expect the same of others. They strive to carry out the duties and responsibilities entrusted to them to the very best of their ability. Their preference is for operating according to plan, which is why they usually map out what they intend to do in advance and will often draw up their schedule for the day, either in their minds or on paper, or make a 'to-do' list. As a rule, they adhere to accepted procedures conscientiously and are happy to submit to those in authority, believing this to be indispensable to operating effectively. They are able to spot occurrences of ineffectiveness which have gone unnoticed by others and they set great store by time, doing their utmost to make optimum use of it.

Leisure

Administrators enjoy the simple things in life: spending time with those closest to them, sharing meals, having fun and playing games together. They are capable of relaxing and unwinding, though not when an unfinished task awaits them! In general, they like active leisure pursuits. Prolonged periods of stress cause them to feel alienated and superfluous and they begin to doubt their own worth. At times, tension and friction can lead them to become either withdrawn or dogmatic and stubborn.

Socially

Administrators enjoy being among people and get on well with new faces. Though often formal in their contact with others, they have no problem in establishing relationships with them and are also easy to get to know. They try to be tactful and courteous, but will not allow themselves to be used and never seek other people's sympathy, not at any price. Subjected to pressure and manipulation, they remain unreceptive and unyielding.

As a rule, they have a need to be affiliated to a larger group, often becoming involved in social activities and belonging to all sorts of clubs, associations and communities. Shunning responsibilities would be alien to them and they readily devote their time to accomplishing the aims they identify with. They also set great store by family customs and celebrations, as well as nurturing their relationships with their friends, seizing every possible opportunity of meeting up with them.

Administrators are exceptionally loyal to those close to them Responsibility and duty are the foundations of their creed as far as interpersonal relationships are concerned. They give of themselves unstintingly and expect the same of others. Always ready to come to other people's aid, they are unfailingly generous with their time and energy when it comes to extending a helping hand, providing those who need it with support, infusing them with faith in themselves and assisting them in discovering their talents. They are also unsparing in sharing their own experience.

They are happy when others perceive their dedication and show their thanks. As believers in the maxim that actions speak louder than words, their way of expressing affection and devotion is practical. They rarely show their emotions and are rather scant in their praise. Their inability to read the emotions and feelings of others is also a problem for them; with their direct pronouncements and crisp, explicit comments, there are times when they unwittingly hurt people's feelings.

Amongst friends

Administrators will usually surround themselves with people they can both trust and count on without fail, deriving real joy from spending time with them. Strangers will often perceive *administrators* as formal and strict traditionalists. Their friends, though, know that there is another side to their character and that they are quite capable of having a good time, joking around and being the centre of attention. Although their direct style sometimes intimidates people, it also makes them easy to get to know, since they speak their minds and make no secret of their opinions and points of view. Amongst friends, they neither try to play any kind of role nor to adopt a mask of any sort.

Administrators often make friendships which last a lifetime. As a rule, they integrate rapidly with their colleagues, not only enjoying work-related gatherings and ice-breaking events, but also meeting up outside the workplace. They hold experienced, competent and influential people in esteem and have no liking for those who are flamboyant or eccentric or who go against convention. Finding a common language with people who perceive the world in a wholly different way from theirs is also difficult for them. They most often strike up friendships with *animators*, *inspectors* and *directors* and most rarely with *idealists*, *enthusiasts*, *counsellors* and other *administrators*. Their friends and acquaintances value their devotion and reliability, though at times, despite having known them for a long time, they feel overwhelmed by their self-assurance.

As life partners

To *administrators*, life partnerships are sacred. In general, they give no house room to thoughts of divorce, although if their relationship does collapse, they are able to pick themselves up and move on quite quickly. Family is one of the most important things in their lives and they consider every kind of familial obligation to be of the utmost importance. They are a rock for their nearest and dearest and are always willing to help them out. They consider providing for their family and assuring their security to be their personal responsibility; those closest to them warrant their utmost endeavour and devotion. They show their attachments and dedication in practical ways, involving themselves in family life and fulfilling their duties and obligations.

In taking on responsibility for their nearest and dearest, they will sometimes attempt to instruct and advise them, an approach which generally fails to go down too well with their partners. Neither are they capable of reading and interpreting their partner's feelings and emotions and, as a result, they will sometimes unwittingly hurt them with their blunt comments or remarks. Rarely will an *administrator* show them warmth, and, as a rule, they are unlikely to shower them with compliments either, more often praising them for a concrete achievement. Their partner might therefore be left with a sense that their emotional needs are somehow unfulfilled.

The natural candidates for an *administrator's* life partner are people of a personality type akin to their own: *animators*, *inspectors* or *practitioners*. Building mutual understanding and harmonious relations will be easier in a union of that kind. Nonetheless, experience has taught us that people are also

capable of creating happy and successful relationships despite what would seem to be an evident typological incompatibility. Moreover, the differences between two partners can lend added dynamics to a relationship and engender personal development. Indeed, for many people, this is a prospect that appears more attractive than the vision of a harmonious relationship wherein concord and full, mutual understanding hold sway.

As parents

Administrators take their parental responsibilities extremely seriously. The role of parent comes naturally to them and they invest every effort in bringing their children up to be responsible and independent people. They prefer the traditional model of the family, where the parents represent figures of authority to their children and warrant respect; 'palling around with the kids' is out of the question. Disobedience and the breaking of established rules are not tolerated and they are demanding and capable of applying discipline.

Unstinting in their criticism, *administrators* are also sparing when it comes to praising their children. They are often unperceptive of their emotional needs and fail to demonstrate a sufficient amount of warmth. On the other hand, they are eager to teach them decent behaviour and help them to distinguish between right and wrong, as well as instilling them with a practical, logical and common-sense approach to problems. They will show their impatience when their children continually make the same mistakes or blatantly disregard their duties and obligations. Yet they are highly devoted to their offspring and unstinting in giving them their time and energy. Later in life, their children appreciate them first and foremost for their ready dedication, for being their support and for inculcating them with the rules that make the world go round.

Work and career paths

Administrators are titans at work and engage to the full in accomplishing the tasks entrusted to them. They are incapable of working to less than their maximum potential. They cope superbly with practical tasks and are able to comply with complex procedures and conform with top-down guidelines and instructions. Their preference is for stable surroundings and they have no liking for frequent change.

As part of a team

Administrators believe that it is only by carrying out one's duties conscientiously, collaborating and sticking to the established rules that a given goal can be achieved. They make for trouble-free subordinates who can be relied on and are capable of working harmoniously with others. It is rare for them to question the instructions of those in charge or ignore the requisite procedures.

Organisation at work

Administrators need no reminders, urging, supervision or checking up on, since they are self-motivating and derive great pleasure from a job well done.

They are ideally suited to tasks demanding organisational skills and a love of orderliness. They are unrivalled when it comes to drawing up all kinds of plans of actions, schedules, systems, charts, diagrams and other graphic representations, to say nothing of putting them into practice. When they are charged with managing a team of employees or a system, then rest assured! The requisite procedures will be observed, the deadlines will be met and the job will be done effectively, efficiently and without disruptions.

Administrators have no understanding of people who fail to apply themselves to the tasks entrusted to them or to follow through on earlier undertakings or who consciously disregard regulations. They feel a sense of injustice when reliable employees are treated the same as those whose approach to their duties lacks diligence. They are definite supporters of remuneration on the basis of achievement and, in their view, 'fair' is not in the least synonymous with 'equal'.

Tasks

Administrators prefer practical tasks with a short time span. They enjoy solving tangible and concrete problems and like their work to have visible results. It gives them enormous satisfaction to see a system which was previously defective begin to function efficiently or resources which were being wasted now being put to more effective use or newly organised working procedures and practices giving rise to measurable savings of time. They cope less well in situations which demand thinking ahead into the future, reference to theory, improvisation or relying on intuition.

Companies and institutions

Administrators like the people in charge to respect their subordinates, value their experience and reward their achievements. Given their reliability, loyalty and predictability, they have a predisposition for jobs in administrative fields, both in state institutions and businesses. They enjoy the stability and prestige which goes hand in hand with working in large public organisations or enterprises with an established position. As employees, they are extremely loyal and fit in well in hierarchies and corporate structures providing the possibility of promotion. They will often spend the best part of their lives with one employer, steadily climbing the career ladder and, quite often, making their way to the very top. They also cope well with competition and rivalry.

In positions of authority

Administrators have a natural talent for leadership and are capable of organising and supervising the work of others. They enjoy making decisions, influencing the course of events and getting involved in settling practical problems. They are less good at coping with issues of a theoretical nature and strategic planning.

As leaders, they will more often perform the role of manager than of visionary and their preferred style for dealing with their subordinates is official and formal. While they are normally critical and demanding in their appraisals, they are also unusually objective and fair. They fix priorities and set clear goals, making it easy for them to evaluate the achievements of the employees they supervise. In general, they tend to be impatient, wanting to see tasks which are waiting to be carried out accomplished as soon as possible. Knowing that there is work outstanding or that a job may not be done on time causes them a definite sense of unease.

In focusing on urgent jobs, they often lose sight of crucial tasks, particularly when a longer time span is involved. They can also become overburdened with duties, since they have a problematic tendency to exercise excessive supervision over their subordinates and may thus fail to delegate sufficiently. This springs from their conviction that they will do the job quicker and better themselves, which is, indeed, very often the case. However, this *modus operandi* discourages those they supervise from working independently and deprives them of the privilege of learning from their mistakes.

Professions

Knowledge of our own personality profile and natural preferences provides us with invaluable help in choosing the optimal path in our professional careers. Experience has shown that, while *administrators* are perfectly able to work and find fulfilment in a range of fields, their personality type

41

naturally predisposes them to the following professions and fields:

- administrator
- auditor
- banking
- bookkeeper
- chef
- clerk
- detective
- director
- economist
- engineer
- office manager
- inspector
- insurance agent
- IT
- judge
- lawyer
- librarian
- manager
- pharmacist
- police officer
- politician
- project coordinator
- public administration
- referee/umpire
- sales representative
- scholar
- soldier
- sports coach
- teacher
- technician
- tertiary educator

Potential strengths and weaknesses

Like any other personality type, *administrators* have their potential strengths and weaknesses and this potential can be cultivated in a variety of ways. Their personal happiness and professional fulfilment depend on whether they make the most of the 'pluses' offered by their personality type and face up to its inherent dangers. Here, then, is a SUMMARY of those 'pluses' and dangers:

Potential strengths

Administrators are enthusiastic, friendly and ready to extend a helping hand to others. In terms of their work, they are self-motivating and have a sense of duty. Energetic, decisive and matter-of-fact, they are happy to accept responsibility for accomplishing tasks. With their natural leadership skills, they are capable of heading up teams and supervising others. They are able to evaluate impartially and objectively and are logical, rational and practical. They will always speak their mind and are direct in their contact with others, accept criticism well and are also capable of carrying out critical appraisals.

As a rule, they are highly perceptive, have good memories and are able to assimilate large amounts of detailed information. When they can see the potential for streamlining a system, improving its effectiveness and efficiency or putting a stop to waste, they feel stirred to take action. Capable when it comes to drawing up plans and establishing procedures, they will spot flaws and shortcomings imperceptible to others. They are hard-working, responsible and extremely loyal and complete the jobs they are given on time or, indeed, quite often before the deadline. They are incapable of consciously working to less than their full potential. With their love of order and organisational flair, they are excellent and capable resource managers and superb system organisers and administrators. Characterised by their independence and resistance to manipulation, they are true to their convictions and, no matter what the prevailing opinion might be, they stick to their own principles.

Potential weaknesses

As a rule, *administrators* assume that they are right. They will often shut out points of view which differ from their own, and as a result they narrow their own field of perception. With their natural inclination to instruct and advise, they will sometimes behave condescendingly and try to exert pressure on others. They have a tendency to focus excessively on details, which often means that they fail to perceive the bigger picture. Digesting theories and predicting the future consequences of present decisions and events comes hard to them. They feel that they are on very uncertain ground in situations which demand that they think ahead into the future or rely on intuition or improvisation. They have an inclination to concentrate on urgent tasks at the expense of important ones. Two problems that frequently crop up are their failure to delegate sufficiently and their habit of interfering in the work of their subordinates or colleagues. They are highly demanding, their expectations can be unrealistic and they can give the impression of being almost impossible to satisfy.

Reading the emotions and feelings of others is difficult for them, which often means that they unwittingly upset people. They have little awareness of the fact that their bluntly expressed opinions and jokes might be hurtful to others. Their mode of communication may not always be appropriate to the situation and circumstances in which they find themselves. Expressing their own emotions and demonstrating warmth towards others is also hard for them. In general, they are sparing in their praise and generous with their criticism. Being somewhat inflexible by nature, they find it difficult to cope with change. They can be stubborn, dogmatic, impatient and irritable and may be overly focused on immediate benefits, social status and material possessions.

Personal development

Administrators' personal development depends on the extent to which they make use of their natural potential and surmount the dangers inherent in their personality type. What follows are some practical tips which, together, form a specific guide that we might call *The Administrator's Ten Commandments*.

Be more understanding

Show more patience towards children, young people and those who have less experience or are less able. Not everyone is skilled in the same fields. If others are unable to cope with a task, this is not always a sign of their ill will or laziness.

Listen

Demonstrate an interest in others, even when you disagree with them or are convinced that they are wrong. Save your response until you have heard them out. The ability to listen could well revolutionise your relationship with others!

Accept change

When you look at ideas which might bring about change or undermine the current order and discard them in advance, you are throwing away the opportunity for development and depriving yourself of countless valuable experiences. Change always brings risk, but it will usually be rather less than you expected.

Admit that you can make mistakes

Always being right is neither obligatory nor likely. Sometimes you might be mistaken. At times, reality is more complex than you thought and both sides may be right, at any rate partially. Avoid assuming that no one else knows about a given matter as well as you do; this, in itself, is a mistake!

Praise others

Make the most of every occasion to appreciate other people, say something nice to them and praise them for something they have done. At work, value people not only for the job they do, but also for who they are. Then wait and see. The difference will come as a pleasant surprise!

Criticise less

Not everyone has your ability to handle constructive criticism. In many cases, being openly critical can have a destructive effect. Studies have shown that praising positive behaviour, albeit limited, motivates people more than criticising negative conduct.

Treat others kindly

People have a desire to be seen as something more than just tools serving to accomplish a goal. They long for their emotions, feelings and enthusiasms to be perceived. Mix with people, communicate with them, try to put yourself in their shoes and understand what they are going through, what fascinates them, what worries them, what they fear …

Leave some things to take their natural course

There is no way you can have everything under your personal control and no way you can manage to be in command of absolutely everything. Leave less important matters to take their natural course. Lay less crucial decisions aside. Stop putting all that effort into reforming other people. You will save energy and avoid frustration.

Stop blaming others for your problems

Your problems may not only be caused by others – they might also be caused by you! You, too, are capable of oversights and mistakes. You, too, can be the root of a problem.

Control your emotions

If you feel that you might well explode, then try to relax, wind down and think about something else for a moment. Outbursts of anger help neither you nor the people around you.

Well-known figures

Below is a list of some well-known people who match the *administrator's* profile:

- **Carry Nation** (1846-1911); an American temperance activist.
- **Bette Davis** (Ruth Elizabeth Davis; 1908-1989); an American stage and screen actress whose films include *All About Eve*. The winner of numerous prestigious awards, she is considered one of the greatest actresses of all time.
- **Harry S. Truman** (1884-1972); the 33rd president of the United States.
- **Billy Graham** (William Franklin Graham, Jr; 1918-2018); an American Baptist preacher, one of the most famous evangelists in the world and the author of a number of books, including *Peace with God*.
- **Sandra Day O'Connor** (born in 1930); an American lawyer and the first female judge to be

appointed a Justice of the Supreme Court of the United States.

- **George W. Bush** (born in 1946); the 43rd president of the United States.
- **Susan Sarandon** (Susan Abigail Tomalin; born in 1946); an American screen actress whose films include *Dead Man Walking*.
- **John de Lancie** (born in 1948); an American screen actor whose films include *Star Trek*.
- **Bruce Willis** (born in 1955); an American screen actor whose films include *Armageddon*, he is also a singer.
- **Mickey Rourke** (born in 1956); an American screen actor whose films include *Animal Factory*, he is also a screenwriter.
- **Laura Linney** (born in 1964); an American screen actress whose films include *Mystic River*.
- **Brendan Fraser** (born in 1968); an American-Canadian screen actor whose films include *The Mummy*.
- **Daniel Craig** (born in 1968); an English stage and screen actor who took on the role of James Bond in 2005. His first Bond movie was *Casino Royale*.

The Advocate (ESFJ)

The Personality in a Nutshell

Life motto: How can I help you?

In brief, *advocates* …

are well-organised, energetic and enthusiastic. Practical, responsible and conscientious, they are sincere and exceptionally gregarious.

Advocates are perceptive of human feelings, emotions and needs. They value harmony and find criticism and conflict difficult to bear. With their sensitivity to any and every manifestation of injustice, prejudice or detriment to another, they are genuinely interested in other people's problems and take real delight in helping them and tending to their needs, while often neglecting their own. They have a tendency to do everything for others and can be vulnerable to manipulation.

The *advocate*'s four natural inclinations:

- source of life energy: the exterior world
- mode of assimilating information: via the senses
- decision-making mode: the heart
- lifestyle: organised

Similar personality types:

- the Presenter
- the Protector
- the Artist

Statistical data:

- *advocates* constitute between ten and thirteen per cent of the global community
- women predominate among *advocates* (70 per cent)
- Canada is an example of a nation corresponding to the *advocate's* profile[3]

The Four-Letter Code

In terms of Jungian personality typology, the universal four-letter code for the *advocate* is ESFJ.

General character traits

Advocates like other people and are genuinely interested in their experiences and problems, with the ability both to be happy for them when good fortune comes their way and to identify with them when they are suffering. They excel at reading human feelings and emotions and are equally well

---

[3] What this means is not that all the residents of Canada fall within this personality type, but that Canadian society as a whole possesses a great many of the character traits typical of the *advocate*.

aware of their own, as well as being capable of expressing them and discussing them. In general, they are very approachable and easy to get to know, being both open and natural. They are quick to establish contact with others and find a common language with them. Their empathy, warmth, solicitude, sincerity and positive energy draw people to them and those who meet them for the first time will often have the impression that they have known them for ages.

Attitude to others

Advocates are quicker than most when it comes to identifying the needs of other people and will unstintingly give of their time and energy in order to help them. They are sensitive to human prejudice and to any and every manifestation of injustice. Their compassion and empathy drives them to act; they will stand in defence of those who have been harmed and try to solve their problems. What they are incapable of doing is passing them by in indifference. Entirely naturally, they will often become advocates for those who are unable to defend themselves … hence the name for this personality type.

Their nature is to see others in a positive light and, at times, they will refuse to take on board any notion of faults or shortcomings in their nearest and dearest, their friends or their colleagues. Indeed, sometimes, they will fly in the face of the evidence, defending them and blindly believing in their innocence to the end.

Perception and thinking

Advocates are splendid observers and outstanding in their perceptiveness, quick to spot and remember details and facts of importance to them. They are interested in the outside world and well-informed, knowing what's going on with their friends and acquaintances and in their immediate vicinity.

Being practical by nature, they learn by doing and by solving problems. Theoretical arguments and abstract concepts detached from reality weary them. They would far rather solve practical issues which concern specific people and offer the chance of improving their quality of life or reduce their suffering. Their character also features a sense of the aesthetic and a love of order and their homes and workplaces are perfect reflections of their personality.

View of the world

Advocates are distrustful of presentiment and intuition, preferring to rely on hard data and facts. Yet this does not make them people who operate solely on the basis of dry logic and calculation. The human aspect is also highly important to them and they will always consider how a given decision or action will affect others and how it will be received. Their surroundings have a considerable impact both on the way they perceive the world and on their viewpoint. However, this in no way categorises them amongst those whose convictions are in a frequent state of flux. In this, as in other areas, they are extremely constant and sometimes, indeed, downright dogmatic. As a rule, they make no secret of their views, expressing them openly, though with uncommon tact. When stating their opinion, they are rarely aggressive or confrontational.

Advocates frequently see reality in terms of black and white, devoid of shades of grey. Their world is exceptionally orderly; things are either right or wrong. In fact, there are times when they are even ready to retouch them slightly in order to be able to assign them to a specific category.

In general, understanding other people's point of view is difficult for them and they will often not even try to look at a problem from their perspective, assuming that their own perception is the correct one and that they are well aware of what will be good for others. This attitude will sometimes end up with their 'making people happy whether they like it or not'.

Decisions

When *advocates* are convinced that a decision is the right one, it will be a decision quickly taken. Sometimes too quickly, in fact. Despite their characteristic pragmatism, they can act under the influence of an emotional impulse and they are not always careful to ponder the far-reaching consequences of their actions, either. Nonetheless, they will always bear in mind the way that a given decision or mode of behaviour will be received by those around them and they tend to discuss important matters with their nearest and dearest or their colleagues and take their opinions into account when deciding. For *advocates*, the most difficult decisions are those which might harm other people or be received unfavourably by the people around them and they will often put off the moment of deciding or quite simply avoid it altogether.

When emotions are voiced and when the prospect of other people's suffering or injured feelings materialises, their decision-making processes will often be overcome by paralysis. Another problem which is widespread among *advocates* is their low assertiveness and vulnerability to being manipulated and used by others. On the other hand, their perseverance is one of their strengths. Once a decision has been taken and they start work, one thing is certain. They will see the task through, surmounting any hurdles and overcoming any adversities they encounter along the way.

In the face of change

Advocates have no fondness for change. They do, however, cope well with the practical consequences, such as reorganisation at work, but, being sentimental by nature, they see any change as the end of a stage of their lives, a point of no return and, as a rule, they require more time than many others to become accustomed to it. In situations of that kind, talking to other people helps them, as does the opportunity to share their thoughts and fears with someone else.

It is their nature to like stability, predictability, an orderly daily rhythm and even routine, all of which give them a sense of security and continuity. They dislike sudden changes of plan and any rapid *volte-face*. In life, they prize the timeless and immutable; for instance, they respect institutions or organisations with a long pedigree.

As others see them

Advocates have a reputation as practical, active and enterprising and are usually perceived to be sincere, caring and full of warmth. Others know that they can be counted on, although their want of flexibility does irritate some people, as does their loquaciousness, their excessive enthusiasm for proffering good advice and their reaction to criticism, which is sometimes considered to be disproportionate.

In turn, *advocates* themselves are annoyed by unpleasantness, laziness, sloppiness, scruffiness, carelessness, perfunctoriness and unreliability in others.

Problem solving

Advocates enjoy solving tangible and concrete problems and willingly help others. The prospect of positive change in people's lives spurs them into action. They are quick to identify human problems and involve themselves in lending a helping hand, quite often neglecting their own needs in the process. As a rule, they find it easier to help others than to ask for help in solving their own problems.

They have no liking for tasks of a theoretical and abstract nature; being characterised by pragmatism, all that interests them are effective solutions to real problems. They enjoy creating logical, orderly systems and are often the authors of solutions which provide genuine assistance to specific people or communities. However, their preference is for tried and tested methods of action and they can be mistrustful of innovative and experimental solutions. To those who happily reach for alternative methods, they may seem inflexible and over-traditional in their approach to problems.

In general, *advocates* do their best to avoid confrontations. When conflict looms, they will yield or withdraw from the field, rather than face strife, disputes and feuds. Nevertheless, once they spot gross injustice or harm being done to others, they are capable of entering the fray in defence of legitimate issues. They will often act on behalf of others, taking the side of the injured parties and serving as a voice for those who, for various reasons, are unable to defend their own interests. They are more active than most in signing on to the work of organisations dedicated to the social good or in spontaneously offering a helping hand to those in need. Doing so gives them genuine joy; the awareness that they have been able to help someone, that they have given them heart, that they have changed someone's life for the better is a source of happiness and personal satisfaction for them. Just as the liking, recognition and appreciation of others charges them with energy, so human ingratitude and untapped potential depresses them. They have difficulty in coming to terms with the fact that someone will not allow themselves to be helped and has no wish to grasp the hand held out to them.

Communication

Advocates are open in expressing their convictions and, as a rule, they have no fear of stepping into the public eye, being well able to speak out in a group or run a meeting. At the same time, they are masters of the diplomatic, knowing what to say and when to say it. They are extremely tactful and considerate; when presenting their views, they do so in a way that will not hurt or offend others, and even when their comments are critical they will strive for a subtle touch and phrase their remarks kindly in order to avoid upsetting people. If the people they are in conversation with are less sensitive and accustomed to more direct modes of communication, they might well actually fail to spot the criticism within their words.

Advocates are genuinely happy at the success of others and have no hesitation in voicing their esteem and admiration. They are unstinting in their praise of other people and their frank and sincere appreciation provides its recipients with a shot of energy and self-confidence. In the same way, a kind word from others gives *advocates* strength; what clips their wings is hostility, ingratitude and unpleasantness from other people.

In the face of stress

Advocates enjoy activity and practical undertakings. They are capable of working well and are just as good at having fun. In general, they are very busy, not only with their professional work, but also with helping others and they will often take on more of a burden than they are able to bear. When overloaded and stressed, they can become caustic or start bemoaning their fate, adopting the role of victim and martyr, for instance. They may well also lose their sense of self-worth and start composing pessimistic scenarios for the future in their heads. Criticism is a source of stress to them, as are repudiation, a lack of acceptance and even the common-or-garden indifference of others.

Socially

Advocates like people. Warm, friendly and harmonious relationships matter to them and they are incapable of understanding those who deliberately foul the atmosphere by making unpleasant comments or openly criticising others. People who manage to spend months talking about their aims and the tasks that need to be done, but fail to take any practical action whatsoever, are another source of puzzlement to them. *Advocates* esteem those who are down-to-earth, strong on substance and conscientious, who are not afraid of hard work and who, on seeing a problem, exert themselves to meet it head on. They respect their attitude, even when their activities fail to produce the desired outcome. This is because, as they see things, it is not only results that count, but also willingness and commitment. The people they cannot understand are those who, in the face of a challenge, are quick to give up without really even trying. They are also irritated by laziness and perfunctoriness.

Advocates feel responsible for others. They enjoy representing them, helping them and acting on their behalf. They will sometimes step into the role of advocate for other people, even if those people actually have no desire for someone to represent them, help them or expend enormous effort on reforming their lives.

In general, they are inclined to yield to other people for the sake of avoiding tension and are also capable of giving up their own pleasures for the good of others. When grappling with their own problems they will often give no sign of it, not wishing to burden other people with their troubles. As a rule, they will not express their dissatisfaction or discontent outwardly, and have a tendency to bottle up their emotions. However, after keeping them firmly suppressed for a long time, they might give way to an uncontrolled explosion, much to the astonishment of those around them.

Advocates are inclined to idealise their nearest and dearest, their friends and their colleagues. Rejection or betrayal on the part of someone they hold dear can be a genuine tragedy for them and, at the given moment, it may well seem to them that their entire world has come tumbling down. They also find being isolated and alone for any length of time hard to handle.

Amongst friends

Advocates are sincere and empathic. They are genuinely interested in others, highly affectionate and devoted and make faithful friends who can always be counted on for support and unselfish assistance, since they will never treat friendship like an object, using it as a form of self-advertising, for instance, or as a tool for building a career.

They prize honesty and openness greatly, perceive the positive potential in others and are able to elicit the best in them, all of which draws people to them and makes them widely popular. They will generally be surrounded by friends and acquaintances and will readily devote time to them, sometimes leaving none too much for themselves and, indeed, even neglecting their own needs.

Friends are a crucial part of their lives, second only to their family in importance. To a large extent, their own happiness depends on that of their friends and on healthy bonds with them. If possible, they will open up their homes to them. They love spending time with them and, if deprived of that contact, they feel cut off from their source of energy. They enjoy getting together with friends and other people are equally as happy to spend time in their company, gaining self-confidence, a sense of being accepted and a feeling of being stronger and better from their presence.

Just as they show others their respect, warmth, genuine interest and acceptance, so they look for a similar attitude towards themselves. The awareness that they are liked and valued gives them a boost and is a source of joy to them. On the other hand, they can scarcely bear indifference and criticism levelled at them by other people. Various personality types can be encountered amongst *advocates'* friends and acquaintances. However, they most frequently strike up a friendship with *presenters*, *protectors*, *counsellors* and other *advocates* and, most rarely, with *logicians*, *innovators* and *strategists*.

As life partners

Advocates value stability and the family is one of the most important things in their lives. Healthy family bonds form one of their foundations and give them a sense of security.

They take their obligations very seriously and marital vows are sacred to them. They love their family home and spending time there, adore family gatherings and make superb hosts and MCs. As a rule, they are attached to the traditional division of roles and cope splendidly with daily household duties.

The ideal they strive for is a peaceful and harmonious family life and the happiness of their nearest and dearest, and they invest enormous energy in accomplishing this. Even when they are overburdened with obligations, something which unfortunately happens all too often, they will never neglect their family or lose sight of those dearest to them. The people they love are their highest priority in life; they are unstinting in showering them with compliments, warm words and kind gestures and will never forget their birthdays and other important anniversaries. They too need warmth, closeness and signs of affection and take coolness, indifference and criticism very badly.

In general, they avoid touching on thorny subjects, preferring to remain silent about problems, bearing them patiently or pretending they don't exist. They also have a tendency both to idealise their nearest and dearest, failing to see their faults and to blame themselves for troubles within the family. The natural candidates for an *advocate's* life partner are people of a personality type akin to their own: *presenters, protectors* or *artists*. Building mutual understanding and harmonious relations will be easier in a union of that kind. Nonetheless, experience has taught us that people are also capable of creating happy and successful relationships despite what would seem to be an evident typological incompatibility. Moreover, the differences between two partners can lend added dynamics to a relationship and engender personal development.

As parents

Advocates are remarkably solicitous parents who take their parental responsibilities extremely seriously, wrapping their children in warmth, care and endearment and capably fulfilling their emotional needs. What they desire is to raise them to be sensitive and responsible people and they strive to make them receptive to the needs of others.

In general, they run their homes along lucid principles, thanks to which their children have a sense of security. They show their offspring love and acceptance, but expect their respect. The partnership style of parenting finds no favour with them; they establish clear rules and require them to be followed. However, they are not always successful in enforcing them.

Advocates have a tendency towards overprotectiveness, doing too much for their offspring and exercising excessive control, which often gives rise to problems with teenagers. Their children, in turn, are inclined to use and manipulate them, since they know that their *advocate*-parent will do anything for them and will always get them out of trouble if the need arises. Later in life, they will have happy recollections of the warmth of their family home and will appreciate the parental solicitude, endearment and devotion they received, as well as the clear principles which at the time might have seemed restrictive, but which gave order to their world and taught them to recognise what is important in life.

Work and career paths

Advocates enjoy working in a secure and stable environment where harmony prevails and will readily choose a profession which assures them of constant contact with other people.

Organisation at work

Advocates like things to be orderly and well-organised and favour established working procedures and a clear division of responsibilities and duties. In their opinion, all these factors help to get the job done effectively and enable the goals which have been set to be achieved. They find it hard to cope with working in disorderly and chaotic surroundings and are equally as irritated by poorly organised work, vague divisions of responsibilities and duties, wastefulness and ineffectiveness.

They dislike work which demands constant change and flexibility and rarely question the existing order. Respect for established rules and time-honoured traditions is part of their nature and so they won't generally challenge the legitimacy of the solutions adopted by their employer, even when they are anachronistic and not wholly suited to new needs and requirements.

As part of a team

Advocates enjoy teamwork and readily support other employees, bringing energy, a cordial atmosphere and practical ideas to the team. Their genuine praise and compliments have a motivating effect on others and they set great store by healthy and friendly relations. They find the company of people who are cold, reserved and reticent hard to bear and have a liking for hard-working, well-organised and predictable colleagues, finding it difficult to understand those who fail to apply themselves to their tasks and disregard their duties.

Views on workplace hierarchy

Advocates appreciate superiors who provide them with clearly defined expectations and lucidly specified goals and who evaluate them in terms of their achievements and the degree to which they accomplish their tasks. They fit in well in hierarchical organisations with a fixed structure. What they expect from those over them is genuine care for their subordinates and appreciation of their commitment.

They are deeply unhappy in an organisation where the employees are perceived as components of the system. When they hold a supervisory position, they will endeavour to consult their subordinates on decisions concerning their work, are interested in their opinions, motivate them to act and are able to boost their self-confidence. They give committed subordinates a sense of being genuinely appreciated.

Relationships with colleagues

In their pursuit of high effectiveness and the best possible use of time, *advocates* are liberal with their advice and instructions to employees. At the same time, they have a tendency to do too much for them, as well as being inclined to over-supervise and exercise too much control, which discourages others from experimenting, makes it more difficult for them to learn from their mistakes and restricts their independence.

Advocates believe that traditional structures and formal relations help to maintain harmony and stability and thus expect not only conscientiousness and commitment from employees, but also loyalty and respect. They find situations where pleasing everyone concerned will be impossible or where it becomes necessary to take difficult and unpopular decisions challenging. Disciplining employees or drawing their attention to inappropriate behaviour is also a serious problem for them.

Professions

Knowledge of our own personality profile and natural preferences provides us with invaluable help in choosing the optimal path in our professional careers. Experience has shown that, while *advocates* are perfectly able to work and find fulfilment in a range of fields, their personality type naturally predisposes them to the following fields and professions:

- acting
- barrister
- bookkeeper
- the clergy

- customer services
- educator
- estate agent
- financial advisor
- human resources
- kindergarten teacher
- manager
- marketing
- nurse
- optician
- paramedic
- personal development coach
- pharmacist
- physician
- physiotherapist
- public relations
- receptionist
- restaurateur
- sales representative
- sales assistant
- speech therapist
- teacher
- therapist
- travel agent
- welfare work

Potential strengths and weaknesses

Like any other personality type, *advocates* have their potential strengths and weaknesses and this potential can be cultivated in a variety of ways. *Advocates'* personal happiness and professional fulfilment depend on whether they make the most of the 'pluses' offered by their personality type and face up to its inherent dangers. Here, then, is a SUMMARY of those 'pluses' and dangers:

Potential strengths

Advocates like people and are genuinely interested in their experiences and problems. Being highly empathic, they are capable of reading the feelings and emotions of others, and are equally as good at expressing their own. Their warm, sincere interest and solicitude draws other people to them. They create a healthy, friendly atmosphere around themselves and excel when working as part of a group. They are also superb organisers, capable of turning their efforts to common goals. Gifted with the ability to collaborate harmoniously, they take genuine delight in the success of others and, as a motivating force, give other people faith in their own powers and elicit their hidden potential.

They are loyal employees, more focused on accomplishing the tasks entrusted to them than on personal benefits, which is why they are less likely than others to change jobs in search of better terms and conditions. By nature hard-working, energetic and stable, *advocates* are also characterised by their realism, pragmatism and predictability. What interests them are concrete facts and they are attracted by effective and practical solutions which either eliminate real problems or make someone's life easier.

They will finish what they start. Entrust a job to them and, rest assured, they will engage to the utmost in accomplishing it. *Advocates* cope well with tasks which require adherence to strict procedures, involve large amounts of data and demand repetitive activities.

Potential weaknesses

Being oriented towards helping others and low on assertiveness means that *advocates* are not always very good at tending to their own needs or defending their own interests and are also vulnerable to deceit, manipulation and emotional blackmail. They have a tendency to avoid difficult conversations, even when they are essential. Incapable of ending toxic and damaging relationships, they are inclined to blame themselves for any failure in that area of their lives. They fare poorly when dealing with crises and are extremely sensitive to criticism. Working alone comes hard to them and they are dependent on praise and affirmation from other people. When faced with hostility or indifference, they may well lose faith in themselves.

They find it difficult to cope in fields of activity which are completely new to them and are attached to old, tried and tested solutions, which might cause them to regard experiments and innovative methods of operating with scepticism. Being rather inflexible, they rapidly find themselves completely at sea in situations demanding swift decisions and improvisation. They also have a problem with delegating duties and responsibilities, as well as a tendency to do too much for others and help them whether they like it or not. Despite their tremendous openness to people, *advocates* are often sceptical when it comes to points of view other than their own. Indeed, simply encountering those opinions can cause them a deep sense of unease. They are also inclined to negate and reject the new and unfamiliar prematurely and, more often than most, are characterised by dogmatism and an inability to perceive the complexity of events.

Their loyalty towards people can bias them and they have difficulty in accepting that their relatives, friends or colleagues might be in the wrong or at fault. With their focus on current needs, *advocates* may not perceive future challenges and, in concentrating on individual problems, might fail to take note of the wider context.

Personal development

Advocates' personal development depends on the extent to which they make use of their natural potential and surmount the dangers inherent in their personality type. What follows are some practical tips which, together, form a specific guide that we might call *The Advocate's Ten Commandments*.

Stop doing everything for others

You may long to help people, but if you do everything for them, they will never learn anything new for themselves and you will be perpetually overburdened. When you give others a helping hand, let them take responsibility for their own lives, make their own mistakes and draw their own conclusions for the future.

Leave some things to run their natural course

There is no way you can have everything under your personal control. There is no way you can manage to be in command of every matter. Leave those less important matters to run their natural course. You will save energy and avoid frustration.

Stop fearing other people's ideas and opinions

Being open to the viewpoints of others is not synonymous with discarding your own. Stop fearing ideas and opinions which are different from yours. Before you reject them, give them some consideration and try to understand them.

Look at problems from a wider perspective

Always try to see the wider context, the bigger picture. Try to look at problems from every angle and with other people's eyes. Reach for their opinions, give thought to various points of view. When you engage with something, take all the different aspects of the matter into consideration.

Stop being afraid of conflict

Differences of opinion do arise, even in our closest circles. Conflict need not necessarily be destructive. In fact, it very often helps us to expose problems and solve them! So, when conflicts emerge, stop hiding your head in the sand and, instead, express your point of view and feelings about the situation openly.

Learn to say 'no'

When you disagree with something, why be afraid to speak out? When you are simply unable to take yet another task onto your shoulders, just say so. Learn to say 'no', particularly when you feel that someone is abusing your help or trying to land you with everything.

Stop being afraid of new experiences

Try something new every week or every month. Go somewhere you have never been before, talk to people you have never got to know before, undertake tasks you have never done before. It will give you a host of valuable ideas and mean that you start seeing the world from a wider perspective.

Be good to yourself

Try to help yourself with the same solicitude that you give to the happiness and well-being of others. Be more understanding of yourself. Try to get away from your responsibilities and duties once in a while and relax; do something for the sheer pleasure and fun of it.

Stop fearing criticism

Quell your fear of expressing your own critical opinions and of accepting criticism from others. Criticism can be constructive. There is no law which says that this has to mean attacking people or undermining their worth.

Accept help from others

You operate in the belief that you should be helping other people and that others usually seek support from you. Well, when you have a problem, turn the tables on that assumption! Stop hesitating, ask others to help you and then grasp the hand they extend. The ability to accept help is every bit as valuable as the ability to give it.

Well-known figures

Below is a list of some well-known people who match the *advocate*'s profile:

- **Louis Burt Mayer** (Eliezer Meir; 1882-1957); an American entrepreneur of Jewish origins. A film producer and distributor, he was one of the co-founders of film studio giant, Metro-Goldwyn-Mayer.
- **Ray Kroc** (1902-1984); an American entrepreneur and the founder of McDonald's Corporation, he is known as 'the hamburger king'.
- **Sam Walton** (1918-1992); an American entrepreneur, the founder of Wal-Mart, the largest retail chain in the world at the time of going to press.
- **Mary Tyler Moore** (1936-2017); an American screen actress whose films include *Ordinary People*.
- **Bill Clinton** (born in 1946); the 42nd president of the United States.
- **Danny Glover** (born in 1946); an American screen actor whose films include *Lethal Weapon*, he is also a producer and director.
- **Sally Field** (born in 1946); an American screen actress, whose films include *Forrest Gump*.
- **Eddy Murphy** (born in 1961); an American comedian and screen actor whose films include

Beverly Hills Cop, he is also a producer, screenwriter and director.

- **Lars Ulrich** (born in 1963); a Danish drummer, co-founder of American heavy metal band Metallica.
- **Björk Guðmundsdóttir** (born in 1965); an Icelandic singer, lyricist, composer and actress.
- **Geri Halliwell** (Geraldine Estelle Halliwell; born 1972); an English pop singer of Spanish-Swedish descent, she was one of the Spice Girls 'girl band'.
- **Elvis Stojko** (born 1972); a Canadian figure skater, Olympic medallist and three times world champion.
- **Linda Park** (born in 1978); an American screen actress of Korean descent, whose filmography includes the *Star Trek. Enterprise* TV series.
- **Samaire Armstrong** (born in 1980); an American screen actress of Scottish-Italian descent, whose filmography includes the TV series *The O.C.*

The Animator (ESTP)

THE ID16™© PERSONALITY TYPOLOGY

The Personality in a Nutshell

Life motto: Let's DO something!

In brief, *animators* …

are energetic, active and enterprising. Fond of the company of others, they have the ability to enjoy the moment and are spontaneous, flexible and open to change.

Animators are inspirers and instigators, spurring others to act. Being logical, rational and pragmatic realists, they are wearied by abstract concepts and solutions for the future. Their focus is on solving concrete problems in the here and now. They have difficulties with organising and planning and can be impulsive, acting first and thinking later.

The *animator's* four natural inclinations:

- source of life energy: the exterior world
- mode of assimilating information: via the senses
- decision-making mode: the mind
- lifestyle: spontaneous

Similar personality types:

- the Administrator
- the Practitioner
- the Inspector

Statistical data:

- *animators* constitute between six and ten per cent of the global community
- men predominate among *animators* (60 per cent)
- Australia is an example of a nation corresponding to the *animator's* profile[4]

The Four-Letter Code

In terms of Jungian personality typology, the universal four-letter code for the *animator* is ESTP.

General character traits

Animators are active and spontaneous. They focus on today and have the ability to enjoy the moment, preferring to make the most of what life offers them here and now, rather than being the kind of person who spends much of their time wondering what the future will bring. With their liking

---

[4] What this means is not that all the residents of Australia fall within this personality type, but that Australian society as a whole possesses a great many of the character traits typical of the *animator*.

for variability and the unexpected, they will readily get involved in anything new that comes their way.

Animators have difficulty staying in one place and continually hunger for new impressions and experiences. Once they have delved into a field of knowledge and found the answers to a question that has been nagging them or acquired new skills, they are off again, spotting new challenges and problems to be solved. As a rule, they have no difficulty in adapting to new circumstances and find changes easy to handle. In fact, they look forward to them!

Perception

In general, *animators* are pragmatists and realists, relying on what can be touched, seen and heard. Splendid observers and outstanding in their perceptiveness, they distrust presentiment and intuition. *Animators* learn by practical action, finding theoretical arguments and abstract concepts wearisome. Open by nature, they are tolerant and understanding both of others and of themselves. They have the ability to forgive themselves a great deal and are not given to torturing themselves with recollections of past mistakes or poor choices.

Decisions

When *animators* make decisions, they are guided by logic. Rational arguments and evidence speak louder to them than their personal feelings and intuition. Their decisions are usually reactions to situations and needs which have emerged and more rarely the result of conscious and planned preparation for something they anticipate in the future. They will often 'think out loud'; discussing problems with other people and putting various possibilities into words helps them to arrive at a solution.

When they decide to act, they pay little attention to how people around them will respond to what they do. First and foremost, they follow their own convictions, which are grounded in rational and objective facts. Faith in their own principles is not only more important to them than satisfying other people, but even takes precedence over observing prevailing norms and customs.

As others see them

Other people see *animators* as compassionate, spontaneous and open. In general, they are considered to be energetic, active, practical and extremely direct; indeed, some people find them too direct. They are often viewed not only as very welcome company when it comes to having a good time, but also as people whose help can be relied on when problems suddenly crop up. Much more rarely will they be perceived as experts in tasks demanding good planning and sensible organisation; in fact, they sometimes have a reputation for being disorganised, if not chaotic. Those who are devoted to the unselfish service of others or focused on the life of the spirit often take *animators* to be superficial people with their interest fixed on building a career and material things.

In turn, *animators* have trouble understanding those who are fascinated by abstract theories or concepts. Fans of sentimental novels, melodramas and soap operas are also a source of bewilderment to them.

Problem solving

Being practical by nature, *animators* have no liking for lengthy digressions on the theme of what should be done, but would rather just roll up their sleeves and get straight on with things. They prefer practical, concrete tasks and will often subconsciously monitor their surroundings, seeking out problems that require solving. On the whole, they need little time to prepare, being always 'on their marks, set and ready to go'. They excel at coping in circumstances demanding fast reactions, flexibility and improvisation. While others are overcome by emotion or paralysed by fear in emergency situations – such as search and rescue actions, for instance – *animators* keep their heads and stay cool, evaluating the situation rapidly and objectively and taking whatever action is vital. In addition, their reactions keep pace with changing circumstances and new factors and they have the ability to shift the thrust of their activities and adapt them to fresh conditions in a flash.

They cope less well with tasks which demand planning and lengthy preparation. In situations of that kind, they will try and save the day by means of that superb talent for improvisation which is so typical of the *animator*. Nonetheless, it can happen that, as a result of their problems with planning and their rather deficient organisation of their work, they end up losing out on all sorts of opportunities and failing to make the most of myriad 'chances of a lifetime'.

Animators are prone to overestimating what they can manage; for instance, they might underrate the amount of work necessary to accomplish a task. They will thus sometimes leave too much until the last minute, putting their colleagues and their nearest and dearest through a host of stressful experiences. Planning and organisation may not be numbered among their strengths, but even so, with a little effort, they are capable of developing those skills to a considerable extent.

Communication

Animators dislike expressing their thoughts in writing and much prefer the spoken word. They have a colourful turn of phrase and the gift of persuasiveness. Being more ready to speak than to listen, they are usually impatient. As such, they might well interrupt the people they are in conversation with, without letting them finish. However, their openness, optimism and sense of humour make other people happy to listen to them. All of this, in conjunction with their active nature and enthusiasm, means that, where an *animator* goes, others will follow. They are often the instigators and animators of all kinds of activities … hence the name for this personality type.

When they set out on a new venture, they have the ability both to infuse others with faith in its success and to encourage them to act. However, by nature, they are better at initiating an activity than seeing it through to the end. They have more problems than most with keeping their promises and sticking to previous arrangements; when a new challenge appears on the horizon, their enthusiasm for the things they have already started doing will simply vanish. This attitude will sometimes cause disappointment to those who, encouraged by their initial commitment, joined them in an activity they initiated.

In the face of stress

Animators are capable of working well and are just as good at relaxing. They have the ability to 'switch off' and give themselves over completely to unwinding or having fun without feeling the slightest pang of conscience on that account. They will often have a particular love of sport and active leisure pursuits. As a rule, they cope well with stress in situations of conflict. If the tension drags on, though, it can lead to their exhaustion, loss of energy and withdrawal. When wearied and fatigued, they may seek powerful sensory experiences, turning to substances or looking for thrills in gambling or risky financial speculations.

Socially

Animators are open to people, which makes them approachable and easy to get to know. They will usually win the liking of those around them and are able to fit in with a new 'crowd' and adapt to whatever situation they find themselves in. They are known for the way they can regale people for hours with amusing stories and for their ability to come out with witty comments on reality. Their very presence alone will often be enough to take the strain out of a tense atmosphere. Remarkably direct in their dealings with others and prone, in general, to speaking their mind, they can also be impulsive and explicit. Indeed, their critical remarks might be hurtful to people who are more sensitive and emotional.

Being impervious to criticism and pressure from those around them, *animators* are unlikely to waste time on inquiring about what others think of them and how they perceive them. They are capable of influencing people and even of manipulating them in order to achieve goals they consider to be important.

Although they brighten things up for the people who spend time with them and are often the life and soul of the party, they frequently have problems with deeper interpersonal relationships. If they are forced to enter the world of emotions and feelings, their 'inner compass' fails them and, in no time at all, they are hopelessly lost. As a rule, they find it easier to forge bonds when the focal point is having fun or tackling problems together; developing relationships rooted in feelings comes much harder to them. As a result, family relations can pose a greater challenge to them than professional ones.

Amongst friends

Where's the action? Wherever it is, that is where *animators* will want to be. They like the company of others, love having fun with them and are always up for any kind of 'team' venture, as well as being quick to adapt and feel at home with new people, and in new surroundings and circumstances. Others appreciate their enthusiasm, optimism and sense of humour and will happily spend time with them. They are usually seen as gregarious, spontaneous and uncomplicated.

Animators like striking up acquaintanceships. Happy to get to know new people, the focus of their friendship shifts more often than in others. After a brief conversation, they will already have sized up the potential of people they have only just met. The problems start when it comes to reading their emotions and feelings. Their spontaneity and impulsiveness mean that other people quite often take them to be emotional. In reality, though, they are guided first and foremost by logic and common sense.

When it comes to spending time with others, variety is most certainly the spice of an *animator's* life. Spontaneous and quick to make decisions, they would definitely rather see everyone up and doing something together; in the long run, sitting around a table and chatting bores them to tears. *Animators* are a prime example of people who prefer deeds to words and their family and friends know that, if a practical problem needs a fast solution, they can always count on their help. Practical action is their way of expressing their friendship and affection. They most often make friends with *administrators*, *practitioners*, *innovators* and other *animators* and, most rarely, with *mentors*, *counsellors* and *idealists*.

As life partners

Animators are dynamic, energetic and sensual, with a spontaneity and sense of humour which make it impossible to be bored in their company. As a partner, they bring vitality and energy to the relationship; life will never be dull with an *animator* around. In general, they set great store by freedom and find restrictions hard to endure. By the same token, they impose no restraints on their partners, but give them free rein.

Animators care deeply about their partner's needs and are highly supportive. However, actions speak louder than words in their case and it is practical needs, rather than emotional, which carry more weight with them, since they themselves have few of the latter and thus have difficulty perceiving them in their nearest and dearest. As a rule, they also have trouble with reading and showing feelings, though with a modicum of effort, they are able to develop those skills over time. The nature of their romantic disposition can mean that their partner feels hurt by the lack of compliments, affection and endearments and might also suffer on account of the *animator's* critical remarks and unkind jokes.

In general, *animators* will have no truck with talking about feelings and relationships, finding discussions of that kind not also tiresome but also a waste of time that would be better spent doing something concrete. To a sensitive and emotional partner, the *animator's* conversations with them might appear shallow and superficial, while their responses can give the impression of being rather too terse.

A powerful new stimulus will normally rivet the *animator's* attention so firmly that, as they become absorbed in the latest challenge, their previous undertakings may well fly right out of their minds. Once an insoluble problem or unexplored puzzle intrigues them, there is very little that can stop them from becoming engrossed in it and, as a result, they often have trouble with keeping previous promises. This will sometimes evoke a sense of frustration in their partner, particular when they do not share the *animator's* enthusiasm or have no understanding of the essence of whatever is currently absorbing them.

Animators live for the moment, which is why the vow "to have and to hold (...) till death do us part" might represent a considerable challenge to them. Their nature is to view undertakings of that kind as decisions which are made anew on a daily basis. Life with an *animator* may be a constant adventure, thanks to their spontaneity and love of change, but those same characteristics can sometimes be a threat to the stability of their relationships. Their perpetual fascination with new acquaintances and their inclination to flirt are also potential hazards.

The natural candidates for an *animator's* life partner are people of a personality type akin to their own: *administrators*, *practitioners* or *inspectors*. Building mutual understanding and harmonious relations will be easier in a union of that kind. Nonetheless, experience has taught us that people are also

capable of creating happy and successful relationships despite what would seem to be an evident typological incompatibility. Moreover, the differences between two partners can lend added dynamics to a relationship and engender personal development. Indeed, for many people, this is a prospect that appears more attractive than the vision of a harmonious relationship wherein concord and full, mutual understanding hold sway.

As parents

The *animator* parent treats their children as independent people, asking for their viewpoints, counting on their opinions and being ready to admit that they are right and even to learn from them. They encourage their offspring to explore the world and make active use of their free time. Partnership parenting is their preferred style and they are more like friends than mentors, searching for the answers to questions and discovering the world together with their children.

Rather than adopting the role of experts proffering ready answers to just about anything, they are not embarrassed to admit to not knowing something. In general, they are tolerant, uncomplicated and understanding, though they can sometimes be impulsive and impatient and their efforts at raising their children are often lacking in cohesion and inconsistent. If the other parent is unable to operate in a more organised fashion, their children might lack a sense of security and stability, as well as clear rules establishing how the world is run.

Animators often have problems with disciplining their offspring, a duty which they are only too happy to cede to their partner. On the other hand, they love playing and having carefree fun with them, deriving just as much joy from it as the children. Indeed, they will sometimes be so involved that all thought of their other responsibilities vanishes from their minds. By the same token, though, when they are engrossed in some other activity, it is their children who are well-nigh forgotten.

It can sometimes be difficult for children to understand their *animator* parent and their switchback tendency to focus entirely on playing with them some of the time and be utterly inaccessible on other occasions. Another cause of problems in parent-child relationships is the difficulty *animators* have with reading and expressing feelings. They are not, by nature, the kind of parents who shower their children with endearments and wrap them in warmth on a daily basis. Their natural mode for showing their love is their solicitude for their offspring's needs, particularly in the practical sphere, a responsibility they take extremely seriously. When their child is facing some kind of trouble, they are capable of swinging straight into action, doing whatever is necessary without delay. For instance, if they hear of any problems occurring in their children's school, they will not only be the first to intervene, but will also spur other parents to act as well.

Once adults, their children are grateful to their *animator* parent for allowing them so much freedom, encouraging them to explore the world and getting them out of trouble when things got difficult. They will also have fond recollections of all the crazy fun they had together.

Work and career paths

Wherever the action is, that is where *animators*, with their love of variety, will be happy to work. They fit in well in organisations which value activeness and enterprise and give their employees a free hand in accomplishing their tasks, but handle strict supervision and constantly being checked up on very badly and dislike immovable deadlines, rigid structures and bureaucratic procedures. When they are convinced they are in the right, they are capable of consciously ignoring the relevant instructions or regulations, just as long as they accomplish a goal which matters to them.

Preferences

Animators cannot bear routine and repetitiveness. When they have to carry out a monotonous and repetitious task, they will try to lend variety and attraction to the job by introducing elements of variety and diversity to it. A great many of them, intent on avoiding a lifetime spent at a desk or under the eagle eye of the boss, will consciously choose work which takes them out and about, demanding travel and meetings with contractors and clients, but providing a greater degree of freedom. Their innate activeness, enterprise, liking for risk and thirst for independence mean that many *animators* set up their own companies and become successful in the business world.

Skills and stumbling blocks

As a rule, *animators* do better at tasks requiring spontaneity and fast reactions rather than good planning, sensible organisation and methodical execution. As a result, when they hold supervisory or managerial positions, they need the strong support of assistants or secretaries to whom they can assign all their practical, routine duties. Problems where emotions and feelings play a large part are also a stumbling block. Since they feel on very uncertain ground when they enter areas demanding intuition and empathy and requiring them to read human emotions, they will do everything they can to avoid situations of that kind.

As part of a team

To *animators*, a good boss is a boss who sets out the general course of action for their subordinates and then leaves them alone to get on with the job. They are happy to work as part of a group, contributing optimism, enthusiasm and a practical approach to problems. They are natural inspirers and initiators and will often be the first to get to work, spurring others to follow suit. Their fervour, enthusiasm and engagement are a positive inspiration and motivating force. They themselves will most happily work with people whose openness and spontaneity is similar to their own and who are gifted with a sense of humour and the ability to enjoy life.

Animators suffer when they have to cooperate with people who are incapable of taking responsibility for their own lives or who see the world in gloomy hues. They fail to comprehend those who manage to spend months chewing over a problem without taking so much as a single practical step aimed at solving it. To *animators*, theoretical debate is not only stupendously tiresome, but is also unproductive, signifying a waste of time and energy. In turn, their own actions can be perceived as hasty, ill-conceived, premature and chaotic.

Professions

Knowledge of our own personality profile and natural preferences provides us with invaluable help in choosing the optimal path in our professional careers. Experience has shown that, while *animators* are perfectly able to work and find fulfilment in a range of fields, their personality type naturally predisposes them to the following fields and professions:

- acting
- animateur
- anti-terrorism
- bodyguard
- the construction industry
- crisis management
- driver
- electrician
- electronics
- engineer

- entrepreneur
- estate agent
- financial advisor
- firefighter
- insurance agent
- lifeguard
- locksmith
- logistics
- metalworker
- photographer
- physiotherapist
- police officer
- radio presenter
- sales assistant
- sales representative
- security guard
- soldier
- sportswoman/sportsman
- television presenter
- tour guide
- tourist/holiday resort representative
- sports coach
- travel agent

Potential strengths and weaknesses

Like any other personality type, *animators* have their potential strengths and weaknesses and this potential can be cultivated in a variety of ways. *Animators'* personal happiness and professional fulfilment depend on whether they make the most of the 'pluses' offered by their personality type and face up to its inherent dangers. Here, then, is a SUMMARY of those 'pluses' and dangers:

Potential strengths

Animators are open, optimistic and quick to establish contact with others. They hold no grudges, but are able to forgive both other people and themselves. They live for today, enjoying the here and now and not tormenting themselves with thoughts of past mistakes. Splendid observers, with excellent memories, they are characterised by their uncommon flexibility and spontaneity, find change easy to handle and adapt rapidly to new circumstances. Being unusually logical and rational, they enjoy tackling practical problems and have no fear of 'insoluble' tasks. They have the ability to size up a situation rapidly and, with their extraordinary gift for improvisation, to respond appropriately to problems and changing circumstances as they crop up. Efficient, enterprising and energetic, they cope well in situations of conflict, are impervious to criticism and, when convinced that they should take a particular action, they are capable of doing so regardless of the views and opinions of others. Dissuading them is something of a challenge.

By nature bold and unafraid of risk, *animators* infect others with their enthusiasm and faith that their undertakings will succeed. They initiate all kinds of activities and motivate others to work. Capable of investing their entire energy in a task that matters to them, they are just as good at relaxing. As a rule, they are superb oral communicators, keeping their listeners riveted with their colourful, witty and fascinating way with the spoken word. They also possess the gift of persuasiveness.

Potential weaknesses

Animators have a problem with defining priorities and with operating methodically and systematically, being prone to act impulsively. Their activities are usually reactions to immediate problems and challenges; they will rarely be the result of planned actions taken with the future in mind.

Focused as they are on the here and now, they have trouble identifying future opportunities and threats, as well as with foreseeing the consequences of their actions and their impact on other people. They are easily distracted. When they catch sight of a new challenge, their enthusiasm for things they have already started doing dissolves and, as a result, they have problems with keeping their promises and seeing things through to the end. Their poor planning and time management skills can sometimes mean that they fail to organise their tasks properly, missing deadlines as a consequence.

Animators cope badly with tasks requiring them to work alone and demanding lengthy preparation by way of reading large amounts of material, for instance, or drawing up a detailed plan of action. In general, they do no better when it comes to routine tasks and repetitive activities and anything which entails abstract thinking or looking ahead to the future will also be a problem for them. By nature impatient and quick to tire of situations, they are also frequently characterised by an inclination towards risk and dicing with danger. Their self-assurance usually helps them to succeed; however, on occasion, it can lead them to overestimate their capabilities or underrate the seriousness of a problem. Despite their excellent interpersonal relationships in the social sphere, *animators* have difficulty both in reading the emotions and feelings of others and in expressing their own. It can happen that they hurt other people with their explicit or critical remarks, while they themselves remain completely unaware of the impact of their words.

Personal development

Animators' personal development depends on the extent to which they make use of their natural potential and surmount the dangers inherent in their personality type. What follows are some practical tips which, together, form a specific guide that we might call *The Animator's Ten Commandments.*

Admit that you can make mistakes

Things may be more complex than they seem to you. You may not always be in the right. Bring that thought to the forefront of your mind before you start accusing others or pointing out their mistakes and reproaching them.

Learn to set priorities and manage your time

Enthusiasm is your main driving force. Nonetheless, listing priorities, establishing time frames and planning out a job are not at all the same thing as forging chains to shackle your creativity, fetter your activities and encumber you as you carry out the task. Perish the thought! They are tools and when you use them properly, they will help you achieve the goals you are aiming for.

Praise others

Make the most of every occasion to appreciate other people, say something nice to them and praise them for something they have done. At work, value people not only for the job they do, but also for who they are. Then wait and see. The difference will come as a pleasant surprise!

Be more understanding

Show others more warmth. Remember that not everyone should be assigned the same tasks, because not everyone is skilled in the same fields. If someone is unable to cope with a task, this is not always a sign of their ill will or laziness.

Appreciate the worth of creative ideas

Operating solely on the basis of dry facts and hard data brings a whole range of restrictions in its wake. Many a problem can only be solved by intuition, an innovative approach and thinking creatively. So stay open to them all!

Give some thought to the future

With most of your attention focused on current tasks and immediate goals, you might well be overlooking future opportunities. Why miss out? To make the most of them, all you need do is give some thought to what you want to achieve over the next year, the next five years and the next decade.

Keep your impulsiveness reigned in

Before you make a decision or commit yourself to a venture, devote a little time to gathering some relevant information and analysing it. When you take that approach, you will most likely find yourself with less to do and, more to the point, you will end up doing it better.

Criticise less

Not everyone has your ability to handle constructive criticism. In many cases, it can have a destructive effect. Studies have shown that praising positive behaviour, albeit limited, motivates people more than criticising negative conduct. When you comment on the behaviour and viewpoints of others, exercise more restraint.

Finish what you start

You launch into new things enthusiastically but have problems with finishing what you have already started, a *modus operandi* which usually produces mediocre results. Try sorting out what is most important to you and deciding how you want to accomplish it. Then knuckle down and turn your back firmly on all those tempting distractions!

Remember important dates and anniversaries

Arrangements to meet people, the birthdays of those closest to you and family anniversaries may seem like rather trivial matters to you in comparison to whatever it is you are involved in. They matter a great deal to other people, though. So if you are incapable of remembering them, jot them down somewhere handy ... and then remember to check those notes!

Well-known figures

Below is a list of some well-known people who match the *animator's* profile:

- **Sir Winston Churchill** (1874-1965); a British politician, orator, strategist, author and historian. He served twice as prime minister of the United Kingdom and wrote numerous outstanding historical works, winning the Nobel Prize for Literature.
- **Ernest Hemingway** (1899-1961); an American author whose works include *The Old Man and the Sea*, he was awarded the Nobel Prize for Literature.
- **Evita** (María Eva Duarte de Perón; 1919-1952); an Argentinean screen and radio actress also famed as a political and social activist.
- **Mikhail Kalashnikov** (1919-2013); a Russian weapons designer and the creator of the AK-47 automatic assault rifle, widely known as the 'Kalashnikov'.
- **Peter Falk** (1927-2011); an American screen actor whose filmography includes the title role in the *Columbo* TV series.
- **Jack Nicholson** (born in 1937); an American screen actor whose films include *One Flew Over the Cuckoo's Nest*, he is also a director, screenwriter and

producer and the holder of numerous prestigious awards.

- **John Rhys-Davies** (born in 1944); a Welsh screen and voice actor whose films include *The Lord of the Rings*.
- **Madonna** (Madonna Louise Veronica Ciccone; born in 1958); an American singer, songwriter and actress of Italian and French-Canadian descent, she has won numerous prestigious awards.
- **Antonio Banderas** (José Antonio Domínguez Bandera; born in 1960); a Spanish screen actor whose films include *Desperado*, he is also a director and producer and the winner of numerous prestigious awards.
- **Jeremy Clarkson** (born in 1960); an English print and media journalist and television presenter whose TV shows include *Top Gear*.
- **Michal J. Fox** (born in 1961); a Canadian-American film actor, author and producer whose films include *Back to the Future*.
- **Mike Tyson** (Michael Gerard Tyson; born in 1966); an American boxer and former world heavyweight champion, now retired from the ring.
- **Matt Damon** (born in 1970); an American film actor whose films include *Good Will Hunting*, he is also a screenwriter and producer.
- **David Tennant** (David MacDonald; born in 1971); a British stage, screen and voice actor whose filmography includes the title role in the *Doctor Who* TV series.
- **Britney Spears** (born in 1981); an American pop singer, dancer and screen actress.

The Artist (ISFP)

THE ID16™© PERSONALITY TYPOLOGY

The Personality in a Nutshell

Life motto: Let's create something!

In brief, *artists* …

… are sensitive, creative and original, with a sense of the aesthetic and natural artistic talents. Independent in character, they follow their own system of values and are optimistic in outlook, with a positive approach to life and an ability to enjoy the moment.

Helping others is a source of joy to them. They find abstract theories tedious and would rather create reality than talk about it, although starting on something new comes more easily to them than finishing what they have already started. They have difficulty in voicing their own desires and needs.

The *artist's* four natural inclinations:

- source of life energy: the interior world
- mode of assimilating information: via the senses
- decision-making mode: the heart
- lifestyle: spontaneous

Similar personality types:

- the Protector
- the Presenter
- the Advocate

Statistical data:

- *artists* constitute between six and nine per cent of the global community
- women predominate among *artists* (60 per cent)
- China is an example of a nation corresponding to the *artist's* profile[5]

The Four-Letter Code

In terms of Jungian personality typology, the universal four-letter code for the *artist* is ISFP.

General character traits

Artists possess a sunny disposition and a refined sense of humour. They follow their own system of values and are insusceptible to external pressure, although the opinion of others also matters a great deal to them. When they evaluate themselves, they do so through the prism of other people's

---

[5] What this means is not that all the residents of China fall within this personality type, but that Chinese society as a whole possesses a great many of the character traits typical of the *artist*.

views and assessments of them and, by the same token, are highly sensitive and easily hurt.

Interior compass

Artists have the ability to live for today and enjoy the moment, rarely eating their hearts out over the past or worrying about the future, but living out their lives in the here and now. They love liberty and the sense of freedom; their perception of the world is as a place of limitless possibilities and they are fascinated by its beauty. With their dislike of abstract theories and concepts which are difficult to apply in practice, they would rather experience life than spend time describing it or speculating about it. They strive to live in accordance with the values they hold; acting against their own convictions causes them an enormous sense of uneasiness. The world of the spirit attracts them and, if they profess no particular faith, they tend to be beset by an intense feeling of emptiness, of something lacking.

Healthy relationships with their nearest and dearest are also vital to *artists* and, without them, they are incapable of being happy and enjoying life to the full. They like to live to their own rhythm, finding uniformity and conformity hard to bear. Unyielding to pressures which affront their principles, they will sometimes have problems with accommodating the prevailing norms and have no liking for bowing to requirements they deem inexplicable, either. They often have a dread of being pigeonholed and restricted and, as a result, will sometimes fear responsibilities and obligations, as well as being concerned that they will lose the chance of being themselves, making their own decisions and choices.

Attitude to others

Artists believe that every person has the right to be themselves, should be accepted as they are and possesses positive potential. They have the ability to spot the good in those who have been rejected and written off by society as a whole. With their uncanny gift for empathy, they are able to help other people, giving them heart and faith in their own powers. They put the needs of others first and express their acceptance of them more or less unconditionally, just so long as their attitude agrees with their own system of values and convictions. They believe that if we all showed one another more love, the world would be a far better place.

They are incapable of understanding people who have a liking for attacking and criticising others and are equally as bewildered by those who flaunt themselves or try to pretend to be something other than they really are, finding the motives for behaviour of that kind incomprehensible. They themselves prize authenticity and exert themselves in the cause of other people's well-being. Endeavouring to make an impression on people is alien to their behavioural repertoire, as is the pursuit of power and influence. They neither impose nor intrude and they make no attempt to exert pressure on others or to persuade them to adopt their own points of view. Sharing their thoughts and reflections is something they do most willingly in the family and among close friends.

As others see them

Other people see *artists* as pleasant, compassionate, calm and modest, but as people who are, nonetheless, difficult to get close to, since they can appear eccentric and mysterious. They themselves are unaware of the fact that this is how they are sometimes perceived. They intrigue those around them because describing and pigeonholing them unequivocally is an elusive affair. In general, they are reserved and withdrawn, although they will sometimes come out of their shell, happily engaging people in conversation and showering them with compliments. At times, they can give the impression of being either flighty or passive, indecisive and bent on avoiding responsibility.

In reality, though, they take life very seriously and, contrary to the opinions of some, are not antisocial, but simply like doing things 'their way', in their own time and at their own pace. They also prefer operating individually to taking part in joint actions and group undertakings of various kinds. Other people will sometimes find their desire to help others hard to understand and, rather than believing that they really are acting without self-interest, seek hidden motives in what they do.

Aesthetics

Artists are usually nature lovers. They have a liking for life in the bosom of nature and adore virgin landscapes, undefiled by civilisation. Aesthetically tuned, they have a feel for beauty and an artistic spirit. They love harmony and natural simplicity and have a superb sense of space, colour, hues and sounds. They are not simply connoisseurs of beauty, but also its creators, possessed of the ability to play with matter and create stunning compositions, images and objects from it. Ever ready and glad to immerse themselves in art, they are often artists … hence the name for this personality type. In general, they are quick to spot new trends in fashion, design and art and, indeed, they are often the trendsetters themselves.

Work style

Artists operate under the sway of the creative impulse, without devoting overmuch time to preparation and deliberation. When an idea pops into their head, they simply go ahead and set about turning it into reality. With their sweeping range of interests, they love turning their hand to trying out something new. Once absorbed in something, they are quite capable of forgetting the entire world, becoming utterly engrossed in their work and losing all track of time. On the other hand, when something else excites their curiosity, they are equally as capable of discarding their current task and giving themselves over completely to the new one.

Artists are highly flexible and capable of adapting to changing circumstances. Their work style often poses something of a puzzle to those around them, since, being easily distracted and having a tendency to immerse themselves in other things, they can give the impression that they fail to make good use of the time they have to carry out their tasks. Despite this, though, they normally manage to meet their deadlines.

Studying

Artists are practical by nature and view theories and concepts which cannot be applied to life as valueless. Rather than theorising on the topic of reality, they prefer to create it.

They often have fairly painful memories of lessons at school. They love learning new things, but find dry, monotonous and theoretical lectures wearisome, learning best and most readily by doing. The very creative process itself is a source of enormous joy to them; indeed, they will often rate it as more important than the end result.

Decisions

When *artists* are solving a problem, they are capable of making a rapid assessment of the situation, taking all the measures and means available to them at the given moment into account and making an on-the-spot decision which meets the occasion. They follow their own system of values and apply a healthy dose of common sense when making their choices. However, reaching a decision analytically and rationally is generally beyond them; as a rule, their consideration of a situation involves thinking about the real people it will affect and about what they will experience and feel. They also reflect on how they themselves will feel if they make this or that decision.

Communication

Artists tend to be reticent, particularly amongst larger groups of people. It may even be that, paralysed by a dread of misunderstanding or criticism, they are frightened of expressing their thoughts openly. As a result, those around them are often unaware of their views, their opinions and their likes and dislikes. In general, they assume that actions speak louder than words, which is why they prefer to convey their feelings and emotions by doing something concrete.

They also have a very low tolerance threshold when it comes to being criticised and, indeed, will often perceive criticism where none was intended. There are times when they may well treat opinions which differ from their own convictions as an attack on their system of values, an attitude which can mean that, on occasion, they will shut out information at variance with their views and thus, in turn, limit their own perceptions.

In the face of stress

To a large extent, *artists'* sense of well-being is dependent on their environment. When surrounded by beauty and harmony, as well as love, warmth and acceptance from others, they are happy, whereas criticism, discord and conflict trigger their sense of being under threat. Their reaction to prolonged periods of stress is to withdraw, give up or escape. Contact with nature and animals has a soothing effect on them, as does immersing themselves in art. As a rule, they love relaxing and unwinding in the open air and have the ability to find joy in the small things in life.

Socially

Artists need space and privacy, which is why they sometimes give the impression of being rather withdrawn and mysterious. Yet their relationships with others are actually of fundamental importance to them and they find it hard to enjoy life if they cannot count on the acceptance and support of those closest to them. They are extraordinarily loyal, take their responsibilities extremely seriously and their friendships are stable and enduring.

In general, they exert themselves in the cause of other people's well-being and will do anything to avoid conflicts. They tread carefully in order not to hurt, distress, sadden or discourage anyone. Although they will happily help others to solve their problems, they distrust people who try to dominate or use them.

Artists are usually reserved towards strangers and take their time in building new acquaintanceships. It is rare for them to express their desires openly and they are reluctant to share their personal problems, an attitude which is often interpreted as a sign that they are distant and withdrawn. Amongst larger groups, they can sometimes be dominated by others, or pushed to the margins or even, quite simply, ignored, which might lead to their becoming embittered and increasingly isolated.

Amongst friends

Artists are seldom numbered among people who have plenty to say for themselves. However, when they do talk to someone, they engage in the conversation to the full, listening attentively and asking questions as and when appropriate, as well as applying their ability to read non-verbal signals. They are genuinely interested in their friends' lives, experiences and personal histories – and they actually remember them! They know who is interested in what and are aware of their likes and dislikes, their passions and their problems. Altruists by nature, they readily hold out a helping hand without ulterior motive; this more often than not takes the form of doing something concrete, rather than talking.

Artists enjoy spending time with like-minded people who accept them for what they are and make no attempt either to change them or to pressurise them. They themselves are both exceptionally tolerant and extremely sensitive to the needs and feelings of others. Faithful and highly devoted, they involve themselves in their relationships wholeheartedly, giving their time and energy to their friends unstintingly. They willingly support others, showing them understanding and providing practical assistance.

They will usually go through their entire lives surrounded by the same group of close friends, amongst whom the most frequently encountered personality types will be *protectors*, *presenters*, *idealists* and other *artists*, while those which feature most rarely will be *directors*, *strategists* and *innovators*.

As life partners

Artists expect trust and understanding from their partners and they themselves also endeavour both to understand them and to respond to their needs. They long for profound relationships and constancy and, at one and the same time, for tolerance and a lack of constraints. Indeed, a mutual respect for the other person's freedom lies at the very core of their relationships.

They seek affirmation of their own worth in their partner's words and gestures. Rarely do they speak of their emotions and feelings; those closest to them are often unaware that, in fact, *artists* are intensely emotional and sensitive people. Always striving for harmony in their relationships and showing their partners immense love and warmth, they, too, have a deep-seated need for endearments, gestures of affection and closeness. When their partner fails to perceive their needs, *artists* may well feel used, superfluous and unattractive. They handle indifference badly and find open criticism even more difficult to cope with, reacting to it by becoming withdrawn and increasingly embittered, as well as by losing all faith in themselves.

The natural candidates for an *artist's* life partner are people of a personality type akin to their own: *protectors*, *presenters* or *advocates*. Building mutual understanding and harmonious relations will be easier in a union of that kind. Nonetheless, experience has taught us that people are also capable of creating happy and successful relationships despite what would seem to be an evident typological incompatibility. Moreover, the differences between two partners can lend added dynamics to a relationship and engender personal development.

As parents

Artists adore children, so the role of parent gives them tremendous joy. They will always find time for their children and every moment with them, every second of fun and every family expedition is something they enjoy to the full. They have an extraordinary and singular bond with their offspring, building it from their earliest years and nurturing it throughout their lives. Their children's individuality is something they respect and they make no attempt to shape them in accordance with their own notions. They will point their children in the right direction, but impose no rigid frameworks, encouraging them to be themselves, pursue their own enthusiasms, live out their own dreams and make the most of their own strengths. In general, *artists* are none too demanding as parents and find it difficult to be tough disciplinarians.

Their flexibility, openness and tolerance may well trigger unlooked-for side effects, since their children sometimes have problems in distinguishing good and desirable behaviour from what is bad and reprehensible. As parents, *artists* are ready to devote their all. As a result, it might be that they spoil their children, fulfilling their every whim and inundating them with presents. Later in life, their offspring appreciate their *artist* parents first and foremost for their acceptance, their warmth and the respect they showed for their decisions and choices.

Work and career paths

Artists can perform a wide range of tasks successfully. However, what gives them the greatest satisfaction is work which enables them to put the values they hold dear into practice. The key to their thriving professionally is their passionate commitment. When they are engaged in something which arouses their enthusiasm, they can move mountains. However, the results they achieve when they find something boring or of little value are somewhat less than impressive and nothing will change that, not even the most remarkable of motivational programmes.

Environment

On the whole, *artists* cope rather less than well in positions demanding that they carry out numerous routine activities and tasks. A formalised environment where everything is bureaucratised, where a host of rigid procedures have to be observed, where detailed guidelines have to be put into practice and where everything has to be done according to plan and within fixed deadlines is torture to them. It is simply not their world.

Artists will often try and plan their careers in a way which means that what they do in life is something which interests them and is important to them. In their case, work is more than a means of earning a living and success is not synonymous with holding a high position and being admired by those around them. They fit in well in institutions where the driving purpose is helping other people and solving their problems and they also enjoy work which offers them contact with nature and animals.

Work style

Artists make for reluctant leaders, since they cope badly when it comes to disciplining people, calling their attention to poor achievements, giving instructions and enforcing duties. They like operating behind the scenes, although this may not always be possible; for instance, if they are artists by profession, they are condemned to being the centre of attention. When they do have to play a leading role, they will get themselves out of the spotlight's glare as quickly as possible.

After they have completed a task, they will happily step back into the shadows. Peace, quiet and time on their own enables them to recharge their batteries and they also have a need for feedback and confirmation that they have done a good job. The opinion of others matters a great deal to them. They themselves tend to be extremely self-critical and to assess what they have done very harshly, often being highly dissatisfied with the results of their work, despite the positive evaluation of those around them.

Other people appreciate *artists* for their practical ideas for solving problems, their flexibility and their improvisational skills when unplanned events and situations crop up without warning. The ability to react rapidly to changing circumstances makes them ideal candidates for rescue work and positions in crisis management centres.

Views on workplace hierarchy

Artists esteem superiors who give their employees freedom, allowing them to be themselves and to carry out their tasks in the way that works best for them. In their opinion, bosses are there to support the people they are in charge of, particularly during difficult moments and crises in people's lives. They like professional relationships to be based on trust and place a high value on a friendly and healthy atmosphere in the workplace. Believing that praise, encouragement and a kind word will achieve more than criticism, discipline and strict supervision, they are happy when their superiors let them know they are satisfied with their work.

On the other hand, they have no liking at all for treating people uniformly or pigeonholing them, and find being told what to do and how they 'should' behave fairly intolerable.

By the same token, they themselves neither exert pressure on others nor instruct them, considering that everyone should have the freedom to make their own decisions about their own lives. This approach means that they are unsuited to working in fields where persuasive skills and the ability to pressurise people are a prerequisite, such as jobs involving canvassing for business or soliciting clients, for instance.

Professions

Knowledge of our own personality profile and natural preferences provides us with invaluable help in choosing the optimal path in our professional careers. Experience has shown that, while *artists* are perfectly able to work and find fulfilment in a range of fields, their personality type naturally predisposes them to the following fields and professions:

- artisan
- the arts
- botanist
- chef
- craftsperson
- crisis management
- early primary-level teacher
- fashion designer
- florist
- forester
- gardener
- graphic artist
- hairdresser
- interior decorator
- interior designer
- kindergarten teacher
- lifeguard
- mechanic
- musician

- natural historian
- pet grooming
- photographer
- physician
- psychologist
- social welfare
- stylist
- therapist
- life coach
- travel agent
- vet
- visual artist
- waiter / waitress

Potential strengths and weaknesses

Like any other personality type, *artists* have their potential strengths and weaknesses and this potential can be cultivated in a variety of ways. *Artists'* personal happiness and professional fulfilment depend on whether they make the most of the 'pluses' offered by their personality type and face up to its inherent dangers. Here, then, is a SUMMARY of those 'pluses' and dangers:

Potential strengths

Artists are optimistic by nature, with a positive approach to life. They are exceptionally sincere and are characterised by their openness to people and their tolerance. Being aesthetically inclined, they have a feel for beauty, an artistic spirit and a superb sense of space, colour, hues and sounds, as well as the ability to take whatever tools and materials are available to them and use them to create stunning compositions, images and objects. They are quicker than most to spot new trends in fashion, design and art. When they are working on tasks they believe in, they are capable of investing enormous effort and energy in them. They learn fast by doing. *Artists* are genuine altruists; they take a sincere interest in other people's experiences and problems and long to help them. They are able to show others warmth and care and respect their individualism. Superb listeners, they will find a positive potential and good in everyone.

With their uncanny gift for empathy, they are able to help other people, giving them heart and faith in their own powers. They are independent, following their own system of values and remaining insusceptible to pressure. Speculations about the future fail to absorb them and worrying over past mistakes is alien to them; they have the ability to focus absolutely on immediate and current problems. Being highly flexible, they find change easy to handle and adapt rapidly to new circumstances, responding to them quickly. They know how to make the most of a situation's potential and, when the need arises, they can improvise brilliantly.

Potential weaknesses

As a rule, *artists* cope none too well with tasks stretching over a lengthy time span and demanding planning, preparation and thinking ahead. Motivating them to do jobs where the results will only become apparent at some distant moment in time is a challenging undertaking. They have a tendency to act and make decisions impulsively and are better at starting something new than at finishing what they have already begun. Analytic and rational decision-making in detachment from real people and situations is difficult for them. In general, they evaluate themselves through the prism of other people's views and assessments of them; by the same token, they are highly sensitive and easily hurt. This might give rise to major problems in the lives of *artists* who are operating in an environment hostile to their nature, for instance among people who are very sparing in their praise or generous in their criticism. They are inclined to have low self-esteem and it is all too easy to undermine their faith in themselves. Openly voicing their thoughts and desires is something they often dread.

Artists have a very low tolerance threshold when it comes to being criticised and may perceive criticism even where none is intended; they are also liable to take opinions which run contrary to their own as an attack on their system of values. This can lead to their shutting out information at variance with their views and limiting their own perceptions as a result. They frequently have problems with assimilating theories and grasping concepts unsuited to practical application. Their individualism and fondness for doing things 'their way' hampers them when it comes to teamwork. When carrying out management functions, they have difficulty in disciplining people, calling their attention to poor achievements, giving instructions and enforcing duties.

Personal development

Artists' personal development depends on the extent to which they make use of their natural potential and surmount the dangers inherent in their personality type. What follows are some practical tips which, together, form a specific guide that we might call *The Artist's Ten Commandments*.

Finish what you start

You launch into new things enthusiastically, but have problems with finishing what you have already started, a *modus operandi* which usually produces mediocre results. Try sorting out what is most important to you and deciding how you want to accomplish it. Then knuckle down and turn your back firmly on all those tempting distractions!

Stop being afraid of conflict

When you find yourself in a situation of conflict, stop hiding your head in the sand and try voicing your point of view and feelings openly instead. Conflict very often helps us to expose problems and solve them.

Don't condemn others to relying on guesswork

Tell people how you feel, what you're going through and what you desire. Stop dithering over whether or not to express your opinions, feelings and emotions and just go for it. You will be helping your colleagues and your nearest and dearest immensely when you do.

Stop fearing ideas and opinions which are different from yours

Before you reject them, give them some consideration and try to understand them. Being open to the viewpoints of others is not synonymous with discarding your own.

Stop fearing criticism

Quell your fear of other people's critical comments. Criticism can be constructive. There is no law which says it has to mean that you are under attack or that your worth is being undermined.

Accept help from others

You operate on the assumption that you should be helping other people and that others seek support from you. Well, when you have a problem, don't hesitate! Ask others for their help and then grasp the hand they offer!

Set yourself free from other people's opinions

You accept others, don't you? So start accepting yourself and stop evaluating yourself on the basis of what other people have to say about you. They could be wrong. They could even be lying. When it comes to making decisions about your life, who could possibly be more competent than you?

Keep your impulsiveness reigned in

Before you make a decision or commit yourself to something, devote a little time to gathering some relevant information, analysing it and evaluating the situation coolly and objectively. That way, you will most probably not only cut down on the number of things you have to do, but will also ensure that you do them more effectively.

Banish those gloomy thoughts

Stop assuming that you are bound to be misunderstood, that you will come a cropper or make a fool of yourself. An attitude to life like that can paralyse you. You will achieve a great deal more by assuming that everything will go swimmingly and focusing on the positive.

Learn to say 'no'

When you disagree with something, why be afraid to say so? Say 'no', particularly when you feel that someone is abusing your help or trying to make you do everything.

Well-known figures

Below is a list of some well-known people who match the *artist's* profile:

- **Wolfgang Amadeus Mozart** (1756-1791); an Austrian composer and musician of the Classical period, one of the three outstanding composers often referred to jointly as the First Viennese School.
- **Fyodor Dostoyevsky** (1821-1881); a Russian writer whose works include *Crime and Punishment*, he is considered one of the world's greatest authors of psychological prose.

- **August François-René Rodin** (1840-1917); a French Symbolist and Impressionist sculptor and precursor of modern sculpture.

- **Vincent van Gogh** (1853-1890); a Dutch painter of the Post-Impressionist school.

- **Marilyn Monroe** (Norma Jean Mortensen/Baker; 1926-1962); an American screen actress and cinema legend whose filmography includes *Some Like It Hot*.

- **Elizabeth Taylor** (1932-2011); a British-American actress whose filmography includes *Cleopatra*, she received numerous awards, including two Oscars.

- **Bob Dylan** (Robert Allen Zimmerman; born in 1941); an American musician, vocalist, composer and writer, he is one of the most important figures in the popular music of the second half of the twentieth century and has won numerous awards, including Grammys, an Oscar and a Pulitzer.

- **Paul McCartney** (born in 1942); an English composer, multi-instrumentalist and songwriter, co-founder of the legendary group the Beatles and holder of numerous prestigious awards.

- **Steven Spielberg** (born in 1946); an American director whose filmography includes *Schindler's List*, he is also a screenwriter and producer and the winner of numerous prestigious awards.

- **Jean Reno** (Juan Morenoy Jederique Jiménez; born in 1948); a French screen actor whose films include *Leon*.

- **Christopher Reeve** (1951-2004); an American actor whose filmography includes the title role in *Superman*, he was also a director and writer.

- **John Travolta** (born in 1954); an American film actor whose movies include *Saturday Night Fever*, he is also a singer and dancer.

- **Kevin Costner** (born 1955); an American actor and director whose filmography includes *Dances with Wolves*, he is also a producer.
- **Earvin 'Magic' Johnson** (born in 1959); a professional American, NBA basketball player and Olympic medallist.

The Counsellor (ENFJ)

The Personality in a Nutshell

Life motto: My friends are my world

In brief, *counsellors* …

are optimistic, enthusiastic and quick-witted. Courteous and tactful, they have an extraordinary gift for empathy and find joy in acting for the good of others, with no thought of themselves. They have the ability to influence other people, inspiring them, eliciting their hidden potential and giving them faith in their own powers. Radiating warmth, they draw others to them and often help them in solving their personal problems.

 Counsellors can be over-trusting and have a tendency to view the world through rose-tinted glasses. With their focus on other people, they often forget about their own needs.

The *counsellor's* four natural inclinations:

- source of life energy: the exterior world
- mode of assimilating information: intuition
- decision-making mode: the heart
- lifestyle: organised

Similar personality types:

- the Enthusiast
- the Mentor
- the Idealist

Statistical data:

- *counsellors* constitute between three and five per cent of the global community
- women predominate among *counsellors* (80 per cent)
- France is an example of a nation corresponding to the *counsellor's* profile[6]

The Four-Letter Code

In terms of Jungian personality typology, the universal four-letter code for the *counsellor* is ENFJ.

General character traits

Counsellors are energetic, nimble-witted and optimistic. They find joy in helping others and excel at reading their feelings and emotions. When they observe people, they spot things that remain hidden to others. With their extraordinary

---

[6] What this means is not that all the residents of France fall within this personality type, but that French society as a whole possesses a great many of the character traits typical of the *counsellor*.

intuition and empathy, they are capable of lifting other people's spirits, inspiring them and motivating them to act.

Attitude to others

Counsellors have a healthy sense of their own worth, but are ready to surrender their needs and adapt to others if doing so will enable them to provide the necessary help or support. The problems experienced by their family and friends affect them deeply and they are often so focused on other people that they have no time to reflect on their own lives. Indeed, sometimes they even have difficulty in defining their personal aims in life or their needs.

Others perceive them as superb teachers and mentors and as people in whom they can confide, appreciating them for their help and turning to them for advice in difficult situations. By profession, *counsellors* are often providers of good counsel ... hence the name for this personality type. Nevertheless, regardless of what they do for a living, they will be a source of such counsel for their friends and relations and will often help them to solve their personal problems. Their insights, which strike *counsellors* themselves as absolutely natural and self-evident, are a source of tremendous inspiration to others and prompt them to view a situation with a fresh eye and in a new way.

Although other people's problems absorb a considerable amount of their time, the awareness that they can help someone gives *counsellors* immense joy. In general, they feel responsible for others and find it impossible to stand indifferently by in the face of another person's troubles. At times, they might try to improve other people's lives whether they want it or not, or to do everything for them.

Thinking and perception

Counsellors' thoughts are turned towards the future and they rarely reflect on past failures. Their thinking is global and far-reaching and they derive joy not only from accomplishing their plans, but also from the very process of planning and then proceeding towards the goal. The future excites them more than the present and they look at problems from a broad perspective, perceiving various aspects of the issues they are involved with. They also have an inbuilt capability to multitask.

Counsellors dream of a better world and believe in the possibility of turning those dreams into reality. Their vision spurs them to act and injects them with energy. In general, they like change and new challenges and adopt innovative concepts and ideas with an enthusiasm which can, at times, be indiscriminating. They are often interested in the reality of the spirit and social problems also move them. By nature, *counsellors* are egalitarians. On occasion, they might well subordinate their lives to one idea and work to accomplish it in a way which is almost fanatical.

Interior compass

Counsellors follow the values they profess in life and are mistrustful of decisions taken solely on the basis of logical and rational arguments. When someone attacks their system of values or behaves in a manner which affronts their convictions, they are capable of protesting sharply, much to the astonishment of those around them, since their usual tendency is to step aside for others and avoid confrontations. In extreme cases, they are even ready to take up cudgels and fight for what seems to them to be right and just. However, given that they are, by nature, inclined to leave their own rights bringing up the rear, it will be a fight in defence of principles and standards of behaviour which, in their opinion, are incontrovertible.

As others see them

As a rule, *counsellors* are widely liked and have an uncommon power to draw others to them. Even the coldest and most rigorously conservative of people rarely remain indifferent to their charm, warmth, sincerity and wide range of interests. They are considered to be people who can always be counted on. Their advice helps others to see problems in a new light and talking to them spurs people to act and augments their faith in their own powers. To some people, though, the *counsellor's* optimism seems suspect, while they themselves appear overly enthusiastic and out of touch with reality, sometimes even to the point of naïvety and gullibility.

Counsellors, in turn, are irritated by scepticism in others, as well as by chronic pessimism, lethargy, stagnant attitudes and a lack of faith in the potential for change. They find those who indifferently pass by another person's suffering and ignore the feelings of others incomprehensible. In their eyes, a life devoted only to satisfying one's own needs is a life impoverished and devoid of values. Equally as bewildering to them are people for whom an atmosphere of harmony and warmth is of no account, as are those who consciously pursue confrontation. They themselves are highly sensitive to criticism and will do anything they can to avoid conflicts and unpleasant situations.

Communication

Counsellors display extraordinary tact and intuition in their interpersonal communication. They are masters of the diplomatic, with the gift of always knowing what to say in a given situation and an ability to influence people, shape their behaviour and even to manipulate them when the cause is a good one. As a rule, they are highly communicative and persuasive.

They prefer to communicate directly and orally. Being well aware of the immense power of words, they keep the language they use under firm control. Indeed, they will sometimes give prior thought to what to say in a given situation and, when an essential conversation awaits them, they may even play it out in their minds first. They are usually unafraid of speaking in public and have the ability to present their viewpoints clearly and comprehensibly. There is one exception to this, though. When they evoke the values they profess, they mistakenly assume that they are generally shared by other people and then what they are saying can often be obscure.

In the face of conflict

As *counsellors* see it, healthy relations with other people are the key to happiness in life and at work. When they are aware of an unresolved conflict, they are unable to function normally within their family or focus on what they are doing at work. With their need for warmth, acceptance, endearment and sincerity, they also dislike being alone. Nevertheless, since they derive joy from giving, they are capable of living a happy life even when their needs are unmet.

Their exceptionally low threshold of tolerance for criticism and tendency to avoid any and every kind of unpleasant situation mean that they will often surrender in the face of conflict, either giving up the fight entirely or agreeing to unfavourable conditions simply in order to put an end to an uncomfortable situation. Unfortunately though, in taking that course of action, they expose themselves to similar, equally distressing experiences in the future.

Challenges

Counsellors usually lead active lives and rarely have time to relax. In their free time, they are frequently involved in activities geared towards helping either society or their friends and acquaintances. This may give them great joy, but their low assertiveness and inability to say 'no' means that they take on too many responsibilities and are often overburdened as a result. With their desire to respond to every need that arises, they are frequently distracted and they lack the ability to focus on priorities.

They like being among people, but are highly sensitive and vulnerable to hurt. With their low threshold of tolerance for criticism, they take every unfavourable remark to heart and any unflattering comment whatsoever affects them deeply. By the same token, they are incapable of availing themselves of help from others. They find being alone for any length of time hard to bear, as well; when they are cut off from other people, they are swept by despondency and apathy.

Socially

Counsellors feel thoroughly at home among people. Social relationships are one of the most important things in their lives; they invest a great deal of energy in them and are unusually loyal. They value acceptance, honesty, intensity and warmth in interpersonal relations and are quicker than most to perceive the feelings, emotions and needs of others. Being exceptionally sensitive, they take coolness, indifference and criticism extremely badly.

As a rule, *counsellors* are very outgoing and friendly. They have the ability to express their emotions and feelings and readily share them with their friends. Their attitude to others is highly positive and enthusiastic; they believe in people and genuinely hope for their happiness, identifying with them and sharing in their joys and sorrows. They often feel the suffering of another almost to the point of physicality, while other people's joy means that they themselves are happy.

When they are among other people, they give them their full attention and it is rare indeed for them to focus on thrusting themselves forward or advertising their own points of view, although they are fully capable of articulating them clearly as and when the need arises.

Amongst friends

Counsellors are brimming with of energy and optimism and have an abundant and sparkling sense of humour. They are widely liked, draw others to them and can always be counted on. Their behaviour is natural, they are good listeners and are genuinely interested in other people's experiences and problems. All these qualities make them perfect friendship material. Their acceptance, understanding and sincere interest mean that the people in their company feel better about themselves and their worth.

Counsellors are extremely faithful friends and those who confide in them can be assured of their trustworthiness. They lift their friends' spirits and give them faith in their own powers, perceiving their hidden potential and making them aware of their inherent possibilities. They see helping their friends as something utterly natural and it gives them immense joy to do so. However, their positive attitude to others means that they are not always able to refuse them and they allow themselves to be used as a result.

They usually forge healthy and friendly relationships with everyone, regardless of personality type. However, they most frequently strike up a friendship with *enthusiasts*, *mentors*, *advocates* and other *counsellors* and, most rarely, with *practitioners*, *animators* and *inspectors*.

As life partners

Counsellors treat their relationship with their life partner as precisely that: a relationship for life. They bring a massive dose of warmth, tenderness and acceptance to it, along with their abundant sense of humour, and expect the same in return, suffering if their partners fail to show them love and affection. On the whole, though, they tend not to make too much of it, since they derive joy from giving and the happiness of their nearest and dearest will also be their happiness in some measure. They are faithful, loyal and exceptionally devoted.

Counsellors see the best in their partners, accepting them, supporting them and, on many an occasion, making excuses for them. However, the balance between giving and receiving in their relationships often slips out of kilter, given that, by nature, they give much more than they take. With their focus firmly on the happiness of their partner, they seldom fight for their own rights or shine a light on their own needs. They regularly 'monitor' the status of their mutual relationships and their partner's emotional state, for instance by asking how they are feeling, which some people may well find tiresome.

Their low threshold of tolerance for criticism is an ever-present problem for *counsellors*. Blunt remarks and direct comments from a less sensitive partner will hurt them and they will do anything they can to avoid conflicts and unpleasant conversations. In general, they would rather suffer than call other people's attention to their inappropriate behaviour and they also have problems in withdrawing from destructive relationships, often remaining in them for a very long time as a result. Faced with trouble in their relationship, they are ready to work at it and make sacrifices. If their efforts fail to produce results, they have a tendency to blame themselves for the lack of success and, if a relationship falls apart, they give their minds over to pondering the mistakes they made. However, on the whole, it will not be long before they shake themselves out of their reflections and come to terms with parting.

The natural candidates for a *counsellor's* life partner are people of a personality type akin to their own: *enthusiasts*, *mentors* or *idealists*. Building mutual understanding and harmonious relations will be easier in a union of that kind. Nonetheless, experience has taught us that people are also capable of creating happy and successful relationships despite what would seem to be an evident typological incompatibility.

As parents

Counsellors make responsible parents, taking their duties in this respect very seriously and being well aware of the importance of having proper relationships with their children. They endeavour to pass on the values which they themselves believe in and truly wish to be a good example. They show their children warmth, tenderness and care. Unstinting in their praise and words of encouragement, they accept them as they are and make that plain to them. Nonetheless, they are capable of applying discipline and inculcating their offspring with the standards and principles which give order to their world, since they earnestly wish for them both to perceive the difference between desirable and reprehensible behaviour and to be able to make the right choices. *Counsellor* parents take good care to ensure that their children want for nothing and they are a steady presence in their offspring's lives, empathising with them and, as and when the circumstances demand, offering comfort, encouragement, motivation or ideas. They will always be by their side at difficult moments and it is a rare event for them to miss the fact that they are wrestling with a problem.

Counsellors have the ability to influence their children's behaviour, something which they normally employ for worthy ends, such as increasing their faith in their own powers. However, at times, they may attempt to manipulate them. They also have a tendency to do everything for them, thus depriving them of the chance to experiment and learn from their mistakes. At times, older children will complain that their *counsellor* parent is interfering too much in their lives and, fed up with parental over-protectiveness and what they perceive to be excessive control, they will occasionally envy their peers' freedom and lack of restrictions. Looking back, though, they are grateful to their *counsellor* parent for surrounding them with love, being their support and teaching them to distinguish right from wrong.

Work and career paths

Counsellors cope very well with change, are happy to learn something new and enjoy challenges. They are able to put their whole heart into accomplishing purposes they believe in. Although they have no fear of innovative tasks and pioneering ventures, they like order, structure, proper organisation and clear, comprehensible rules. Sparking their enthusiasm for work on a project when they are not properly prepared or where the aim is only fuzzily defined will be difficult. They prefer straightforward solutions and will thus do their best to simplify complicated procedures and strip complex systems down to the essentials. Good organisers themselves, they like working according to plan and take their responsibilities extremely seriously. When they make decisions, they take into consideration not only the relevant objective reasoning or the economic score, but also the potential impact on people's lives. In general, they believe that changes which will affect employees should be agreed with them or that there should, at the very least, be a consultation process.

As part of a team

Counsellors derive great satisfaction from jobs requiring contact with people and are happy to work in companies and institutions where the driving purpose is to solve human problems or improve lives. They are tailor-made for customer service departments and advice or welfare centres, coping excellently with tasks demanding interpersonal skills. When they work as part of a team, they are pillars of support for their colleagues; indeed, they go well beyond the call of duty in this respect.

Counsellors have the ability to create a warm, friendly atmosphere and to engender comprise, as well as having a positive influence on their colleagues, motivating them, inspiring them and infecting them with optimism and faith in their success. They are unhappy both in soulless corporations where the emotions, feelings and needs of the employees count for nothing and in institutions where people perform the function of 'cogs in the machine'. Open, honest, natural and direct relationships with their colleagues are crucial to them and they dislike environments where mutual contact between staff members is formalised and the exchange of information only takes place within rigorously defined procedures. They will have difficulty fitting in with teams dominated by cool, reticent employees and they also have no liking for tasks which demand a host of routine activities, adherence to detailed instructions and the processing of huge quantities of data. On the whole they are easily distracted; if someone diverts their attention from their work and asks for advice, they are capable of completely forgetting the task they were engaged in and giving themselves over absolutely to the conversation.

Views on workplace hierarchy

Counsellors appreciate superiors who behave in line with the principles they profess, give their subordinates freedom in accomplishing their tasks and respect their individual style of working. When they themselves are given a position of authority, which occurs quite frequently, they behave in the same way. In their case, working in management positions usually incurs a great deal of stress, since they not only have to confront unpleasant situations head on, while their nature dictates that they avoid them, but are also obliged to be guided primarily by the company's economic interests, something which will not always be favourable as far as their subordinates are concerned. They feel a tremendous sense of discomfort on this account. Their tendency to make decisions prematurely might also prove to be a potential source of problems.

Professions

Knowledge of our own personality profile and natural preferences provides us with invaluable help in choosing the optimal path in our professional careers. Experience has shown that, while *counsellors* are perfectly able to work and find fulfilment in a range of fields, their personality type naturally predisposes them to the following fields and professions:

- acting
- advisor
- clergy
- life coach
- consultant
- diplomat
- editor
- human resources
- manager
- marketing
- musician
- paramedic
- physician
- police officer
- politician
- psychiatrist
- physiotherapist
- psychologist
- public relations
- rehabilitation
- reporter
- sales representative
- scientist
- social welfare
- supervisor / head of a team
- teacher
- therapist

- tertiary educator
- travel agent
- vocational training
- writer

Potential strengths and weaknesses

Like any other personality type, *counsellors* have their potential strengths and weaknesses and this potential can be cultivated in a variety of ways. *Counsellors'* personal happiness and professional fulfilment depend on whether they make the most of the 'pluses' offered by their personality type and face up to its inherent dangers. Here, then, is a SUMMARY of those 'pluses' and dangers:

Potential strengths

Counsellors are energetic and optimistic. Loyal and faithful, they can always be relied on. They are conscientious, responsible, orderly and well-organised. Their thinking is global and far-reaching and they look at problems from a broad perspective, perceiving various aspects of the issues they are engaging with. They live in accordance with the values they profess and, when the situation demands, they will stand in their defence without regard for the consequences. They voice their feelings and emotions openly and have excellent oral skills, with the ability to express their thoughts intelligibly and persuasively. However, imposing their views on others is alien to them, as is making themselves the focal point. Their focus is on other people; *counsellors* give of their time unstintingly and are ready to adapt to others and their needs if doing so will enable them to provide help in solving their problems or changing their lives for the better.

They display extraordinary tact and intuition in their interpersonal communication and are masters of the diplomatic. Their 'people skills' are outstanding and they have an immense gift both for empathy and for perceiving the feelings and emotions of others. They are very open towards other people, with a genuine interest in their problems and a sincere eagerness to help. With their highly developed intuition and perceptiveness, they are able to divine other people's thoughts, intentions and motives and are also quick to spot problems in interpersonal relationships. Being people of compromise and endowed with the gift of persuasion, they have the ability to build understanding and play an instrumental part in finding solutions which are favourable to all concerned. They are quick-witted, courteous and full of humour.

Counsellors are also excellent conversationalists, with the rare skill of listening to other people and the ability to elicit the best in them, spotting the potential and possibilities that have gone unremarked by others. Talking to *counsellors* inspires people to act, motivates them, lifts their spirits and sets them believing in their own powers. *Counsellors* also have a natural gift for drawing others to them; they are sought-after friends and colleagues. Their charm, warmth and sincerity, their natural attitude of acceptance and their wide range of interests mean that others enjoy being in their company, which gives them a sense of worth and a feeling of being appreciated. They are also natural leaders; where they go, others will follow, infected by their vision and faith that the venture will succeed.

Potential weaknesses

Counsellors are characterised by an extreme optimism and idealism. They usually see reality through rose-tinted glasses and have a tendency to marginalise negative occurrences, limitations and dangers; indeed, they might well fail to spot them at all. They quite often lose touch with reality as far as their ideas are concerned and are liable to subordinate their entire life to accomplishing one ruling notion, a course of action which may well narrow their world and cramp their perceptions. They can be critical and suspicious of opinions and viewpoints which diverge significantly from their own. With their inclination to do too much for others and even, at times, to manipulate them, they can also be overprotective or invasive.

Counsellors cope very badly with situations of conflict and have an exceptionally low threshold of tolerance for criticism levelled at them by others. They often prefer to keep quiet about their troubles or someone else's inappropriate behaviour rather than engage in a difficult conversation about the problem. They will do everything within their power to avoid unpleasant situations and their tendency to throw in the towel prematurely, yield and give up the fight for their own rights may manifest itself as a result. Ending destructive and toxic relationships is also something which frequently causes them difficulty. They have little appreciation for their own achievements and play down their role in successes; on the other hand, they are inclined to pin the blame for failures on themselves. They can have problems with accommodating themselves to socially accepted norms and conventions.

As a rule, *counsellors* are rather inflexible and find situations demanding improvisation hard to handle. They also have difficulty in making decisions on the basis of purely rational and logical premises, without reference to the social context. The awareness that a given decision may have an unfavourable impact on the lives of other people will often leave them paralysed and render them incapable of assessing a situation coolly and taking whatever action might be essential. The problems they sometimes have with carrying out objective evaluations stem from the same cause. Their sensitivity to the opinions and appraisals of others makes it difficult for them to function in an unfriendly environment and even more of a struggle in an outright hostile one. They incline towards perfectionism and this can reduce the efficacy of their activities, since they may well spend time improving things which suffice as they are. In general, they devote too little time to reflecting on their own lives and priorities and, in focusing on other people, they often forget about their own needs.

Personal development

Counsellors' personal development depends on the extent to which they make use of their natural potential and surmount the dangers inherent in their personality type. What follows are some practical tips which, together, form a specific guide that we might call *The Counsellor's Ten Commandments*.

Keep your focus fixed

You simply cannot help all of the people all of the time, any more than you can solve all of their problems. Keep your eyes firmly fixed on whatever is most crucial to you and stop letting yourself be distracted by less important matters. Do that and you will find yourself avoiding frustration and achieving more.

Stop fearing criticism

Quell your fear of expressing your own critical opinions and of accepting criticism from others. Criticism can be constructive. There is no law which says that it has to mean attacking people or undermining their worth.

Give some thought to yourself

Give some consideration to your own needs and find the time to reflect on your own life. Stop letting yourself be used and start learning to say 'no'. If you really want to help other people effectively, you also have to look after yourself.

Stop agonising over the plan and get going on the action

Instead of nit-picking over how you can improve on what you intend to do, simply get going and do it. Otherwise the day will come when you realise that you have spent your entire life perfecting your plans. Surely setting out to accomplish them and doing things well, but not necessarily to the point of sheer perfection, would be better than never doing anything at all?

Stop being afraid of conflict

Controversy does arise, even in our closest circles. Conflict need not necessarily be destructive. In fact, it very often helps us to identify problems and solve them! So, when conflicts emerge, stop hiding your head in the sand and, instead, express your point of view and feelings about the situation openly.

Be more practical

You have a natural inclination to come up with idealistic notions which sometimes have little in common with real life. Give some thought to the practical aspects and to how they can actually be accomplished in this imperfect world we live in.

Admit that you can make mistakes

None of us is infallible. Other people might well be absolutely right, or partially right and you might be partially or absolutely wrong. Accept that fact and learn to admit your mistakes.

Ask

Stop assuming that, if other people are silent, it means that they are indifferent or hostile. If you really want to know what they think, ask them.

Stop doing everything for others

Go ahead and help people to discover their potential and motivate them to act all you like – but then let them get on with it. You cannot live their lives for them, so allow them to take matters into their own hands, do things for themselves and learn from their own mistakes.

Take some time out

Try to get away from your responsibilities and duties once in a while and do something for the sheer pleasure, relaxation and fun of it. It will help you get a better perspective on things and when you go back to your tasks your mind and your thinking will be refreshed.

Well-known figures

Below is a list of some well-known people who match the *counsellor's* profile:

- **Abraham Maslow** (1908-1970); an American psychologist and the creator of 'Maslow's Hierarchy of Needs', he is considered to be one of the most important figures in the development of humanistic and transpersonal psychology.
- **Abraham Lincoln** (1809-1865); the 16th president of the United States.
- **Ronald Reagan** (1911-2004); the 40th president of the United States.
- **François Mitterrand** (1916-1996); the 21st president of France, he held office from 1981 to 1995.
- **Pope John Paul II** (Karol Jozef Wojtyla; 1920-2005); a Polish Roman Catholic priest, he became Archbishop of Krakow in 1964, was made a cardinal in 1967 and was elected to the papacy in 1978.
- **Sean Connery** (1930-2020); a Scottish screen actor whose filmography includes *The Name of the Rose*, he is the holder of numerous prestigious awards.
- **Mikhail Gorbachev** (1931-2022); a Russian politician and reformer, he was the last General

Secretary of the Central Committee of the Communist Party of the Soviet Union and the one and only person to hold office as president of the USSR.

- **Tommy Lee Jones** (born in 1946); an American screen actor whose filmography includes *Men in Black*.
- **Samuel Leroy Jackson** (born in 1948); an American screen actor whose filmography includes *Jurassic Park*, he is also a producer.
- **Kirstie Alley** (1951-2022); an American screen actress and comedian whose filmography includes *Look Who's Talking*.
- **Patrick Swayze** (1952-2009); an American screen actor whose filmography includes *Dirty Dancing*, he was also a dancer, singer and choreographer.
- **Tony Blair** (Anthony Charles Lynton Blair; born in 1953); a British politician and former leader of the Labour Party, he held office as prime minister of the United Kingdom three times in succession.
- **Barack Obama** (born in 1961); the 44th president of the United States.
- **Johnny Depp**, (John Christopher Depp II; born in 1963); an American screen actor whose filmography includes *Pirates of the Caribbean*.
- **Ben Stiller** (born in 1965); an American screen actor whose movies include *Meet the Fockers*, he is also a producer and director.

The Director (ENTJ)

THE ID16™© PERSONALITY TYPOLOGY

The Personality in a Nutshell

Life motto: I'll tell you what you need to do.

In brief, *directors* ...

are independent, active and decisive. Rational, logical and creative, when they analyse problems they look at the wider picture and are able to foresee the future consequences of human activities. They are characterised by optimism and a healthy sense of their own worth and are capable of transforming theoretical concepts into concrete, practical plans of action.

Visionaries, mentors and organisers, *directors* possess natural leadership skills. Their powerful personalities and direct and critical style can often have an intimidating effect, causing them problems in their interpersonal relationships.

The *director's* four natural inclinations:

- source of life energy: the exterior world
- mode of assimilating information: intuition
- decision-making mode: the mind
- lifestyle: organised

Similar personality types:

- the Innovator
- the Strategist
- the Logician

Statistical data:

- *directors* constitute between two and five per cent of the global community
- men predominate among *directors* (70 per cent)
- Holland is an example of a nation corresponding to the *director's* profile[7]

The Four-Letter Code

In terms of Jungian personality typology, the universal four-letter code for the *director* is ENTJ.

General character traits

Directors are independent, active and energetic. Their intuition is their guide and they have great faith in it. They are shrewd and clear-headed, with the ability to relate disparate facts and formulate apt generalisations. When

---

[7] What this means is not that all the residents of Holland fall within this personality type, but that Dutch society as a whole possesses a great many of the character traits typical of the *director*.

tackling problems, they analyse them from various angles and take the broad view.

Perception and thinking

Directors are quick to spot shifts in their surroundings and changing circumstances. Being exceptionally logical and rational, they excel at assessing a situation coolly, objectively and impartially. They think ahead, taking various possible scenarios into consideration and making the most of their ability to foresee the long-term consequences of a given course of action. Optimists by nature, they believe in their own capabilities and assume that they will succeed in doing whatever they undertake to do. This does not make them dreamers, though. On the contrary, they are very well aware of the effort required to accomplish the task in question. They prefer preparing thoroughly before tackling a job and cannot abide improvisation.

Decisions

Directors have the ability to transform theoretical and general concepts into concrete plans of action. They are visionaries and their vision serves them as a shot of energy and a motivating force. When faced with the necessity of making a decision, they like to have time to think it through, weighing up the various possibilities and then selecting the ones that seem to them to be the most logical and rational. Once the decision is made, they roll up their sleeves and get going without further ado.

As others see them

Other people perceive *directors* as powerful personalities, energetic, firm and decisive. They are widely appreciated as reliable and hard-working, though they can also have a reputation for being rather unapproachable and difficult to get close to. Their directness frequently intimidates and even antagonises or alienates others and they are sometimes deemed to be overly critical and demanding. Indeed, on occasion, their colleagues or their nearest and dearest will complain that satisfying them completely is "next to impossible".

Interior compass

Directors are highly independent, following neither prevailing views nor general trends. Their own thoughts and conclusions count for more with them than the opinions of other people and whether or not others share their convictions is a matter of indifference to them. They are strongly wedded to their own principles and outlook and present their opinions and viewpoints as something patently obvious.

As a rule, *directors* assume in advance that they are right and, indeed, that assumption often proves to be correct! Nonetheless, they are capable of verifying their views in the light of new data or changing circumstances. They like challenges and find repetitive and routine activities tedious to a fault. Being of an enquiring disposition, when a concept interests them they make an effort to go into it thoroughly and understand it properly, as well as giving thought to the possibilities of putting it to practical use. In general, they will acquire a wide range of interests in their youth and, over the course of time, will enrich and systemise their knowledge, constructing an internal map of the world which is completely their own and enables them to comprehend reality and the phenomena that occur in it.

Organisational modes

Directors have a tremendous thirst for knowledge and will pose themselves questions and then seek the answers to them. Identifying cause-and-effect relationships comes easily to them, as does discerning the principles which govern the world and human behaviour. Rational arguments are what carry weight with them and they have zero tolerance for logical inconsistency or incoherence in a concept, internal contradictions in a system and overlapping areas of authority, not to mention inefficiency, in an organisation. They have a remarkable love of order and dislike wastefulness and chaos.

Perfectionists by nature, *directors* are quite capable of working incessantly to improve everything they come into contact with. They make highly effective use of their time and have an inbuilt ability for multitasking; watching television and reading a book at one and the same time, for instance, is a piece of cake for them. When they undertake a task, they endeavour to carry it out in the best possible way; consciously doing anything to less than their full capabilities is completely beyond them. They see things through to the end and successfully finishing a job gives them a sense of satisfaction – and liberation, since they are then free to involve themselves in the next task!

Attitude to others

Directors are exceptionally independent, assertive and immune to attempts to manipulate or pressurise them. Other people's criticism rolls off them like water off a duck's back. They are quite capable of saying 'no' and will not allow themselves to be used. When they are convinced of something, the thoughts of others on the subject are of no concern to them whatsoever, although they do make an exception in the case of prominent figures and authorities who enjoy widespread recognition.

They often demonstrate a dismal failure when it comes to comprehending opinions that oppose their own. Discerning other people's feelings is also problematic for them and they are normally unaware of the fact that their critical remarks and bluntly expressed opinions are frequently hurtful to the person at whom they are levelled.

Leisure

Directors are titanic workers and generally incapable of relaxing. Passive leisure is foreign to their nature and even if they happen not to be engaged in a physical activity, their brains will be beavering away nineteen to the dozen, constantly analysing new possibilities and ideas and pondering over how to turn them into reality. They enjoy learning new things and broadening their horizons, so they will happily spend their free time augmenting their knowledge and acquiring new information.

In the face of stress

In the face of prolonged periods of stress, *directors* will sometimes lose faith in themselves and become highly critical of their own achievements. At that stage, they tend to feel swamped by their responsibilities and duties, as well as fearing that they have lost control of the situation. In their efforts to relieve their stress, they may then turn to using substances.

Socially

Directors rarely show their own emotions and are rather sparing in their praise, often coming across as cold, reserved and unapproachable. In reality, though, they are capable of opening up to people to whom they have given their trust.

They can also be highly sentimental and sensitive, despite giving no outward sign of what they are feeling. Indeed, those around them have difficulty in discerning that aspect of their personality – or even, perhaps, in believing that it exists at all!

The company *directors* value most highly is that of intelligent and competent people from whom they can learn something. They respect those who are able to prove the legitimacy of their arguments and can both support their own convictions and defend them vigorously. By the same token, they will often ignore people who fail to rise to that challenge, since they have no grasp of the fact that not everyone shares their relish for disputes and confrontations, but wrongly assume that the inability to voice one's beliefs openly and an unwillingness to fight in defence of one's reasoning is tantamount to a lack of personal points of view.

Directors expect rational and sensible behaviour from others and are incapable of understanding those who are guided by anything other than logic. They dislike repeating themselves and, if other people reject their viewpoint at the outset, they will make no effort to convince them otherwise. They prize freedom, which is why they will sometimes avoid relationships which place limits on their independence. They themselves accord freedom to others and have no inclination to be invasive.

Amongst friends

Contrary to the suppositions of many, good relationships with others matter greatly to *directors*. However, they operate on the premise that any such relationship should serve a concrete purpose, such as solving problems, for instance, or carrying out tasks or helping others to discover their potential.

Spending time amongst people infuses *directors* with energy and they will most readily strike up a friendship with those who share their outlook and convictions or who will broaden their horizons by providing them with new information and experiences. Other people also perceive them as interesting conversationalists and are often inspired and spurred into action by an encounter with them. However, some people are either intimidated or antagonised and alienated by their self-assurance and the firmness with which they voice their views. These two aspects of their character are often taken as arrogance, especially since they usually say what they think, heedless of the circumstances and the feelings of others. They are often just as direct in their questions, which distresses or embarrasses a great many of the people they talk to, some of whom, overwhelmed by their categoric statements, find themselves incapable of voicing their views or thoughts in their presence.

Directors themselves feel absolutely at home in the company of other strong personalities, even when their opinions differ. They appreciate people who are capable of articulating their convictions clearly and have no fear of confrontation. They most often make friends with *innovators, strategists, administrators* and other *directors,* but struggle to find a common language with *artists, presenters* and *protectors.*

As life partners

Directors take their responsibilities in a life partnership extremely seriously. Within the family, they will normally assume the role of leader and sentinel. Actions speak loudest to them, so they show their devotion not so much by way of tender gestures and warm words as through doing something concrete.

Their nature renders them both very insensitive to their partner's feelings and completely unaware of their emotional needs; they may love them dearly and yet, at one and the same time, have absolutely no grasp whatsoever of what they are experiencing and feeling or of their emotional state. However, with a little effort, they can change this and if they are in a relationship with a person of romantic disposition, then making that effort is an absolute must! *Directors* themselves have few emotional needs. They like to know that they are important to, and loved by, their life partner, but they do not, as a rule, expect endearing words, compliments and frequent assurances of love and affection. Their devotion and sense of responsibility for their family is a strong bonding element in their relationships.

Mutual respect is a characteristic feature of *directors'* life partnerships, as is supporting one another's personal growth. They value a relationship which serves as their mainstay and inspiration, and if it stops living up to their expectations they will often walk away from it. Another potential threat is their propensity for workaholism. Usually successful in their professional lives, they are sought-after employees. In many cases they will frequently be away from home and, when they actually are there, will often be absorbed in work-related matters, a state of affairs which normally gives rise to all kinds of tension. The positive attitude *directors* have towards confrontations, disputes and criticism, which they view as factors conducive to self-development and learning, can be a serious problem for romantically inclined and sensitive partners.

The natural candidates for a *director's* life partner are people of a personality type akin to their own: *innovators, strategists* or *logicians*. Nonetheless, experience has taught us that people are also capable of creating happy and successful relationships despite what would seem to be an evident typological incompatibility. Moreover, the differences between two partners can lend added dynamics to a relationship and engender personal development. Indeed, to *directors*, this is a prospect that appears more attractive than the vision of a harmonious relationship in which concord and full, mutual understanding hold sway.

As parents

Directors take their role as a parent just as seriously as their life partnership. They help their children to understand the world, teaching them to think for themselves, nurturing their development and placing great emphasis on their education. However, they also make heavy demands of them, as well as expecting respect, obedience and compliance with the rules they set. In extreme cases, they might adopt a high-handed attitude or even operate like overbearing dictators. As a rule, they are unstinting in their criticism of their offspring, but reserved in their praise, and they are also often unperceptive of their emotional needs.

Directors are usually impatient with their children's repeated mistakes and oversights, while sometimes failing to perceive that their expectations go beyond what a child is capable of and that, when the results are poor, this may not be the outcome of laziness, thoughtlessness or a frivolous attitude. Their offspring normally strive to live up to their expectations and avoid inadvertences in order to escape being exposed to their criticism. However, with puberty, a time of crisis often emerges; at that stage, teenage children cease to accept their *director* parent's rules and usually revolt against their discipline and regulations. *Directors* themselves struggle to come to terms with their offspring's ever burgeoning independence.

When *directors* succeed in avoiding those mistakes, they are superb parents and excellent figures of authority to their children. They are also instrumental in their development, encouraging them to explore the world, acquire knowledge and face up to challenges. As a result, their offspring usually grow up to become responsible, creative and independent adults with no fear of taking up the gauntlets that life throws at their feet.

Work and career paths

Their professional career is a vital element of *directors*' lives and they are generally devoted to their work and frequently ascend to the highest of posts.

Quick to identify new challenges and problems, they are just as fast in tackling them and equally swift when it comes to spotting potential and doing something about it. Their thinking is global and far-reaching and they are visionaries, first delineating their goals and then applying themselves zealously to accomplishing them. When seeking solutions, they usually take the long-term view; their thinking goes beyond the current situation and they have the ability to foresee factors which may appear in the future. All of this, combined with their reliability, responsibility and predisposition for hard work, makes them sought-after employees. They are able to devote all their energy to accomplishing tasks they believe in. On the other hand, they are incapable of committing themselves wholeheartedly to undertakings which they believe to be unrealistic, fuzzy or incoherent.

Views on workplace hierarchy

Directors appreciate competent superiors who have got where they are on merit and have concrete achievements under their belt. They also value those who give their subordinates freedom in carrying out the tasks assigned to them.

As part of a team

When *directors* work as part of a team, they seize the initiative and, willingly or not, take responsibility on their shoulders. As such, they are perceived as natural leaders and, indeed, where they go, others will follow. They have the ability to motivate other people and put them in the frame of mind to achieve the goals that have been set, firing them with optimism and faith in their success. They are also capable of drawing out the best in others and of helping them realise their potential. However, their method of assistance is extremely unlikely to involve providing ready-made solutions or doing everything for them; as a rule, they will throw people in at the deep end.

Superb mentors and coaches, they assist people in identifying their long-term aims and then transforming them into short-term action plans. In positions of authority, they keep their subordinates informed both of impending changes in their environment and of future challenges, and they keep a firm eye on the effectiveness and efficiency of the company or the department for which they are responsible.

Tasks

When *directors* begin work on an undertaking, they define the measures necessary to accomplish it and then find the right people to carry it out while they move on, eager to devote themselves to the next new task. They are excellent at handling the kind of complex problems which other people are only too happy to avoid like the plague and are also good strategists, with the ability to define priorities with pinpoint accuracy.

Companies and institutions

Directors fit in well in corporations and businesses which provide prospects for promotion, apply clear rules for the game and reward their employees for concrete achievements. On the other hand, they will be restless and unhappy in companies where compliance with the accepted regulations or detailed procedures takes precedence over creative ideas and results.

Work style

Directors make for ideal managers in fields demanding organisational skills and strategic planning, such as creating new systems from scratch or implementing innovative solutions, organising teams and managing companies in the throes of transformation. Their ability to multitask means that they are also capable of coordinating a host of different ventures and projects at one and the same time.

They will very often make it to the very top of their company's hierarchical tree and are thus often directors ... hence the name for this personality type. They like working with people they can rely on and who fulfil the tasks assigned to them, sharing their enthusiasm and zeal for work with them. By the same token, they find passiveness, lethargy and a lack of commitment intolerable. Impatient with those who fail to keep pace, drag out their tasks or continually make the same mistakes, they are capable of being direct, sometimes to the point of brutal frankness, when evaluating their achievements, paying no regard to the fact that they might hurt or offend them. They also have no difficulty in parting company with employees who fail to live up to their expectations. Other people's feelings are rarely a matter of concern to them; making the right decision matters more to them than winning and keeping the favour of those around them. A want of order, waste, excessive bureaucracy and overly complex procedures all irritate them immensely.

When *directors* look at problems, they do so objectively, with no concern for sentimental or emotional considerations. They have no attachment to particular solutions either, and are ready to discard them the moment they fail to perform as required. Who introduced them and how long they have been in place is of no great significance to them and they are capable of coldly eliminating any that are impractical or ineffective. Indeed, they are able do away with time-honoured work methods, practices and habits in one fell swoop and, when they are convinced that their ideas are the way forward, they may well set out to accomplish them at any price – by violating procedures and paying no heed at all to the human cost.

Professions

Knowledge of our own personality profile and natural preferences provides us with invaluable help in choosing the optimal path in our professional careers. Experience has shown that, while *directors* are perfectly able to work and find fulfilment in a range of fields, their personality type naturally predisposes them to the following fields and professions:

- administrator
- artistic director
- CEO
- computer systems analyst
- credit analyst

- development director
- entrepreneur
- executive director
- human resources
- IT specialist
- journalist
- judge
- lawyer
- life coach
- loans and credit
- manager
- marketing
- marketing director
- musician
- politician
- project coordinator
- investor
- psychologist
- public administration
- public relations
- scientist
- urban / rural planning
- tertiary educator
- writer

Potential strengths and weaknesses

Like any other personality type, *directors* have their potential strengths and weaknesses and this potential can be cultivated in a variety of ways. *Directors'* personal happiness and professional fulfilment depend on whether they make the most of the 'pluses' offered by their personality type and face up to its inherent dangers. Here, then is a SUMMARY of those 'pluses' and dangers:

Potential strengths

Directors have a healthy sense of their own worth and possess natural leadership skills. Capable of firing others with optimism and faith in their success, they themselves brim with energy, enthusiasm for work and the ability to put their whole heart into accomplishing tasks they believe in. Their vision gives them energy and they are thus able to work extremely hard in order to accomplish it. They are characterised by a positive attitude to tasks and problems, being well aware of the potential difficulties but believing that they will succeed in meeting the challenge. With their serious approach to their responsibilities, one thing is certain: once they take on a job, they will see it through to the end. Fresh concepts and ideas interest them and they are open to new solutions, possessing the ability to assimilate them and apply them when accomplishing their own tasks.

Independent, active and creative, they have the ability to transform theoretical and general concepts into concrete plans of action. They approach their work very seriously and expect the same of others. Their focus is on the merits of the matter and they refuse to allow less crucial aspects to distract them. When analysing facts and data, they are cool and objective, giving emotion and bias short shrift. They are able to manage money and other resources effectively and efficiently and are well-organised and extremely hard-working, as well as being direct and straightforward; no one will ever need to spend time wondering what their opinion on a given topic might be. *Directors* say what they think. They are good oral communicators and public speaking and debate pose no major problems for them.

By nature, they interested in self-development, acquiring knowledge and self-improvement in various areas of their lives. With their powerful, assertive personality, they cope well in difficult situations of conflict and are capable of putting an end to friendships and acquaintanceships if they become uncomfortable or destructive. They are open to constructive criticism. Given their love of order, they make superb organisers, as well as excelling in orchestrating the work of others, having a flair for creating systems which function effectively and efficiently and being good strategists, with the ability to define priorities with pinpoint accuracy.

Potential weaknesses

Directors pursue confrontation. Their love of tough polemics and dispute means that they are seen as difficult and critical conversationalists, while their powerful personalities often have an intimidating effect on others and can even arouse anxieties and fears. When they argue a point with other people, they strive to prove that they are absolutely right and completely 'wipe the floor' with their opponents; rarely will they be able to admit that someone who holds a different view could be right, even if only in part. They have difficulty in understanding the needs of others when they differ from their own and, by their very nature, are insensitive to other people's feelings and reactions. Expressing their own feelings and emotions comes just as hard to them and they are at rather a loss in situations demanding that they read those of others. They fare no better when it comes to listening, and have a tendency to criticise any opinion whatsoever if it fails to concur with their own point of view.

Highly demanding of themselves, they are no more sparing in the high standards they require others to meet, even though they generally set the benchmark too high for many. When they call other people's attention to wastefulness, perfunctoriness or other oversights, they are often extremely severe and can even be harsh to the point of roughness. At the same time, they are very stinting in their praise when things are going well, setting no store by positive reinforcement in the form of encouragement, approval and rewards. Seizing the initiative comes naturally to them and they are reluctant to share responsibility with others, as well as displaying a frequent tendency to make premature and ill-considered decisions. In extreme cases, their pursuit of authority can see them acting dogmatically and high-handedly towards those they seek to oversee; on occasion, they may well even humiliate them. When they find themselves in stressful situations, they are liable to explode in anger and manifest other forms of aggressive behaviour. They may also endeavour to relieve their tension by overeating or abusing alcohol.

The dogmatism and extremely rational approach to life exhibited by directors, together with their inability to identify other people's needs, are all characteristics which often cause them problems and can lead to a specific form of social isolation, whereby they are highly valued at work but have no friends to speak of. With no real grasp as to why this should be, they will sometimes begin to suspect other people of wishing them ill or conspiring against them. Those who are either incapable of adapting to their ideas and plans or have no wish to do so are another frequent source of frustration to them.

Personal development

Directors' personal development depends on the extent to which they make use of their natural potential and surmount the dangers inherent in their personality type. What follows are some practical tips which, together, form a specific guide that we might call *The Director's Ten Commandments*.

Admit that you can make mistakes

Things may be more complex than they seem to you. You may not always be in the right. Bring that thought to the forefront of your mind before you start accusing others or pointing out their mistakes and reproaching them.

Criticise less

Not everyone is able to handle constructive criticism. In fact, dispensing it frankly can have a destructive effect in many cases. Studies have shown that praising positive behaviour, albeit limited, motivates people more than criticising negative conduct.

Praise more

Make the most of every occasion to appreciate other people, say something nice to them and praise them for something they have done. At work, value people not only for the job they do, but also for who they are. Then wait and see. The difference will come as a pleasant surprise!

Stop trying to control absolutely everything

Eagerness to control everything will only lead to your eventual frustration. Keep your eye on the most important things and leave less crucial matters to others – or even just let them run their own course.

Listen to people

Show an interest in other people, even when you disagree with them or are convinced that they are wrong. Save your response until you have heard them out. The ability to listen could well revolutionise your relationship with others.

Stop blaming others for your problems

Your problems may not only be caused by others; they might also be caused by you! You, too, are capable of oversights and mistakes. You, too, can be the root of a problem.

Treat others kindly

People want to be treated as something more than simply the performers of tasks. They long for their emotions, feelings and enthusiasms to be perceived. Mix with people, communicate with them, try to put yourself in their shoes and understand what they are going through, what fascinates them, what worries them and what they fear.

Control your emotions

If you feel that you might well explode, then try to relax, wind down and think about something else for a moment. Outbursts of anger help neither you nor the people around you.

Be more understanding

Show others more warmth. Remember that not everyone should be assigned the same tasks, because not everyone is skilled in the same fields. If others are unable to cope with a task, this is not always a sign of their ill will or laziness.

Learn to take things easy

Taking time out is not synonymous with wasting precious hours, minutes and seconds and there is no legislation requiring you to feel guilty if you set work to one side and relax or do something for the sheer pleasure of it. What will actually happen is that your batteries will be recharged in the process; and that can only make you more efficient and effective at work!

Well-known figures

Below is a list of some well-known people who match the *director's* profile:

- **Jack London** (John Griffith Chaney; 1876-1916); an American writer whose works include *The Call of the Wild*, he was also a naturalist and was deemed one of the most romantic figures of his time.
- **Franklin Delano Roosevelt** (1882-1945); the 32nd president of the United States.

- **Edward Teller** (1908-2003); a Hungarian physicist of Jewish origins, he was a member of America's Manhattan Engineer District, better known as the Manhattan Project, which researched and developed the first atomic bombs.

- **Benny Goodman** (1909-1986); an American jazz musician, clarinettist and bandleader, he was dubbed 'the King of Swing'.

- **Richard M. Nixon** (1913-1994); the 37th president of the United States.

- **Margaret Thatcher** (1925-2013); a British politician and leader of the Conservative Party, she held office as prime minister of the United Kingdom three times in succession, from 1979 to 1990, and earned the nickname of 'the Iron Lady'.

- **Patrick Stewart** (born in 1940); a British stage and screen actor whose filmography includes *Star Trek*.

- **Harrison Ford** (born in 1942); an American screen actor whose filmography includes the *Indiana Jones* series.

- **Hillary Clinton** (born in 1947); an America political activist, former Secretary of State and US senator, she is married to the 42nd president, Bill Clinton.

- **Al Gore** (born in 1948); the 45th vice-president of the United States.

- **Bill Gates** (born in 1955); an American entrepreneur and philanthropist, co-founder of the Microsoft company and one of the richest people in the world.

- **Whoopi Goldberg** (Caryn Elaine Johnson; born in 1955); an American screen actress, comedienne, political activist, writer and television host whose filmography includes *Ghost*, she has won some of America's most prestigious entertainment industry awards.

- **Steve Jobs** (1955-2011); an American entrepreneur and co-founder of the Apple company.
- **Quentin Tarantino** (born in 1963); an American director, screenwriter, cinematographer, producer and actor whose filmography includes *Kill Bill*.

The Enthusiast (ENFP)

THE ID16™© PERSONALITY TYPOLOGY

The Personality in a Nutshell

Life motto: We'll manage!

In brief, *enthusiasts* …

are energetic, enthusiastic and optimistic. Capable of enjoying life and looking ahead to the future, they are dynamic, quick-witted and creative. They have a liking for people in general, value honest and genuine relationships and are warm, sincere and emotional. Criticism is something they handle badly. With their gift for empathy and ability to perceive people's needs, feelings and motives, they both inspire others and infect them with their own enthusiasm.

They love to be at the centre of events and are flexible and capable of improvising. Their inclination leads towards idealistic notions. Being easily distracted, they have problems with seeing things through to the end.

The *enthusiast's* four natural inclinations:

- source of life energy: the exterior world
- mode of assimilating information: intuition
- decision-making mode: the heart
- lifestyle: spontaneous

Similar personality types:

- the Counsellor
- the Idealist
- the Mentor

Statistical data:

- *enthusiasts* constitute between five and eight per cent of the global community
- women predominate among *enthusiasts* (60 per cent)
- Italy is an example of a nation corresponding to the *enthusiast's* profile[8]

The Four-Letter Code

In terms of Jungian personality typology, the universal four-letter code for the *enthusiast* is ENFP.

General character traits

Enthusiasts love life and have the ability to enjoy every moment. Wherever the action is, that is where *enthusiasts* like to be. Optimists by nature, they view the future with hope and have faith in people. They like change and fresh experiences and constantly hunger to explore new concepts, discover new places and meet new people.

---

[8] What this means is not that all the residents of Italy fall within this personality type, but that Italian society as a whole possesses a great many of the character traits typical of the *enthusiast*.

Enthusiasts will always make an effort to be at the centre of things and they need contact with other people. When they are condemned to being alone and cut off from the world, they descend into a state of apathy. They value good relationships with other people and the liking of those around them matters a great deal to them. Nonetheless, it is not something they will pursue at any price, such as behaving in a way which flies in the face of their convictions. They dislike being subjected to pressure, controlled, checked on and pigeonholed and, by the same token, they themselves respect the freedom and independence of others.

Perception and thinking

Enthusiasts are curious about the world, constantly seek fresh sources of inspiration and are usually interested in new concepts and stimulating ideas. They have no difficulty in assimilating complex notions and abstract theories. Their approach to problems and tasks is creative and often innovative. Once they have identified the connections between disparate facts and occurrences, they are quicker than most to reach a solution. They will sometimes discern hidden meanings and signs in the events and situations around them. As a rule, they are original, inventive and orientated towards the future and are also characterised by incredible optimism and enthusiasm … hence the name for this personality type.

Their attitude inspires others and gives them faith that they will succeed, while they themselves are usually firmly convinced that any venture they undertake will prosper. Obstacles and setbacks thus have no power to perturb or discourage them. When they are aware that an opportunity has appeared, they are ready to take a risk and launch themselves into uncharted waters, just as long as there is a chance of making the most of it. Indeed, they find the very thought of unexploited chances difficult to bear.

Attitude to others

Enthusiasts have an ability to influence other people's behaviour and even to manipulate them. They usually put this skill to positive use in encouraging others to discover their talents, for instance, or motivating them to act or building up their faith in themselves.

When they tackle problems, they are capable of getting to the crux of the matter without being deceived by outward appearances or illusions. They are characterised by their remarkable empathy, which enables them to read other people's feelings, emotions and even their hidden motives, to say nothing of the fact that they are often capable of describing someone else's situation, feelings and needs better than that person can themselves. On occasion, they may well take on the role of 'spokesperson' for others. As many people see it, their extraordinary interpersonal skills, such as their ability to fathom out someone else's secrets, seem to verge on the magical. There is nothing supernatural involved, though: *enthusiasts'* intuition is, quite simply, highly developed and they are masterly observers, paying attention not only to words, but also to non-verbal signals.

Helping others is a source of enormous joy to them and they are genuinely delighted when, thanks to their assistance, people begin to make the most of their potential and gain faith in their own powers. On the other hand, when their efforts fail to produce results or when people are either unwilling or unable to avail themselves of their own possibilities, they will be thoroughly downcast.

They are not reclusive by nature; other people are a part of their lives and thus occupy a great deal of their thoughts. As a rule, they excel at reading people's emotions and feelings – even from afar! When they read a letter or e-mail from someone they know, they are able to put themselves in their shoes, imagining what they are going through and how they are feeling. They will frequently put other people's needs before their own.

As others see them

Enthusiasts' sincerity, warmth and genuine interest acts on others like a magnet, although some people are irritated by their talkativeness and their extreme optimism, which is sometimes taken for naïvety, as well as by their unpunctuality and unreliability.

While it is, indeed, true that, on occasion, they may fail to keep their word, this is neither a conscious action nor is it the deliberate disrespect which some people consider it to be. *Enthusiasts* never make a promise while actually having every intention of breaking it. However, what does happen is that they become so excited by fresh challenges that they are quite capable of completely forgetting their previous undertakings and giving themselves over entirely to new ones, until the next fresh stimulus comes along. At times, this attitude can mean that they are labelled as unreliable, chaotic and lacking in substance.

Enthusiasts themselves are irritated by unnatural behaviour and find it difficult to understand the reasons for which some people try to pretend to be someone other than they are. Passiveness, scepticism and chronic pessimism also set their teeth on edge and they simply cannot comprehend those who are always moaning and complaining about everything, and who invariably take a critical stance towards new ideas and concepts.

Decisions

When *enthusiasts* are faced with making decisions, they will happily turn to others for their opinion, listen to their advice and avail themselves of their experience. In general, they rely on the views of experts and widely acknowledged authorities. They operate on the basis of both their usually unerring intuition and their remarkable 'feel' for a situation. The way in which a given decision or action will be received by those around them is something they never fail to bear in mind, as is its impact on other people. Indeed, not only are they incapable of proceeding without giving due consideration to the human factor, but they also mistrust those who claim to rely solely on hard data and facts.

Organisational modes

In *enthusiasts*, the force driving them to act is, of course, their enthusiasm! They frequently view the world through rose-tinted glasses and fail to discern potential dangers. As a result, they are liable to involve themselves in hazardous ventures and undertake risky activities. Being highly spontaneous and flexible, it is unusual for them to devote overmuch time to deliberation and preparation; once an idea strikes them, they are far more likely to launch into action as soon as they can. On the whole, they cope better with a number of smaller undertakings than with one substantial task demanding months of systematic work and, in general, they have no liking for routine and repetitive activities such as paperwork, cleaning and shopping, perceiving them as restricting, burdensome and a waste of time which would be better spent doing more exciting and creative things.

Enthusiasts are not the best of organisers and planners and their actions tend to be more impulse-led. They often have difficulties in making the best use of their time, as well as in managing money, and their financial situation can often be unstable. It might happen that they will spend large sums on luxury items, only to find themselves needing to borrow money to buy the staples. They are also readier than many to reach for their credit cards.

Communication

Enthusiasts are excellent oral communicators and will readily join in conversations and discussions when they are with a group of people. Speaking in public presents them with no major problems and they are capable of expressing challenging issues clearly and comprehensibly, often bringing interesting stories and colourful examples into play when they do. They also have the gift of persuasion and are capable of convincing others that they are right.

Amongst their friends and acquaintances, they take a delight in telling jokes and amusing stories about their own lives, often with added embellishments! What they have to say brims with emotion and enthusiasm, leading many of their listeners to envy them their adventures and vibrantly fascinating lives. On the other hand, they are frequently wholly unaware of the fact that they might well be dominating a discussion or even, quite simply, taking it over entirely and not letting anyone else get a word in edgeways. On the contrary: even when they are delivering what is, in fact, a monologue, they can be under the impression that they are having an amazing conversation. Their loquaciousness can be another problem, since they are capable of talking for hours on end, holding forth in a veritable river of words, which is something that other people can find fairly unbearable.

In the face of stress

Situations of conflict are often a source of stress to *enthusiasts*, as are displays of indifference or criticism from others. During prolonged periods of tension, they can sometimes become stubborn or start suspecting other people of wishing them ill. Fortunately, though, they are also capable of relaxing 'to the max' and completely wiping their problems, responsibilities and obligations from their minds when they go into 'time-out mode'.

In general, they prefer active leisure pursuits and also greatly enjoy family and social get-togethers, to say nothing of happily organising them themselves. At times, they will try and unload their stress by turning to substances or thrill-seeking.

Socially

Enthusiasts are quick to strike up new acquaintanceships and are extremely outgoing and approachable. As a result, other people will often feel as if they have known them for ages when, in fact, they have really only just met. Highly flexible in their contact with others, they do all they can to respond to their needs, sometimes neglecting their own in the process. All of these characteristics mean that other people feel good in their company.

Enthusiasts themselves love being in the midst of people and the acknowledgement, acceptance and interest of others matters a great deal to them. They approach their interpersonal relationships with extraordinary enthusiasm and have the ability to amuse people and shower them with praise, to say nothing of adding a *soupçon* of coquetry to their dealings with others. However, they also display uncanny intuition, tact and empathy, knowing exactly how to behave in a given situation and possessing the ability to adapt to the circumstances and emotional state of others.

They are eager to meet new people and, with their thirst for bonds which are both genuine and absolute, they have a tendency to seek ideals in terms of the 'perfect friend', or the 'perfect partner for life'. Good relations with others are highly important to them and they will do everything in their power to prevent conflict from raising its head. In general, they are incapable of consciously criticising other people; indeed, they will even struggle when it comes to voicing a critical opinion about someone else's views or calling attention to their inappropriate behaviour, preferring in general to remain silent about the problem and stifle their own negative emotions.

Enthusiasts find indifference and silence on the part of others very hard to bear. They are incapable both of understanding behaviour of that kind and of coping with it. As a rule, they assume, entirely wrongly, that a lack of reaction signifies hostility.

Amongst friends

Enthusiasts prize honest and genuine relationships. Meeting new people, talking to friends and acquaintances and spending time with them make up the essence of their lives, which lose all colour and savour when they are cut off from others.

They are very quick to read other people and, after no more than a few minutes of conversation with someone, will often know that they are simply not on the same wavelength and that a mutual understanding is never really going to happen. Their relationships with others are of the highest importance to them. They usually have a host of friends and acquaintances and are the life and soul of any gathering. People are eager to spend time with them, since *enthusiasts* brim with positive energy and humour, as well as being deeply sincere, showing warmth towards others, respecting their individualism and setting store by their needs. Their acquaintanceships are highly intense, but tend to be short-lived; when they meet new people, they turn the full beam of their attention and energy onto them and will sometimes forget those who came before.

With their outgoing nature, they usually express their emotions openly and are unstinting in their praise of others. They have difficulty in striking up a friendship with people who are disinclined to externalise their feelings or to say what they think and often take that kind of behaviour as a sign of dislike. A cold, unfriendly and inescapable environment, such as a workplace, will cause them enormous discomfort and strain. They find spending time with acquaintances, friends and family the best way to relieve stress.

Enthusiasts are almost always surrounded by people and have a host of friends and acquaintances, although the majority of these relationships are superficial in nature. So many things attract their attention and they are so easily distracted that even their closest acquaintances often feel as if they will never have them entirely to themselves. As a rule, *enthusiasts* have only a few really close friends. They most frequently tend to be *counsellors*, *idealists*, *presenters* or other *enthusiasts* and, most rarely, *inspectors*, *administrators* and *practitioners*.

As life partners

Enthusiasts make highly devoted and caring partners, bringing warmth, enthusiasm, creativity and a sense of humour to their relationships. Their partner's happiness and well-being matter greatly to them and they do all they can to meet their needs, showing them enormous warmth and unstintingly offering them tender words and affectionate gestures.

They, too, need warmth, closeness and acceptance and, given that they are profoundly affected by any kind of cutting remark, unflattering comment or even indifference on the part of their nearest and dearest, they are easily hurt. However, since discussing tough and unpleasant issues is anathema to them, they will try to avoid conflicts and arguments at any price, much preferring to suffer rather than tell their partner that something has upset or distressed them. They will thus often be incapable of withdrawing from bad or destructive relationships.

Enthusiasts keep a constant eye on the state of their relationships and are quick to sense problems. When they do crop up, the *enthusiast* partner will be deeply affected by them and will also feel responsible for them. By the same token, if the relationship ends, they will often reproach themselves for not having done everything within their power to save it. As a rule, they take their responsibilities very seriously, although it can happen that they themselves are the cause of their relationship troubles, since their love of change and experimenting, their dreams of 'perfect love' and their aversion to routine might lead them to seek experiences outside their partnership, this being a particular danger when their 'other half' does not share their fascinations, enthusiasm and curiosity about the world. On the other hand, their care for those they love and their deeply rooted values have an enormous bearing on the permanence of their relationships.

The natural candidates for an *enthusiast's* life partner are people of a personality type akin to their own; *counsellors*, *idealists* or *mentors*. Building mutual understanding and harmonious relations will be easier in a union of that kind. Nonetheless, experience has taught us that people are also capable of creating happy and successful relationships despite what would seem to be an evident typological incompatibility. Moreover, the differences between two partners can lend added dynamics to a relationship and engender personal development. Indeed, for many people, this is a prospect that appears more attractive than the vision of a harmonious relationship in which concord and full, mutual understanding hold sway.

As parents

Enthusiasts take their parental responsibilities extremely seriously. They nurture their offspring's development and pass on the values which they themselves believe in, surround them with warmth, give them faith in their own powers and are unstinting in their affection and praise. At times, their older children, in particular, might well quite simply feel embarrassed by the love and tenderness their *enthusiast* parent lavishes on them, especially in front of their peers. Nonetheless, they appreciate the fact that they can always count on their spiritual and emotional support in difficult moments.

Enthusiasts' inborn aversion to repetitive and routine activities means that helping their children with everyday tasks of a practical nature, such as their homework, presents them with a considerable challenge. Nonetheless, in the majority of cases, their concern for their offspring's well-being wins through and they are able to force themselves to do the kind of tasks they have little liking for.

Their nature usually has something of the child about it and they are great partners-in-fun to their children. They love games, adventures and all kinds of experiments, so 'fun time' spent together is an attraction not only for their offspring, but for the *enthusiast* parents themselves. In turn, their inconsistency and changeability are a source of problems, as they switch from being extremely easy-going and understanding one day to stern and impatient the next, an approach which sometimes means that their children are unable to grasp the behavioural model their parent is following and lose their sense of stability and security. *Enthusiasts* also frequently have problems with disciplining their offspring and ensuring that they do what they are supposed to. However, things are radically different if their children's behaviour violates the principles they themselves profess. When that happens, their reaction will be swift, for *enthusiasts* firmly believe that there are boundaries which should never be crossed.

Once adults, their children have fond memories of the carefree fun they had with their *enthusiast* parent and of the warm and loving atmosphere of their childhood home. They also appreciate the way they respected their choices, demonstrated their support and taught them to care about other people.

Work and career paths

Enthusiasts succeed in all sorts of professions which are as different as chalk and cheese. They usually have a wealth of professional experience, since many of them change jobs relatively frequently and may well switch sectors several times over the course of their working lives. They are most attracted to work which offers possibilities for creativity, experimenting and solving problems. On the other hand, they cannot bear bureaucracy, hierarchies, routine, repetitive tasks and rigid procedures and find cold, hierarchical and formalised corporate environments very hard to handle.

Tasks

Enthusiasts will throw themselves into tasks which provide practical opportunities to give voice to their convictions and put the values they hold dear into effect. They fit in well in institutions geared towards the good of society and bringing about tangible and positive changes in the life of the local community or the country or on a global scale, since they like knowing that their activities have a positive impact on other people's lives and help them to solve their problems. When they are working on a task in which they believe, they will invest all their energy in it, so there will be no need to supervise or motivate them. However, kick-starting them into action on jobs they find tedious or which are inconsistent with their system of values will prove rather a challenge. They also have no liking for working individually and, in professional terms, their worst-case scenario would be a 'static' job, performed alone and demanding long-term focus on a single task. What they enjoy is team work providing movement, variety and frequent change.

Skills and stumbling blocks

Enthusiasts cope excellently with tasks demanding interpersonal skills, inventiveness, flexibility and the ability to improvise. They gravitate towards the action, wherever it might be. In general, they are a pillar of support to their colleagues, readily doing all they can to meet their needs and successfully building compromises. On the one hand, they are highly inventive and creative; on the other, they are quick to become bored and have difficulty in continuing with a task they have already begun once a new and more interesting project appears on the horizon. They often have trouble organising their time, determining their priorities and focusing on what they should be doing. Their propensity is to be easily distracted and, in the battle for their attention, it is usually the newest and most powerful stimulus that will emerge victorious. Uniformity and bureaucracy irritate them immensely and they will sometimes rebel openly against burdensome procedures and regulations which they consider to be unrealistic or impractical. They also find apathy, lethargy, stagnation and passiveness hard to handle.

When working as part of a team, *enthusiasts* value a healthy and friendly atmosphere, feeling themselves to be on very uncertain ground indeed in situations of conflict and struggles for power or authority. They cannot comprehend people who are capable of harming others in their fight for their own interests and find the motives for acting in that manner inconceivable – it is simply not their world.

Views on workplace hierarchy

Enthusiasts appreciate superiors who are flexible and open to innovative solutions and who point their subordinates in the general direction they should take, but afford them freedom in accomplishing their tasks and respect their individual style of working. They favour democratic management principles and give their esteem to bosses who take the employees' opinions into account and give them the opportunity to take part in making decisions which are crucial to the organisation.

Enthusiasts also have natural leadership skills. Where they go, others will follow, inspired and motivated by them. Their enthusiasm and faith in the success of shared undertakings is infectious and they help others to look at problems from a wider perspective and identify future opportunities. Their leadership is grounded in their ability both to identify people's predispositions correctly and to trust them; keeping an iron hand on the reins is not a style they favour. With their knowledge of who will cope best with a given job, they are able to allocate the right tasks to the right person.

In positions at the top of the tree, their management methods involve assistance from other people. At the same time, they avoid unnecessary bureaucracy, prefer a natural, informal approach and will often consult their subordinates about critical decisions. However, they run into problems when it comes to disciplining poor employees, as well as frequently failing to keep their word, which arouses their subordinates' frustration. *Enthusiast* bosses are at their most effective when they can avail themselves of help from assistants who will take on their administrative burden, keep a firm eye on their deadlines and provide them with the support they need in managing their time.

Professions

Knowledge of our own personality profile and natural preferences provides us with invaluable help in choosing the optimal path in our professional careers. Experience has shown that, while *enthusiasts* are perfectly able to work and find fulfilment in a range of fields, their personality type naturally predisposes them to the following fields and professions:

- acting
- advisor
- artistic director
- clergy
- consultant
- diplomat
- editor
- entrepreneur
- events organiser
- insurance agent
- interior designer
- journalist

- manager
- mediator
- musician
- painter
- paramedic
- politician
- psychiatrist
- psychologist
- public relations
- reporter
- sales assistant
- sales representative
- scientist
- speech therapist
- social welfare
- teacher
- therapist
- writer

Potential strengths and weaknesses

Like any other personality type, *enthusiasts* have their potential strengths and weaknesses and this potential can be cultivated in a variety of ways. *Enthusiasts'* personal happiness and professional fulfilment depend on whether they make the most of the 'pluses' offered by their personality type and face up to its inherent dangers. Here, then, is a SUMMARY of those 'pluses' and dangers:

Potential strengths

Enthusiasts are energetic and optimistic. With their positive attitude to other people and sensitivity to their needs, they emanate warmth and sincerity. As a result, they draw others to themselves naturally and people feel good in their company. They have the ability to read human emotions, feelings and motives, obvious and hidden alike, and are quick to discern who they are dealing with. Their intuition is superb and they display an uncanny tact and 'feel' for others in their interpersonal relationships, knowing exactly how to behave in a given situation and having the ability to build compromises. They are tolerant and accept others, respecting their freedom and independence.

Being flexible and possessing the ability to improvise, they cope extremely well with change and respond rapidly to new circumstances. Versatile, nimble-witted and creative, they are quick to assimilate complex concepts and abstract theories. Their oral communication skills are excellent and they are able to express their own thoughts clearly, as well as having impressive powers of persuasion. They are unperturbed by obstacles and setbacks and have no fear of experiments or innovative methods for solving problems. Their thinking is global; they are able to identify the connections between disparate phenomena and look at the bigger picture when considering problems. They have natural leadership skills and are capable of motivating and inspiring people, as well as infecting them with their optimism and faith in their success, drawing out the best in them and helping them to make the most of their potential. Accepting help from others and availing themselves of their experience also present them with no problems.

Potential weaknesses

Enthusiasts often have trouble with determining their priorities and focusing on carrying out their tasks. As a rule, they launch into a job enthusiastically, but are easily distracted and seeing it through to the end is something of a challenge to them. They may well fail to keep their word or meet deadlines and have a tendency to put off doing what has to be done. Managing their time is another problem area for them, as is planning, and they also struggle mightily with repetitive, everyday activities and routine duties in both their private and their working lives. Be it cleaning and shopping or be it compiling reports and accounts, their efforts, such as they are, will probably be dismal.

They are unable to appreciate constructive criticism or benefit from it and will normally perceive it as an attack on themselves personally or an attempt to discredit their values. Being highly dependent on the opinions of others, they cope very badly with unflattering comments and cutting remarks and will also go to any lengths to avoid conflicts and disagreeable conversations, preferring, on the whole, to keep quiet about a problem rather than confront it.

Voicing critical opinions and calling other people's attention to shortcomings or inappropriate behaviour is difficult for them and they tend to clamp the lid down on their negative emotions. In focusing on other people's needs, they often forget about their own, and since they incline towards being over-trusting they will sometimes be used by others. With their enthusiasm and propensity for viewing the world through rose-tinted glasses, they can lose touch with reality on occasion, fail to view potential threats seriously enough and display a tendency to take excessive risks.

Personal development

Enthusiasts' personal development depends on the extent to which they make use of their natural potential and surmount the dangers inherent in their personality type. What follows are some practical indicators which, together, form a specific guide that we might call *The Enthusiast's Ten Commandments*.

Keep your focus fixed

Determine your priorities and make a serious effort to finish what you undertake. Keep your eyes firmly fixed on the most crucial tasks and stop letting yourself be distracted by less important matters. Do that and you will find yourself avoiding frustration and achieving more.

Be more practical

You have a natural inclination to come up with idealistic notions which sometimes have little in common with real life. Give some thought to the practical aspects and to how they can actually be accomplished in this imperfect world we live in.

Stop fearing criticism

Quell your fear of expressing your own critical opinions and of accepting criticism from others. Criticism can be constructive. There is no law which says that it has to mean attacking people or undermining their worth.

Stop blaming others for your problems

Who has the greatest influence over your life? Who is the person most competent to solve your problems? You, of course! Shift your focus away from external obstacles, setbacks and adversities and concentrate on your strengths and making the most of your potential instead.

Stop agonising over the plan and get going on the action

Instead of nit-picking over how you can improve on what you intend to do, simply get going and do it. Otherwise the day will come when you realise that you have spent your entire life perfecting your plans. Surely setting out to accomplish them and doing things well, but not necessarily to the point of sheer perfection, would be better than never doing anything at all?

Give some thought to yourself

Give some consideration to your own needs and find the time to reflect on your own life. Stop letting yourself be used and start learning to say 'no'. If you really want to help other people effectively, you also have to look after yourself.

Stop being afraid of conflict

Conflicts do arise sometimes, even in our closest circles. They need not necessarily be destructive, though. In fact, they very often help us to identify problems and solve them! So, when conflicts emerge, stop hiding your head in the sand and, instead, express your point of view and feelings about the situation openly.

Ask

Stop assuming that, if other people are silent, it means that they are indifferent or hostile. If you really want to know what they think, ask them.

Stop fearing ideas and opinions which are different from yours

Before you reject them, give them some consideration and try to understand them. Being open to the viewpoints of others is not synonymous with discarding your own.

Give voice to your negative emotions

Stop suppressing your irritation, vexation and anger. If a situation or other people's behaviour exasperates you, then say so. The benefits will be twofold. Not only will you help them to understand what upsets you, but you will also help yourself to avoid self-destruction and vehement, uncontrolled reactions.

Well-known figures

Below is a list of some well-known people who match the *enthusiast's* profile:

- **Joseph Haydn** (1732-1809); an Austrian composer of the Classical period and the first of the three who are often referred to jointly as the First Viennese School.
- **Mark Twain**, (Samuel Langhorne Clemens; 1835-1910); an American writer of Scottish origins whose works include *The Adventures of Tom Sawyer* and its sequel, *The Adventures of Huckleberry Finn*.
- **Edith Wharton** (1862-1937); an American writer whose works include *The Age of Innocence*.
- **James Dobson** (born in 1936); an American Christian psychologist and the author of numerous books, including *What Wives Wish Their Husbands Knew About Women*.
- **Cher** (Cherilyn Sarkisian LaPierre; born in 1946); an American singer of Armenian-Cherokee ancestry, she also operates in many other capacities in the entertainment industry.
- **Jonathan Pryce** (Jonathan Price; born in 1947); a Welsh stage and screen actor whose movies include *Pirates of the Caribbean*.
- **James Woods** (born in 1947); an American screen actor whose movies include *Salvador*, he is also a screenwriter and director.
- **Gregg Henry** (born in 1952); an American stage and screen actor whose films include *Body Double*, he is also a musician and singer.
- **Carrie Fisher** (1956-2016); an American screen actress whose filmography includes *Star Wars*.
- **Damon Hill** (born in 1960); a retired British racing driver and former Formula 1 world champion.

- **Heather Locklear** (born in 1961); an American screen actress whose filmography includes the TV series *Dynasty*.

- **Sandra Bullock** (born in 1964); an American screen actress whose filmography includes *While You Were Sleeping*, she is also a producer.

- **Keanu Reeves** (born in 1964); a Canadian film actor whose filmography includes *Matrix*, he is also a director, producer, musician and author.

- **Jason Statham** (born in 1972); an English film actor whose filmography includes *The Transporter*, he is also a producer, martial artist and former competition diver.

The Idealist (INFP)

THE ID16™© PERSONALITY TYPOLOGY

The Personality in a Nutshell

Life motto: We CAN live differently.

In brief, *idealists* …

are sensitive, loyal, and creative. Living in accordance with the values they hold is of immense importance to them and they both manifest an interest in the reality of the spirit and delve deeply into the mysteries of life. Wrapped up in the world's problems and open to the needs of other people, they prize harmony and balance.

Idealists are romantic; not only are they able to show love, but they also need warmth and affection themselves. With their outstanding ability to read other people's feelings and emotions, they build healthy, profound and enduring relationships. They feel that they are on very shaky ground in situations of conflict and have no real resistance to stress and criticism.

The *idealist's* four natural inclinations:

- source of life energy: the interior world
- mode of assimilating information: intuition
- decision-making mode: the heart
- lifestyle: spontaneous

Similar personality types:

- the Mentor
- the Enthusiast
- the Counsellor

Statistical data:

- *idealists* constitute between one and four per cent of the global community
- women predominate among *idealists* (60 per cent)
- Thailand is an example of a nation corresponding to the *idealist's* profile[9]

The Four-Letter Code

In terms of Jungian personality typology, the universal four-letter code for the *idealist* is INFP.

General character traits

Idealists are people whose interior world is a rich one. They thirst to understand themselves and others, pondering over

---

[9] What this means is not that all the residents of Thailand fall within this personality type, but that Thai society as a whole possesses a great many of the character traits typical of the *idealist*.

why people behave in one way rather than another. Although they sometimes give the impression of keeping their distance, they are actually very open to others, with a sincere interest in their problems and the ability to throw themselves wholeheartedly into solving them.

Idealists yearn for harmony; they seek peace and strive to ease conflicts. In leading their lives, they follow their ideals, which are of paramount significance to them – hence the name for this personality type. Their aims in life rarely coincide with those of the majority; material possessions, power, authority and influence completely fail to interest them.

Given the values they profess, *idealists* sometimes have a sense of isolation or alienation, yet they will almost never abandon their ideals, not even when adhering to them costs them dearly. There is simply no other choice for them: they have to be themselves. In their eyes, a life lived in opposition to their values is a life devoid of sense and meaning.

As others see them

Other people perceive *idealists* as unassuming, kind and always ready to offer a helping hand. They can give the impression of being shy, distant and indecisive and are often seen as people who will launch into a host of undertakings, but are incapable of seeing them through to the end. On the other hand, their natural sensitivity to the needs and feelings of others arouses widespread respect.

Idealists have a reputation for calmness. Yet they will never know interior peace, for they are genuinely wrapped up in the problems of the world and highly sensitive to manifestations of injustice. They believe that every human being has the right both to happiness and to be themselves and they yearn for peace, unity and a better world. As they see it, remaining true to their ideals is worth any and every sacrifice and acting at variance with their system of values engenders a deep-seated sense of guilt in them.

World view and priorities

Idealists never cease to delight in the beauty of the world and are unendingly amazed and astonished by the reality around them. They have the ability to see goodness and beauty everywhere and are fascinated by the world and its people alike. Their gaze is turned to the future and they have a driving urge towards self-improvement and self-development. With their love of tapping into the mysteries of life and exploring its meaning, they devote little attention to material concerns. Their most compelling need is to discover the meaning of life, and they are drawn to the world of the spirit. If they profess no particular faith, they tend to be beset by a feeling of emptiness, a sense that something is lacking.

With their inner desire to change reality and help other people, *idealists* often devote their free time to socially oriented activities such as working as a volunteer for charitable organisations. Indeed, they do so regardless of their jobs, even when they are professionally engaged in providing assistance to others. Helping their friends and acquaintances also claims their 'off-duty' hours.

Indefatigable in striving to achieve the aims they identify with, they are equally as persevering in their quest for truth. Before they enter any new information into their internal 'database', they run it through the filter of their system of values. This is their way of assessing whether or not it will prove helpful in seeking the meaning of life, changing the world or helping others. In assimilating new information, they associate and combine it with what they have previously learned and experienced, and they place a great deal of trust in their intuition.

Decisions

Idealists make decisions guided more by their hearts than their heads and, from their point of view, the most important issue is the way in which what they decide will affect their own lives and those of other people. Arguments of a purely logical nature carry no weight with them and they have very little confidence in deliberations conducted rationally and impersonally on the basis of hard facts alone. Before making a decision, they reflect and prepare at length.

They both perceive and value the individuality of every single person. As such, they will never impose their convictions on others and, by the same token, dislike it intensely when someone else makes any attempt to pressurise them or force something on them.

Creativity

In general, *idealists* are highly original and inventive people who derive enormous joy from the act of creating, which is, in fact, more important to them than either the end result of their efforts or other people's perception of it. As a rule, they are seen as remarkable and individual, despite not going out of their way in the slightest to be 'original'; indeed, they are often not even aware that they are perceived in that light.

Perception and thinking

Idealists are open to new ideas and extremely flexible. When they are part of a group, they will let others make the decisions, which might give some people the impression that they are indifferent. However, if it seems that a decision will run contrary to their convictions, they are quite capable of suddenly springing into action, protesting resolutely and even fighting to defend what they consider to be important – much to the astonishment of those around them.

Accommodating themselves to socially accepted norms and conventions can sometimes be a problem for *idealists,* and they also have a tendency to focus on information which concurs with their own world view and 'miss' or ignore data which go against it. When employing their highly particular defence mechanisms, they can become more and more enclosed within their own world and lose the ability to look at problems from a wider perspective. That situation, in turn, can have an adverse impact on their relationships with others, leading to a specific form of self-isolation.

Organisational modes

Idealists rarely pay too much attention to external appearances and the latest trends from the world of fashion do not hold the slightest fascination for them. They may also give the impression of being chaotic and unreliable. However, they take their lives and responsibilities extremely seriously, demand a great deal of themselves and hunger for self-improvement. Nonetheless, they tend to be so absorbed in breathing life into their visions that everyday routine activities may well slip from their minds entirely and their desks will then be left disorderly, their wastepaper bins will overflow and their cars will remain unwashed as a result. They also have no love of administration or paperwork and are far from happy to undertake tasks requiring them to operate on the basis of pure logic and hard facts. Managing their time and organising themselves are also problem areas for them.

Aware of these shortcomings, they make efforts to put various aspects of their lives in order and will normally renew those attempts repeatedly, though with varying results. When they find themselves in a strained or conflict situation, they are incapable of acting rationally and, at a loss as to how to behave, they may well do absolutely anything simply in order to extract themselves from their predicament.

Communication

As a rule, *idealists* are sparing in their use of words; they speak when they have something to say and dislike talking about themselves. On the other hand, they have the ability to describe complex concepts and phenomena simply and comprehensibly and will readily employ colourful comparisons and metaphors. They are well aware of the immense power of words and their potential impact on others.

Idealists love profound conversations with a small group of people. Idle chatter, gossip and exchanges of views about the weather are of no interest to them at all. They dislike crowds and make unwilling public speakers.

They handle the written word masterfully and are also superb listeners, skilled at reading between the lines. As a result, they will be able to say a great deal about someone after meeting them for the first time and are rarely mistaken, at that. Other people frequently find themselves better able to verbalise their own thoughts and feelings when they talk to *idealists*, who, with their ability to put their gift of empathy to good use, can be highly effective mentors. In helping others, they make no attempt to solve problems by logical and rational means such as analysing causes and establishing where blame lies. Instead, they study a given situation through the prism of feelings and endeavour to find a way to extinguish negative emotions, smooth out disputes and work towards a compromise.

In the face of stress

For *idealists*, the combination of their ongoing search for excellence and the uphill task they face in struggling to bring order to certain aspects of their lives, such as organising their time, is a constant source of frustration. On the whole, they cope badly with stress; it causes them to lose faith in their own powers and either leaves them incapable of making a decision or renders them likely to launch impulsively into ill-considered actions. Physical activity is often their favourite way of spending their leisure time.

Socially

Idealists understand others and are able to identify their feelings and motives. Loyal, faithful friends and wonderful listeners, they love helping other people and frequently put the needs of others before their own. They themselves are very unwilling to open up in front of people and, at times, even those closest to them will have trouble working out what is going on inside them.

Idealists believe that other people help us to know ourselves better. Healthy relationships with their nearest and dearest are vital to them; without them, they are incapable of being happy and enjoying life to the full. They set enormous store by symbols and gestures in their relationships and will sometimes also attach great importance to particular, individual modes of behaviour. As they see it, if someone behaves in a way which goes against the rules once, they are liable to behave like that again in the future.

They frequently display a tendency to idealise good people and demonise wrongdoers – their world can often be a clear-cut matter of black or white.

Amongst friends

Idealists are slow to strike up friendship, but the bonds they establish are deep and enduring. They demonstrate great warmth towards others, are extremely sensitive to their feelings and needs, and their attitude is one of acceptance. Ideal relationships matter to them enormously and they are capable of investing tremendous effort in them. They will go to any lengths to avoid conflicts and disagreeable conversations which might hurt someone.

The loyalties and bonds of their friendships remain strong, even when they are apart for a lengthy period. On the whole, they have only a few friends and are always ready to show them support and surround them with care. They value deep, genuine ties and their friendships will often endure for a lifetime. *Mentors, enthusiasts, artists* and other *idealists* figure most frequently as their friends; seldom will *administrators, inspectors* or *animators* number amongst them.

As life partners

Idealists are made for marriage. Their relationships are extraordinarily enduring and they are far less likely than others to remain single by choice. By nature, they are both highly romantic and uncommonly faithful.

Family is one of the most important things in their lives, and they dream of ideal, harmonious and romantic relationships; indeed, they often struggle to reconcile their expectations with reality. They bestow remarkable respect, admiration and trust on their partner, showering them with compliments and showing them immense warmth. They, too, have a profound need for closeness and affection; however, they are neither possessive nor jealous and will never impose themselves or seek to restrict or subordinate their partner or attempt to create a dependency.

They will go to any lengths to ease conflicts within their relationship and avoid unpleasant or awkward subjects, preferring to remain silent about problems rather than air them. They take any critical word whatsoever very personally; even a minor comment or joke can cause them immense pain. To others, their reactions might seem excessive and inappropriate, but *idealists* really do have an extremely low threshold of tolerance for criticism, which is why they are easily hurt. This can constitute a serious problem in relationships with *strategists, inspectors, directors* and *administrators*, for whom criticism, conflict and open confrontation are a normal aspect of interpersonal relations.

The natural candidates for an *idealist's* life partner are people of a personality type akin to their own: *mentors, enthusiasts* or *counsellors*. Building mutual understanding and harmonious relations will be easier in a union of that kind. Nonetheless, experience has taught us that people are also capable of creating happy and successful relationships despite what would seem to be an evident typological incompatibility.

As parents

Idealists take to the role of parents like ducks to water and treat their responsibilities extremely seriously. They provide their children with friendship, a secure environment and a warm-hearted atmosphere, showing them tremendous affection and showering them with praise. Uncommonly devoted, loyal and loving, they protect and support their offspring no matter what the situation. In bringing them up, they tend to employ the positive reinforcements of encouragement and reward, rather than criticism and discipline, resorting to more radical means only when their own system of values is affronted by their children's behaviour. Even so, they are more than willing to leave disciplinary matters to their partner.

Idealists respect their children's individuality and are very unlikely to restrict them. They allow them to take part in making family decisions and respect what they say. Children brought up by *idealists* in a single-parent family, for instance, may sometimes lack clarity when it comes to the rules that make the world go round. However, they will never want for warmth, support, trust or the space to develop and, as adults, that is what they esteem their parents for most highly.

Work and career paths

Idealists are capable of carrying out a diverse range of tasks. However, not everything will provide them with the same satisfaction and they are at their happiest when they can do a job which reflects their personal convictions.

Success

To *idealists*, work is something more than simply a means of earning money. They perceive neither promotion nor high remuneration as synonymous with success, which, as they see it, lies in understanding the meaning of life and the possibility of fulfilling their calling. What they long to do is something they see as profoundly meaningful.

As part of a team

By nature, *idealists* are individualists and are happiest working independently. Nonetheless, if the need arises, they can also fit in with a team. They have no difficulty in adapting to new situations, cope well with change and like new ideas. However, they need some private space and dislike it when someone invades it or interrupts or disturbs them.

When they work as part of a group, they contribute a friendly atmosphere, supporting the other employees and helping the team to succeed in its undertakings. As a rule, they promote the principles of democratic decision making and believe that encouragement and persuasion can achieve more than criticism or pressure. They will do anything they can to avoid conflict within the team and refrain from criticising their colleagues. When forced to call someone's attention to something, they will often tread so carefully and diplomatically that the message they are trying to convey is barely communicated at all.

Companies and institutions

The optimum environment for *idealists* is one where they can proceed in line with their convictions and achieve the aims in which they believe. They fit in well in companies which accept their employees' individualism, but feel stifled in bureaucratic surroundings where the staff's activities are restricted by myriad rigid procedures. In general, they find routine and repetitive tasks hard to handle.

They are happiest working in social organisations or an academic environment and to all intents and purposes are completely unfit for the uniformed services.

Views on workplace hierarchy

Idealists give their esteem to superiors who have a moral backbone, like a creative approach to tasks, support the people they supervise and are not in the least obsessive about procedures, deadlines and formalities. Excessive control irritates them, as does the abuse of authority and power. They chafe at soulless bureaucracy and the treatment of people as cogs in a machine, and cannot abide it when profit and productivity take precedence over the good of the employees.

Preferences

When it comes to *idealists*, stereotyping, the simplification of reality and any attempt whatsoever at uniform treatment are like a red rag to a bull. They are in their element in situations demanding the solution of complex and intricate problems, but dislike working under time pressure; an unmoveable deadline will give them a strong sense of being hampered and restricted.

Professions

Knowledge of our own personality profile and natural preferences provides us with invaluable help in choosing the optimal path in our professional careers. Experience has shown that, while *idealists* are perfectly able to work and find fulfilment in a range of fields, their personality type naturally predisposes them to the following fields and professions:

- acting
- advisor
- artistic director
- blogger

- clergy
- consultant
- editor
- human resources
- interior designer
- journalist
- life coach
- mediator
- multimedia specialist
- musician
- physiotherapist
- psychiatrist
- psychologist
- project coordinator
- publisher
- scientist
- set decorator
- social activist
- social welfare
- teacher
- tertiary educator
- therapist
- translator
- visual artist
- vocational training
- writer

Potential strengths and weaknesses

Like any other personality type, *idealists* have their potential strengths and weaknesses and this potential can be cultivated in a variety of ways. *Idealists'* personal happiness and professional fulfilment depend on whether they make the most of the 'pluses' offered by their personality type and face up to its inherent dangers. Here, then, is a SUMMARY of those 'pluses' and dangers:

Potential strengths

Idealists possess extraordinary warmth and are happy to turn it to 'warming' others. By nature sensitive and caring, they have the ability to identify other people's needs. They are alert to any and every manifestation of injustice and seek to act on behalf of those who are wronged, used or abused. Their stable system of values, uncommon empathy and sincere interest in the fate of others predispose them to acting for the social good. Extremely faithful and loyal, they are able to build profound, stable and enduring relationships. At the same time, they neither impose themselves on other people nor restrict them. On the contrary, they bestow their trust on them and provide them with the space to develop. Being remarkably flexible, they cope extremely well with change.

Their characteristic tolerance and openness to others extends to those whom the majority of society has rejected, and they will find positive potential and good in everyone. With their uncanny gift of empathy, they are able to support other people, giving them heart and faith in their own powers. They are also superb listeners, perceiving the feelings and motives of others. Their skills include the ability to build compromise and mutual agreement, leaving everyone involved with a sense of satisfaction and the conviction that they have succeeded in achieving what they wanted. They have no difficulty in digesting complex theories and concepts and, at one and the same time, are highly creative and open to spiritual and artistic experiences. Indeed, they themselves are often artistically gifted. They are also capable of expressing their thoughts, particularly in writing.

Potential weaknesses

Idealists have a very low threshold of immunity to criticism, especially when it comes from those close to them. Even minor disapproving comments or gently caustic jokes can undermine their faith in themselves and cause them immense pain. Indeed, they will sometimes perceive critical allusions even when none are being made. Their tremendous loyalty and attachment to people means that they will frequently have problems with putting an end to harmful or toxic relationships. Expressing critical opinions and calling other people's attention to shortcomings also comes hard to them and they will sometimes even struggle to present their own point of view. When forced to address an issue critically, they will often tread so carefully that the person or people they are talking to will have difficulty in understanding what it is that they are actually trying to say. They cope extremely badly with situations of conflict and may respond by behaving irrationally or making sudden, ill-considered decisions.

The severity of their self-appraisal and their acute need for affirmation and positive reinforcement from others impedes their ability to function in neutral or cold environments, a situation which is only magnified in situations of open disapproval. They are incapable of keeping a cool head in stressful circumstances and can also be subject to excessive emotional swings. Although their ideas are highly creative, they can sometimes be unrealistic, since they often fail to take into account the limitations and imperfections present in the world, with the human fallibility factor being one such instance. They have a tendency to treat opinions which oppose their own as an attack on themselves and their values and, when it comes to new information, they are inclined only to take it on board if it concurs with their views; should it threaten their outlook, they might well suppress it entirely. This approach will sometimes lead them to isolate themselves and shut themselves off in their own world.

Personal development

Idealists' personal development depends on the extent to which they make use of their natural potential and surmount the dangers inherent in their personality type. What follows are some practical tips which, together, form a specific guide that we might call *The Idealist's Ten Commandments*.

Stop being afraid of conflict

When you find yourself in a situation of conflict, stop hiding your head in the sand and, instead, voice your point of view and feelings openly. Conflict very often helps us to identify problems and solve them.

Look at problems from a wider perspective

Try to look at issues through other people's eyes. Give various points of view consideration and keep different aspects of the matter in mind.

Don't condemn others to relying on guesswork

Tell people how you feel, what you are going through and what you desire. Stop dithering about whether or not to express your opinions, feelings and emotions and just go for it. You will be helping your colleagues and your nearest and dearest immensely when you do.

Be more practical

You have a natural inclination to come up with idealistic notions which sometimes have little in common with real life. Give some thought to the practical aspects and to how they can actually be accomplished in this imperfect world we live in.

Stop agonising over the plan and get going on the action

Instead of nit-picking over how you can improve on what you intend to do, simply get going and do it. Otherwise the day will come when you realise that you have spent your entire life perfecting your plans. Surely setting out to accomplish them and doing things well, but not necessarily to the point of sheer perfection, would be better than never doing anything at all?

Stop fearing ideas and opinions which are different from yours

Before you reject them, give them some consideration and try to understand them. Being open to the viewpoints of others is not synonymous with discarding your own.

Stop fearing criticism

Quell your fear of expressing your own critical opinions and of accepting criticism from others. Criticism can be constructive. There is no law which says that it has to mean attacking people or undermining their worth.

Stop blaming others for your problems

Who has the greatest influence over your life? Who is the person most competent to solve your problems? You, of course! Shift your focus away from external obstacles, setbacks and adversities, and concentrate on your strengths and making the most of their potential instead.

Make time for pleasure

Try to tear yourself away from your responsibilities from time to time and do something for the sheer pleasure, relaxation and fun of it. Physical activity and contact with the arts will help you to avoid reaching exhaustion point – and that can only make you more effective!

Be kinder to yourself

Ask yourself a couple of questions. Do you demand too much of yourself? Are you too severe in your self-appraisal? In both cases, the answer is most probably going to be 'yes'. Be more understanding of yourself and afford yourself the same solicitude that you give to the happiness and well-being of others.

Well-known figures

Below is a list of some well-known people who match the *idealist's* profile:

- **Laura Ingalls Wilder** (1867-1957); an American author whose books include the *Little House on the Prairie* series.
- **Albert Schweitzer** (1875-1965); a German Lutheran theologian, philosopher, music scholar, musician and physician, he founded a hospital in Gabon and was awarded the Nobel Peace Prize.
- **Alan Alexander Milne** (1882-1956); an English author whose works include the Winnie-the-Pooh books for children.
- **Carl Rogers** (1902-1987); an American psychologist, psychotherapist and one of the most important figures in the development of humanistic psychology.
- **George Orwell** (1903-1950); an English novelist, essayist, journalist and critic whose works include *Animal Farm*.
- **James Herriot** (James Alfred Wight; 1916-1995); a British veterinary surgeon and writer whose works include the *All Creatures Great and Small* series.
- **John F. Kennedy** (1917-1963); the 35th president of the United States.

- **Scott Bakula** (born in 1954); an American screen actor whose filmography includes the *Quantum Leap* TV series.
- **Lisa Kudrow** (born in 1963); an American screen actress whose filmography includes the *Friends* TV series.
- **Julia Roberts** (born in 1967); an American screen actress whose filmography includes *Pretty Woman* and *Erin Brokovitch*, for which she won an Oscar.
- **Gillian Anderson** (born in 1968); an American screen actress whose filmography includes *The X Files*.
- **Megan Follows** (born in 1968); a Canadian-American stage and screen actress whose filmography includes the title role in the *Anne of Green Gables* TV mini-series.
- **Fred Savage** (born in 1976); an American screen actor whose filmography includes *The Wonder Years*, he is also a director and producer.

The Innovator (ENTP)

THE ID16™© PERSONALITY TYPOLOGY

The Personality in a Nutshell

Life motto: How about trying a different approach…?

In brief, *innovators* …

are inventive, original and independent. Optimistic, energetic and enterprising, they are people of action who love being at the centre of events and solving 'insoluble' problems. Their thoughts are turned to the future and they are curious about the world and visionary by nature. Open to new concepts and ideas, they enjoy new experiences and experiments and have the ability to identify the connections between separate events.

Innovators are spontaneous, communicative and self-assured. However, they tend to overestimate their own possibilities and have problems with seeing things through to the end. They are also inclined to be impatient and to take risks.

The *innovator's* four natural inclinations:

- source of life energy: the exterior world
- mode of assimilating information: intuition
- decision-making mode: the mind
- lifestyle: spontaneous

Similar personality types:

- the Director
- the Logician
- the Strategist

Statistical data:

- *innovators* constitute between three and five per cent of the global community
- men predominate among *innovators* (70 per cent)
- Israel is an example of a nation corresponding to the *innovator's* profile[10]

The Four-Letter Code

In terms of Jungian personality typology, the universal four-letter code for the *innovator* is ENTP.

General character traits

Perceptive and resourceful, with coruscating minds, *innovators* feel completely at home in a world of complicated

---

[10] What this means is not that all the residents of Israel fall within this personality type, but that Israeli society as a whole possesses a great many of the character traits typical of the *innovator*.

systems and complex theories. A creative approach to problems and the ability to multitask are an inherent part of their nature. Curious about the world and the phenomena which occur in it, every kind of mystery intrigues them. They value concepts and theories which can be translated into practical action, for instance in helping to solve specific problems, simplify life or make it possible to increase the effectiveness of their own or other people's work. By the same token, they have difficulty in understanding those who delight in purely theoretical solutions.

Problem solving

When *innovators* analyse a problem, they study the bigger picture, looking at the issue from various angles. Given their multiplanar analysis, they often perceive more than others and their deliberations and ideas will normally take on the form of cohesive systems. During a crisis, while other people can see nothing but the negative aspects of the situation, *innovators* are capable of spotting the possibilities and opportunities. On the other hand, when the majority are swept up in general euphoria and delight, it will be the *innovators* who display the ability to foresee potential dangers and future problems – and their assessments of the situation in question will usually be spot on.

They identify the essence of problems more clearly than others and derive enormous satisfaction from solving them. Their approach to tasks is innovative and unconventional, while their nature is to strive for thoroughgoing, systemic and far-reaching solutions which get to the crux of the matter. They tend to implement provisional solutions that either camouflage an issue or eliminate it for a while, but fail to address and remove the cause. In general, they are demanding of themselves and of others and will throw themselves wholeheartedly into accomplishing tasks they believe in, without thought of the time they devote to that end.

When they come up against a problem, *innovators* are quick to get to the heart of the issue and take whatever action is necessary. At the same time, they are guided by logical and objective reasoning and are not taken in by appearances. In changing conditions and circumstances, they are equally fast in reacting to a new situation and revising their previous decisions accordingly. When they launch into action, they will sometimes neglect the 'human element' and, while they will give consideration to whether or not they have the right to proceed in a certain way and will also ask themselves if the decision to do so is a rational one, they are less often interested in how their behaviour will be received by other people. This attitude means that, at times, what they do can be perceived as lacking in humanity or unethical. On the other hand, it would be difficult to accuse them of acting irrationally or unlawfully.

View of the world

Innovators are capable of identifying the principles governing the world and the connections linking apparently disparate phenomena. In combining separate elements, they create cohesive systems. They also take note of repetitive patterns of human behaviour and are able to formulate theories explaining those patterns. Viewing life as a jigsaw, they constantly seek the missing parts and are delighted when the separate pieces start coming together to form a whole. By the same token, discovering the hitherto unknown gives them greater satisfaction than the knowledge and experience they already possess. They have the ability to make use both of other people's experience and of whatever means and tools are available to them; however, they will often do so in an innovative and unconventional way. By nature, they are superb strategists and planners.

Thinking

Innovators strive for perfection. With their thoughts fixed firmly on the future, they reflect on existing needs, unsolved problems and potential opportunities. Their minds are always intensively busy, even when they themselves are not, and they are constantly gripped not only by creative tension, but also by a highly particular sense of restlessness – after all, they do have a consuming desire to improve and rationalise existing solutions. New challenges give them added energy and new ideas, and theories which make it possible to take a fresh look at existing problems fill them with excitement. They will always spot potential and opportunity, no matter where or when.

Tasks

As a rule, *innovators* are characterised by their creativity and inventive approach to their tasks, whatever their job may be. New discoveries and pioneering technological solutions fascinate them and they are often bold innovators themselves ... hence the name for this personality type. Quick to warm to new ideas, they have the ability to fire others with their enthusiasm and, as a result, have no difficulty in finding colleagues to support them in bringing venturesome visions and projects to life. At times, though, they tend to overestimate what they can manage to achieve. In general, the newest challenges will exert the strongest tug on their attention, abating their enthusiasm for previous tasks.

A widespread problem amongst *innovators* is the fact that they are easily distracted; their fascination with a whole host of things and their burning desire to bring a mass of ideas to fruition mean that they are sometimes incapable of seeing anything at all through to the end, a situation which often drives them into a state of furious frustration. They are also irritated by everyday routine activities which, in their view, limit them and rob them of valuable time.

Enthusiasms

Innovators are frequently interested in technological novelties. When new devices which have yet to be universally adopted hit the market, *innovators* will reach for them earlier and more readily than others. Among their friends and acquaintances, they are regarded as experts, since, by the time the majority of people have concluded that a new piece of equipment or device is worthy of interest, *innovators* will often already have extensive experience in using it. Moreover, it is rare indeed for them to stick to availing themselves solely of its main functions; they are usually most likely to explore the more advanced options and even experiment in order to try and employ it in ways which are not only unconventional, but may well not have been foreseen by the manufacturer.

This can, of course, lead to their damaging the device, particularly when they are young; though, on the other hand, they often improve on it, introducing valuable innovations or adding new functions. With time, many *innovators* become not only rationalists, but also the creators of projects, as well as designers and inventors. Their innovativeness also makes itself manifest in creating new work organisation systems, new business concepts and new concepts for explaining the phenomena occurring in the world.

In general, *innovators* love travelling and exploring new places, different cultures and diverse ways of looking at the world. They are open to atypical, out-of-the-ordinary and unconventional solutions and adapt with ease to changing circumstances and conditions. New experiences inspire them and spur them to act. They are not afraid to experiment and their approach to tasks is often absolutely new and fresh. By the same token, people who believe that the best way to solve problems is by clinging to orthodox, tried and tested methods are a source of puzzlement to them.

In the face of change

Innovators are drawn to change. The vision and possibility of beginning life afresh, making the most of new chances and grasping new opportunities is something that inspires them. They are more likely than most to carry out a searching revision of their existing system of values, give themselves over to a new concept or switch their lives onto a wholly new course. With no fear of the new and unknown, the fact that no one has ever done what they are doing or that very few share their views is no obstacle to them.

They enjoy being 'the first' and feel completely at home in the role of groundbreaker and guide, blazing the trail, pointing the way and leading others towards new horizons. *Innovators* are simply not numbered among those who are quick to give up without really trying; instead, they see obstacles and limitations as a challenge and an inspiration to take action. Always happy to breathe life into new projects and pioneering solutions, they will pass the baton of post-implementation care on to others, while they themselves turn their focus to the next problem. As a rule, it is the initial, conceptual phase and launching of a project that interest them, and they cope badly with routine work involving repetitive activities.

Attitude to others

Innovators respect others, particularly those who are capable of taking up challenges, wrestling with adversities, confronting difficulties head on, fighting in a just cause and consciously exposing themselves to the criticism, resistance and incomprehension of those around them as a result. They value people who have the courage to introduce unpopular, though essential, changes, shake the existing order and question the *status quo*. However, they have trouble tolerating errors and negligence on the part of others and are impatient with those who have less knowledge and experience than they do and who fail to keep pace with them.

Accepting that other people cannot see what they themselves deem patently obvious is also problematic for them, as is understanding those who are passive and display no initiative. They tend to perceive a lack of enthusiasm as a manifestation of passivity or laziness, a view which is often both erroneous and unjust. Incapable, on the whole, of keeping their calm when they see a job done badly, they will normally call attention to the issue at once, pointing out the mistakes to those responsible and endeavouring to correct their behaviour. Other people's injudicious and illogical decisions are another source of irritation to them.

As others see them

Innovators are perceived as decisive, powerful and sure that they are right. In general, they also have a reputation for being creative, rational and competent. Others know that, in the face of serious problems, they can be counted on to provide help and advice. However, their self-assurance is often taken as arrogance and self-aggrandisement.

A great many people are irritated not only by the fact that *innovators* like to be the centre of attention and have things their own way, but also by their belief that they are always in the right. There are also those who criticise them for their want of empathy, unreasonable demands and insensitivity to the needs of others. Their love of change and unceasing pursuit of the new can sometimes mean that they are seen as inconsistent, chaotic and lacking in perseverance.

Communication

Innovators possess excellent oral communication skills, being able to describe complex problems and theories in a simple, comprehensible fashion. They express themselves extremely precisely, making conscious use of carefully selected words. Generally self-assured, they unhesitatingly voice their convictions in public, even when they are in the minority. They make for difficult partners in polemics, since they are capable of presenting their arguments in a way which is both dazzling and persuasive, and of giving convincing proof of the rightness of their views.

A love of contradicting and polemicising, even for the sheer pleasure of it, is second nature to them. Capable of providing snap answers to questions and refuting arguments, they have no fear of criticism, conflict or unfavourable reactions from others. They are also hard to hurt and, in general, are unaware of the fact that not everyone has the same high threshold of tolerance for critical commentary as they do. As a result, they will often wound people with their bluntly expressed remarks and may well interrupt them in the middle of a sentence. Behaviour of this kind on the part of *innovators* tends to fluster and dishearten those who are less self-assured and engenders a reluctance to enter into conversation with them.

In the face of stress

On the whole, *innovators* derive pleasure from their work. However, the enthusiasm with which they launch themselves into accomplishing a task will frequently disrupt the balance between 'work, rest and play'. Overwork and long-term stress can lead them to become stubborn and unbending and they may well begin to walk all over everyone in their efforts to accomplish what they have planned. They can also react to stress with an exaggerated fear of illness and suffering or with a sense of being isolated, alienated, cast aside and forgotten.

Socially

Open to the world and other people, *innovators* are approachable and easy to get to know. Drawn to wherever the action is, they find being isolated and alone for any length of time hard to bear. They relate to others with ease, spontaneity and flexibility, enjoy getting to know new people and striking up acquaintanceships, and make excellent hosts at get-togethers and gatherings.

Innovators adore surprises and spontaneous fun, adapting to whatever the situation may be with no trouble at all. On the other hand, they are lost in the world of human emotions and feelings and those of a more emotional and affective nature might take them to be cold and insensitive or even accuse them of treating people instrumentally by seeing them as sources of information or problem-solving tools, for instance.

Delighting in disputes and debates, *innovators* handle confrontation well and appreciate those who are capable of fighting in defence of their own views, an attitude which often scares away people who have no driving need of that kind. Seen from the other side of the coin, their unwillingness to engage in confrontation might well be read by *innovators* as a sign of weakness or a lack of conviction in the opinions they profess.

Amongst friends

Good and friendly relations with people are important to *innovators*. What lies at the heart of their bonds of friendship is exchanging information, sharing concepts and ideas and working together to solve problems. Meeting up with other people gives them energy, helps them to develop and acts as a positive spur.

Innovators love inspiring conversations with people who matter to them and are capable of discussing anything and everything; as a rule, they acknowledge no topic as taboo and have no fear that a discussion might take a dangerous turn, such as impelling them to verify their previous convictions, for example. They enjoy spending time with people who have a wide range of interests, help them to look at problems from another angle and, like them, welcome new ideas and challenges. They themselves are equally as happy to share their reflections and knowledge.

Their openness, flexibility and spontaneity make them sought-after conversationalists and company.

Their friendships are most often formed with people who are similar to themselves, distinctive for their intelligence, inventiveness and sparkling minds; they thus tend only to turn their attention to others when they show an interest in their ideas and reflections. Many an *innovator* feels that friendships should enrich people and help them to develop, but that, if they exhaust their potential, they can be brought to a close. *Directors*, *logicians*, *animators* and other *innovators* are most frequently encountered amongst their friends, with *protectors*, *advocates* and *artists* appearing most rarely.

As life partners

As life partners, *innovators* take their obligations very seriously. They bring optimism, enthusiasm and spontaneity to their relationships and, given their love of new experiences and experiments, boredom is unlikely to threaten their partners. Being people of action, they show their devotion not so much by way of tender gestures and warm words as through doing something concrete. Their nature renders them rather insensitive to their partner's feelings and they can often be unaware of their emotional needs; they may love them dearly and yet, at one and the same time, have absolutely no grasp whatsoever of what they are experiencing and feeling, or of their emotional state. However, with a little effort, they can change this and, if they are in a relationship with a person of a romantic disposition, making that effort is an absolute must!

Innovators themselves have few emotional needs. They like to know that they are important to, and loved by, their life partner, but they do not, as a rule, expect endearing words, compliments and frequent assurances of their love and affection. Their positive attitude to confrontations and disputes can be a serious problem for romantically inclined and sensitive partners and it may often be the case that they will hurt those closest to them with their remarks or critical comments, yet have not the slightest idea that they have caused them pain. On the whole, they like to be right and frequently have a problem with admitting to their mistakes or weaknesses. Expressing their own feelings and emotions is also hard for them.

During periods of intensive work or particular stress, they can make difficult partners, as they become stubborn and may fail to take the needs of others into consideration or might even start exerting pressure on them. *Innovators* warm to new ideas rapidly and, once a task has fired their enthusiasm, they will roll up their sleeves and get working on it without further ado. Being capable of devoting all their energy and time to that, what may then ensue are problems in their relationships, particularly when their partner neither shares their enthusiasm nor understands their engrossment. This burning engagement is something they might well carry over into matters of family life; indeed, they have a tendency to treat problems and tasks in that respect as projects which need to be accomplished. What can happen, though, is that their enthusiasm dies down when new tasks and more exciting challenges appear on the horizon. Although sincere in their resolve, they have a struggle in keeping promises they have made and, after ideas have initially fired them up, they find it tough to see them through to the end. At the same time, their characteristic thirst for new impressions and their love of adventure and experiment pose a potential threat to the stability of their relationships. *Innovators* long for good relationships and, as a rule, they will not seek a way out of them. However, they are capable of putting an end to them if, in their opinion, they have become damaging and destructive.

The natural candidates for an *innovator's* life partner are people of a personality type akin to their own: *directors*, *logicians* or *strategists*. Building mutual understanding and harmonious relations will be easier in a union of that kind. Nonetheless, experience has taught us that people are also

capable of creating happy and successful relationships despite what would seem to be an evident typological incompatibility. Moreover, the differences between two partners can lend added dynamics to a relationship and engender personal development. Indeed, for many people, this is a prospect that appears more attractive than the vision of a harmonious relationship wherein concord and full, mutual understanding hold sway.

As parents

As parents, *innovators* have a superb understanding of children's curiosity about the world. In a sense, they themselves always have something of the child in them, and they never lose that curiosity and love of experimentation, adventure and fun. They endeavour to provide their offspring with as many experiences and stimuli as they possibly can, happily organising expeditions and carefree fun with them and deriving just as much joy from the activities as the children do. They will generally instil the ability to think critically in them and will strive to bring them up to become independent, self-sufficient people capable of objectively evaluating facts and making rational and logical decisions.

Their unpredictability can be a problem; they will sometimes make their children a promise or set something up with them, only to face difficulty in following through on it later. They are also easily distracted. When a new vision sweeps them up and they commit themselves wholly to bringing it to fruition, they may well forget their offspring's needs or arrangements they have previously made. Their adult children appreciate the way their *innovator* parent respected their independence, supported them in developing their enthusiasms and taught them to be self-sufficient. They will also have fond memories of family outings and experiments, along with every precious moment spent having fun together.

Work and career paths

Innovators like work which creates an opportunity for experimentation. They excel at pioneering tasks and will often employ methods which others have not dared to try, reaching for new solutions or applying those which already exist in an innovative way and creating an entirely fresh quality as a result. They enjoy 'unconventional' tasks and will readily work in the 'line of fire'.

Skills and stumbling blocks

Motivated by their awareness that unsolved problems and untapped potential opportunities exist, *innovators* face their greatest problem when confronted by work demanding that they perform routine, repetitive and schematic activities. In general, they also have no fondness for tasks which demand a great deal of preparation. On the other hand, they possess excellent improvisational skills and are quick to adapt to new situations. They are capable of multitasking and reconciling various responsibilities. However, with their love of experiment and change, they will often forget about previous arrangements and duties in the face of new and exciting tasks and they also have trouble with working systematically and seeing things through to the end.

As part of a team

Innovators enjoy working in a group. They normally establish good relationships with people and are well liked. However, their preference is for tasks demanding a creative approach and problem-solving skills rather than empathy and the ability to discern human emotions, feelings and needs. They are happiest working with people who are experts in their field and are open both to experiments and to innovative and risky solutions. The reverse side of the coin is the sheer suffering they endure when they have to work with those for whom 'the old ways are the best' and who favour 'tried and trusted' methods and cling tightly to instructions, guidelines and rules.

Tasks

In general, *innovators* find conventional thinking and rigid, fossilised, bureaucratic structures hard to bear. Arguments grounded in tradition carry no weight with them and, if they view a solution as inadequate and insufficiently effective, they are liable to discard it, regardless of who introduced it and how long it has been in place, an approach which sometimes earns them a reputation as dangerous revolutionaries and subversives.

They are usually unwilling to acquiesce to any kind of regulations or instructions and often treat restrictions, be they institutional or legal, as obstacles on the road to achieving their aims; indeed, if they consider a regulation to be unreasonable, pointless or absurd, they are quite capable of consciously ignoring it. They will sometimes mete out the same treatment to people who hamper them in bringing their ideas to life. In fact, when they are firmly convinced that something is essential, they are capable of putting pressure on those who stand in their way. However, despite having a destructive impact on others, their pertinacity frequently determines their success.

Innovators fit in best in companies which give their employees freedom in carrying out their tasks, allow them to experiment, encourage them to seek new solutions, and support creativity and innovativeness. They enjoy environments where discussion on any and every topic is permitted and everyone is free to air their own convictions.

Views on workplace hierarchy

Innovators like and value superiors who provide their staff with freedom of action and single out knowledge, experience, competence and professionalism. Their respect is for people who are true experts in their field and have no fear of experimenting – for instance, by giving up the methods applied thus far in favour of new and more innovative solutions. Their ideal bosses will evaluate employees with due consideration for their creativity, ideas and the tasks they perform, rather than giving weight to the amount of paperwork they get through and their scrupulous adherence to procedures.

In positions of authority themselves, they will apply this method of assessing those under them and will most readily select colleagues who are capable of making independent decisions, know what needs to be done in a given situation and require neither constant instructions and pointers nor close supervision. They find subordinates who constantly need their hands held intensely irritating. *Innovators* are not the kind of people who shower their employees with compliments in order to enhance their sense of well-being and make work a happy place. Nonetheless, they do value their achievements and reward measurable success.

Natural leaders and visionaries, *innovators* are able to point the way, make others aware of existing possibilities, inspire them, give them added courage and infect them with enthusiasm and faith that their undertakings will succeed. However, when they hold supervisory or managerial positions, they need the strong support of assistants or secretaries to whom they can assign all their practical, routine duties.

Professions

Knowledge of our own personality profile and natural preferences provides us with invaluable help in choosing the optimal path in our professional careers. Experience has shown that, while *innovators* are perfectly able to work and find fulfilment in a range of fields, their personality type naturally predisposes them to the following fields and professions:
- acting
- artistic director

- computer programmer
- computer systems analyst
- credit analyst
- engineer
- entrepreneur
- estate agent
- events organiser
- financial advisor
- infrastructure / property developer
- investment and stockbroking
- journalist
- lawyer
- logistics
- marketing
- musician
- photographer
- politician
- press spokesperson
- project coordinator
- psychiatrist
- psychologist
- public relations
- reporter
- sales representative
- scientist
- urban and rural planning
- visual artist
- writer

Potential strengths and weaknesses

Like any other personality type, *innovators* have their potential strengths and weaknesses, and this potential can be cultivated in a variety of ways. *Innovators'* personal happiness and professional fulfilment depend on whether they make the most of the 'pluses' offered by their personality type and face up to its inherent dangers. Here, then, is a SUMMARY of those 'pluses' and dangers:

Potential strengths

Innovators are creative, optimistic and energetic, with the ability both to fire others with enthusiasm and faith in their success and to stir them into action. Nimble-minded, they are logical, rational and insusceptible to manipulation by others. Assimilating complex concepts and theories presents them with no problems. They have a natural curiosity about the world and are able to understand the phenomena which occur in it and the mechanisms driving people's behaviour, to identify the connections and relationships between different events and to look at problems from various angles. When opportunities and possibilities emerge, *innovators* are quicker than most to spot them, just as they are to foresee potential, future dangers.

Enterprising by nature, they like new concepts and pioneering ideas and will readily reach for innovative solutions and methods. Being exceptionally creative and bold, they are able to solve problems in unconventional, original ways and they have no fear of experimenting. They are always happy to learn something new and undertake fresh challenges, enjoy solving complex problems and are not afraid to take risks. Extremely flexible and capable of adapting to new circumstances, they enjoy both the company of others and working in a group. In general, they possess outstanding communication skills, being capable of expressing their thoughts and voicing their opinions clearly and comprehensibly. Neither criticism nor confrontation frightens them and they cope well in difficult, conflict situations. They strive for self-improvement and are always willing to help others to develop.

Potential weaknesses

With their love of change and experiment, pursuit of the new and focus on the latest and most powerful stimuli, *innovators* have far less difficulty in beginning something than they do in seeing it through to the end. They are also easily distracted and their enthusiasm for the tasks they have started vanishes when new problems and challenges appear on the horizon. This means that they drop numerous fascinating ideas at the conceptual stage without even trying to implement them in reality. They also struggle with organising their time, applying self-discipline, making decisions, keeping promises and sticking to deadlines. Defining priorities and then bringing their activities in line with them is also problematic for them. They cope badly with tasks which require them to adhere to strict procedures and follow instructions to the letter.

Another problem which frequently crops up among *innovators* is their impatience with less experienced people who need guidelines, prompting and pointers. Their boldness and unwavering faith that they will succeed may well lead to their making overly risky moves and employing excessively radical solutions. They are liable to overestimate their own possibilities and disregard their limitations. Both their inability to perceive the emotions and feelings of others and the difficulty they have in expressing their own can give rise to problems in their relationships with those closest to them. At the same time, with their confrontational approach, critical comments, general determination to have things their own way and love of dispute and polemic, they are likely to hurt and discourage more sensitive people and may even frighten them away.

Personal development

Innovators' personal development depends on the extent to which they make use of their natural potential and surmount the dangers inherent in their personality type. What follows are some practical indicators which, together, form a specific guide that we might call *The Innovator's Ten Commandments*.

Learn to manage your time and set priorities

Enthusiasm is your main driving force. Nonetheless, listing priorities, establishing time frames and planning out a job are not in the least the same thing as forging chains to shackle your creativity, fetter your activities and encumber you as you carry out the task. Perish the thought! They are tools and when you use them properly, they will help you achieve your sought-after goals.

Be more practical

Give some thought to the practical aspects of your theories and ideas. To make the very most of their potential, try persuading other people to come round to them and considering ways of turning them into reality. Why leave the fruits of your work to languish, neglected and unaccomplished to the full?

When you start something, see it through to the end

You launch into new things enthusiastically, but have problems with finishing what you have already started. Try sorting out what is most important to you and deciding how you want to accomplish it. Then knuckle down and turn your back firmly on all those tempting distractions! Keep your eyes fixed on your priorities and stop letting yourself be distracted by less important matters.

Admit that you can make mistakes

Things may be more complex than they seem to you. You might not always be in the right. Bring that thought to the forefront of your mind before you start accusing others or pointing out their mistakes and reproaching them.

Criticise less

Not everyone has your ability to handle constructive criticism. In many cases, dispensing it frankly can have a destructive effect. Studies have shown that praising positive behaviour, albeit limited, motivates people more than criticising negative conduct.

Stop discarding other people's ideas and opinions

Just because other people's ideas and opinions conflict with your own, this does not automatically mean that they are wrong. Before you judge them as valueless, give them some serious consideration and try to understand them.

Focus on the positive

Instead of concentrating on what is missing, on mistakes, on logical contradictions and on questioning other people's good intentions, learn to identify the positive and turn your gaze to the bright side of life.

Be more understanding

Show others more warmth. Remember that not everyone should be assigned the same tasks, because not everyone is skilled in the same fields. If others are unable to cope with a task, this is not always a sign of their ill will or laziness.

Remember important dates and anniversaries

Arrangements to meet people, the birthdays of those closest to you and family anniversaries may seem like rather trivial matters to you in comparison to whatever it is you are involved in. They matter a great deal to other people, though. So if you are incapable of remembering them, jot them down somewhere handy – and then remember to check those notes!

Praise others

Make the most of every occasion to appreciate other people, say something nice to them and praise them for something they have done. At work, value people not only for the job they do, but also for who they are. Then wait and see. The difference will come as a pleasant surprise!

Well-known figures

Below is a list of some well-known people who match the *innovator's* profile:

- **Lewis Carroll** (Charles Lutwidge Dodgson; 1832-1898); an English writer whose works include *Alice's Adventures in Wonderland*, he was also a mathematician and the author of around two hundred and fifty scholarly works in the fields of mathematics, logic and cryptography.
- **Thomas Edison** (1847-1931); one of the world's best-known and most creative inventors, with more than a thousand patents to his name, including the light bulb and the phonograph, he was also an entrepreneur and the founder of a periodical entitled *Science*.
- **Nikola Tesla** (1856-1943); a Croatian inventor with one hundred and twelve patents to his name, he was also a poet and painter.
- **Theodore Roosevelt** (1858-1919); the 26th president of the United States, he received the Nobel Peace Prize.
- **Buckminster Fuller** (1895-1983); an American designer and architect, he was one of the pioneers of high-tech architecture and the man who developed and patented the geodesic dome.

- **Walt Disney** (Walter Elias Disney; 1901-1966); an American film producer, director, screenwriter, animator, entrepreneur and philanthropist, he founded the Walt Disney Company and Disneyland.

- **Richard Phillips Feynman** (1918-1988); an American theoretical physicist and one of the primary contributors to the development of quantum electrodynamics, he was awarded the Nobel Prize in Physics.

- **Jeremy Brett** (Peter Jeremy William Huggins; 1933-1995); an English stage and screen actor whose filmography includes the *Adventures of Sherlock Holmes* TV series.

- **John Marwood Cleese** (born in 1939); an English actor, comedian, writer and producer whose filmography includes *A Fish Called Wanda*, he was one of the co-founders of the Monty Python team.

- **Roberto Benigni** (born in 1952); an Italian stage and screen actor, comedian, screenwriter and director whose filmography includes *Life Is Beautiful*.

- **James Francis Cameron** (born in 1954); a Canadian film director and producer, screenwriter, editor, engineer, inventor, deep-sea explorer and philanthropist whose filmography includes *The Terminator* and *Titanic*.

- **Tom Hanks** (Thomas Jeffrey Hanks; born in 1956); an American screen actor, director and producer whose filmography includes *Philadelphia*, his extensive list of awards includes Oscars, Golden Globes and Emmys.

- **Jamie Lee Curtis** (born in 1958); an American screen actress whose filmography includes *A Fish Called Wanda*, she is also a children's author and involved in various philanthropic causes.

- **Salma Hayek-Jimenez** (born in 1966); a Mexican-American screen actress whose filmography includes *Desperado*.
- **Celine Dion** (born in 1968); a Canadian singer, songwriter and entrepreneur whose album sales make her one of the best-selling artists in the history of music.

The Inspector (ISTJ)

The Personality in a Nutshell

Life motto: Duty first.

In brief, *inspectors* …

are people who can always be counted on. Well-mannered, punctual, reliable, conscientious and responsible, when they give their word, they keep it. Being analytical, methodical, systematic and logical by nature, they tend be seen as serious, cold and reserved. They prize calm, stability and order, have no fondness for change and like clear principles and concrete rules.

Inspectors are hard-working, persevering and capable of seeing things through to the end. As perfectionists, they try to exercise control over everything within their sphere and are sparing in their praise. They also underrate the importance of other people's feelings and emotions.

The *inspector's* four natural inclinations:

- source of life energy: the interior world
- mode of assimilating information: via the senses
- decision-making mode: the mind
- lifestyle: organised

Similar personality types:

- the Practitioner
- the Administrator
- the Animator

Statistical data:

- *inspectors* constitute between six and ten per cent of the global community
- men predominate among *inspectors* (60 per cent)
- Switzerland is an example of a nation corresponding to the *inspector's* profile [11]

The Four-Letter Code

In terms of Jungian personality typology, the universal four-letter code for the *inspector* is ISTJ.

General character traits

Inspectors are patient, persevering, conscientious, hard-working and, given their natural love of order, well organised. Their sense of duty is their constant companion. They like clearly defined tasks and concrete guidelines, perceiving the world and their surroundings as a highly

---

[11] What this means is not that all the residents of Switzerland fall within this personality type, but that Swiss society as a whole possesses a great many of the character traits typical of the *inspector*.

particular system which depends for its stability and proper functioning on people's acceptance of, and adherence to, the principles and rules in force.

Organisational modes

Inspectors are happy when things are proceeding as they should and thus subject everything within their sphere to unceasing inspection … hence the name for this personality type. They are quick to spot gaps, errors and defects. Capable of seeing things through to the end, they derive great satisfaction from completing a task and only then will they feel able to give themselves over to their next commitment. They have an intense dislike of unregulated duties, uncompleted tasks and unpaid bills, all of which disrupt their peace of mind.

They like life to be orderly and stable and derive great joy from small, simple things. Excellent managers of their time, they more often than not adhere to a fixed and constant 'plan for the day'. Their approach to their work is organised and systematic; they make a note of tasks to be done and are scrupulous about checking that none have been overlooked. It is rare indeed for them to be unprepared or for something to take them by surprise. Armed with a plan of action, they feel secure and ready to confront a variety of duties, responsibilities and challenges. On the other hand, they dislike changes intensely, especially those which have a major impact on their lives.

When it comes to lifestyle, the simple and natural suits them down to the ground. Prizing stability and security, they will do their utmost to avoid risky undertakings. They would rather solve present problems than become involved in predicting those which might arise in the future; their preference will always be for the concrete, the perceptible and the tangible.

Communication

When engaged in a discussion, *inspectors* call upon hard facts, concrete data and logic. Combined with their self-assured attitude, this approach means that they have the ability to convince people that they are right – even when they are wrong! In principle, they operate on the assumption that they are, indeed, in the right and struggle with making room for the notion that they might, in fact, be at least partially mistaken. Nonetheless, they will not attempt to prove their rightness at any price; if they see that doing so might give rise to conflict, they are capable of backing down from the confrontation.

As others see them

Inspectors are perceived as responsible, sensible, courteous and honest people who can always be counted on. The fact that they will always keep their word, their dependability and their punctuality all arouse widespread respect. However, they also have a reputation as being rather unapproachable. Their natural reticence not only makes them difficult to get to know, but also creates a problem when it comes to guessing what they might be thinking and feeling. They are frequently seen as serious, cold and reserved; indeed, some people feel ill-at-ease in their presence, since they often unconsciously engender a sense of inferiority, or even of guilt, in others, triggering a defensive reaction as a result.

Their scepticism and mistrust of new concepts and ideas can also pose a problem. They expect others to provide proof that their proposals for change or new solutions really do have a point. Indeed, when talking to *inspectors*, some people will feel that what they are involved in is less of a conversation and more of an interrogation. Their perfectionism, meticulous focus on detail, urge to control everything within their sphere and conviction that they are always right are also sources of irritation to others.

Aesthetics

Inspectors have no desire either to be surrounded by luxury or to pursue the latest trends, focusing instead on the functional attributes of objects, preferring simple, practical things which are inexpensive to use and prizing their reliability and durability. Elaborate décor, ostentation and sophistication hold no attraction for them; their homes and work stations are usually cared for, functional and tastefully furnished. Tending more towards the traditional in their dress and steering well clear of experiment and flamboyance themselves, they find people who buy clothes or objects simply because they are 'on-trend' a source of utter bewilderment.

Perception and thinking

Inspectors rely on the input of their five senses and are never really guided by emotions, fleeting feelings or impulses. Their decision-making process is logical, rational and grounded in hard data and facts. They are able to express their views clearly and convincingly and will readily do so in writing. The exterior world will never be as important to them as their own, interior one and they generally have a sense of being self-sufficient, assuming that other people have little to offer them. By the same token, understanding opinions and behaviour which differ significantly from their own presents them with a serious problem.

Leisure

Although *inspectors* are devoted to their work, they are also capable of relaxing and are aided in that by their excellent organisational skills. They approach leisure with the same attitude that they bring to their other tasks; their free time is arranged in an orderly fashion and their holidays are thoroughly thought-out and planned, leaving little room for surprises, spontaneity or improvisation.

In the face of stress

Inspectors employ a mechanism inherent to their nature when they attempt to defend themselves against stress; they are, *de facto*, better at avoiding it than they are at coping with it. During particularly tense periods, they tend to sketch out black scenarios in their minds, envisaging their employer collapsing into bankruptcy, while they lose their jobs as a consequence, imagining the onset of disease, be it in themselves or those closest to them, blaming themselves for not having done something as it should have been done or succumbing to an overwhelming sense of their own incompetence and sinking into decision-making paralysis. Under the influence of long-term stress, the spiritual calm so typical of them may vanish, along with their ability to assess situations coolly and logically. They might also experience surges of nostalgia.

Socially

As *inspectors* see it, responsibility and loyalty are the crucial elements cementing interpersonal relations. They themselves express their affection and love through deeds and neither perceiving the emotions and needs of others nor voicing their own comes naturally to them. However, their powerful sense of duty often saves them here; once they become aware of other people's needs, they will view fulfilling them as their bounden duty and they are then capable of showing interest, concern and care.

Although they have an intense dislike of purely social gatherings, they do enjoy family celebrations; indeed, maintaining family traditions matters to them greatly. Amongst family and close friends, they display the ability to joke and amuse others with their conversation. They are exceptionally loyal to their employer, their family and their close friends and are often involved in the life of their neighbourhood or their village, town or city. For *inspectors*, the places that count for the most are their work, their homes and their local community.

Amongst friends

Inspectors feel perfectly at home among other people, though they dislike being the centre of attention. Sparing of words by nature, they find intensive conversations extremely draining and they have an absolute need for solitary moments which will allow them to relax and think current matters over in peace and quiet.

On the one hand, they are perceived as extremely serious; on the other hand, their friends are familiar with another side to their character, as people who know how to have fun and joke around. *Inspectors* see their friendships as highly important and they nurture them solicitously, investing enormous energy in them. However, although they willingly devote themselves to their friends, their family will always come first. They most often strike up friendships with *practitioners*, *administrators*, *strategists* and other *inspectors*. They find the carefree approach exhibited by *enthusiasts*, *idealists* and *counsellors* irritating in the extreme; an aversion which is, in fact, mutual, since those personality types perceive *inspectors* as being overly reserved, rigid and conservative.

As life partners

Care and concern for their nearest and dearest, their security and their material needs are viewed by *inspectors* as their patently obvious duty. In their eyes, the commitments and promises they make are sacred and they consider the vow "until death us do part" in exactly the same way. As a rule, their relationship with their life partner is precisely that: a relationship for life.

Inspectors are not overly burdened with emotional needs. They themselves expect little from their partner in the way of warm words, compliments or gestures of affection and are unlikely to identify those needs in others. Indeed, displaying warmth and affection is problematic for them; their mode of expressing love and attachment is through concrete action and they are numbered among those who tend to buy those closest to them practical gifts, for instance.

The natural candidates for an *inspector's* life partner are people of a personality type akin to their own: *practitioners*, *administrators* or *animators*. Building mutual understanding and harmonious relations will be easier in a union of that kind. Nonetheless, experience has taught us that people are also capable of creating happy and successful relationships despite what would seem to be an evident typological incompatibility. Moreover, the differences between two partners can lend added dynamics to a relationship and engender personal development. Indeed, for many people, this is a prospect that appears more attractive than the vision of a harmonious relationship in which concord and full, mutual understanding hold sway.

Inspectors' diligence and reliability arouses the respect both of their nearest and dearest and of those around them in general. Yet their professional success comes at a cost, since they will normally treat their job as one of their priorities in life and have great difficulty in completely compartmentalising their working and personal lives. Their directness represents another potential problem in their relationships with those closest to them and their critical remarks may well hurt their partner, while they themselves remain absolutely unaware of having done so. In general, they lack the ability both to put themselves in other people's shoes and to predict how a given mode of behaviour or choice of words can upset them.

Whatever their role in society, be it as a child, a life partner, a friend, a parent or a colleague, *inspectors* have a driving urge to perform it in the very best way possible. Given that their sense of responsibility is always their motivating force, their success in any area will invariably depend upon whether or not they consider the matter in question to be their duty. So, once they acknowledge that meeting the emotional needs of their nearest and dearest is their responsibility, they will throw themselves wholeheartedly into their efforts to fulfil it – and to their utmost abilities, at that.

As parents

Inspectors make highly conscientious and devoted parents, ready to invest every effort in bringing up their children in a positive and healthy atmosphere, ensuring that they want for nothing, and providing them with a stable, secure future, seeing this as their natural duty and endeavouring to discharge it to the full. They teach their offspring to perform their social roles and observe the prevailing norms and traditions, require their respect and tolerate neither disobedience nor the breaking of established rules. In general, they make high demands and are capable of severity, viewing discipline as a natural necessity and a tool assisting them to raise their children to be respectable, reliable and responsible adults.

Unstinting in their criticism, *inspectors* are also sparing when it comes to praising their offspring and, being unperceptive of their emotional needs, they tend to fail when it comes to demonstrating a sufficient amount of warmth. What this can generate is not only distance in terms of their parent-child relationships, but also a host of serious emotional problems in the children themselves. Fortunately, in numerous cases, once the *inspector* parent becomes aware of their offspring's needs, they begin to treat encouragement and positive reinforcement as a vital parental task, and that, in turn, serves as a natural spur to putting them into practice.

Their children will often view both the household norms and rules established by *inspectors,* as well as the consistency with which they enforce them, as oppressive, particularly during adolescence. However, those same norms and rules provide them with a sense of security and contribute to their social development. As adults, they appreciate their *inspector* parents for having assured them of a secure home, teaching them to behave responsibly, caring about their future and being ever at the ready in their devotion.

Work and career paths

Inspectors have the ability to perform tasks demanding adherence to complicated procedures, filling in forms and 'communing' with large quantities of numerical data. They will always put duty first and are incapable of relaxing or giving themselves over to pleasure when they have an important job hanging over their heads.

As part of a team

Inspectors like to operate independently and be evaluated on the basis of their own achievements. Nonetheless, if the situation demands it, they are capable of working in a group, though preferably with people who, like themselves, are properly organised and driven by the urge to fulfil their duties to the very best of their abilities.

They appreciate superiors who provide their staff with support and clear guidelines as regards accomplishing their tasks. As members of a team, they nurture a high standard of work and call attention to any details which have escaped the attention of their colleagues. People who fail to throw themselves wholeheartedly into their work and identify with their organisation's aims are a closed book to them. They are also unhappy in the midst of those who are emotional, irritable or given to wasting time on inessential discussions. Equally incomprehensible to them are people who knowingly break the rules, fail to keep their word, fail to return things they have borrowed, fail to fulfil their duties and responsibilities, or are only too happy to air their thoughts on matters which they are, in fact, clueless about.

Work style

Inspectors plan their work scrupulously and then consistently see things through to the end, doggedly making their way towards their goal and refusing to be disheartened by obstacles and difficulties which would discourage many another. Incapable of consciously working to less than their full potential, once a task is finished they will often give way to regret that they failed to do it better.

They prefer to work to step-by-step instructions which set out what needs doing and how it should be done, and they also hold tried and tested procedures and methods in high esteem. Indeed, when their intention is to convince others to employ a particular solution, they will often cite tradition and prior experience: "This is how it's always been done".

Inspectors dislike abstract theories and general concepts which lead to no clear, practical conclusions, and they are no more fond of tasks which are utterly different from what they have done previously and which cannot be solved on the basis of previous experience. They cope badly with radical changes, preferring those which either evolve or are made slowly and steadily. Although reluctant to accept innovation and experiment, they can be persuaded to come round to new methods or solutions if there is convincing proof of their benefits or if they have already been put to the test elsewhere.

Tasks

When *inspectors* are entrusted with a task, rest assured! It will be accomplished in line with the instructions and on time or, more often than not, ahead of time. As they see it, commitments, promises and deadlines are sacred. When they work on a task, they will usually spare neither time nor energy; indeed, even their health then takes a back seat. Their superiors, colleagues and business partners know they can be counted on. At the same time, although they might be overburdened already, *inspectors* will rarely refuse to take on more tasks, viewing their commitment as something absolutely normal. The pursuit of rewards and praise is as alien to them as broadcasting their own achievements. In fact, when they attain something remarkable, they are often completely unaware of having done so.

In positions of authority

Inspectors' commitment, diligence and reliability often pave the way for their promotion and they will frequently work their way up to supervisory and management positions. Once there, they establish clear rules and allocate precisely defined tasks to their staff, exhibit zero tolerance for wastefulness and inefficiency and find carelessness, unreliability and a dismissive or irreverent attitude towards tasks infuriating. When faced with unproductive and poor employees, they are capable of taking radical steps to improve the situation.

Companies and institutions

Inspectors fit in well in institutions with a long tradition, an established position and a fixed order. With their preference for employers who value their dedication, efforts and years of professional experience and who provide their staff with security and financial stability, they can often be found in public administration, large corporations and the uniformed services.

Professions

Knowledge of our own personality profile and natural preferences provides us with invaluable help in choosing the optimal path in our professional careers. Experience has shown that, while *inspectors* are perfectly able to work and find fulfilment in a range of fields, their personality type naturally predisposes them to the following fields and professions:

- administrator
- archivist
- the armed forces
- auditor
- aviator
- bookkeeper
- chartered accountant
- clerk
- computer programmer
- computer systems analyst
- financial controller
- detective
- engineer
- entrepreneur
- executive director
- farmer
- financial director
- inspector
- IT specialist
- judge
- lawyer
- librarian
- logistics
- manager
- mechanic
- pharmacist
- physician
- police officer
- science teacher
- technician

Potential strengths and weaknesses

Like any other personality type, *inspectors* have their potential strengths and weaknesses and this potential can be cultivated in a variety of ways. *Inspectors'* personal happiness and professional fulfilment depend on whether they make the most of the 'pluses' offered by their personality type and face up to its inherent dangers. Here, then, is a SUMMARY of those 'pluses' and dangers:

Potential strengths

Inspectors love order and hold tradition and rules in great respect. True to their word, loyal and steadfast, they take their responsibilities extremely seriously, care for their families and are ready to devote themselves to those closest to them. Their reliability, punctuality and ability to stick to a deadline all arouse the respect of others. Quick to spot gaps, errors and oversights, they are hard-working to a fault and always see things through to the end, without allowing obstacles to discourage them – an attitude which means that they usually attain their goals. They are capable of performing work which demands that they adhere to a host of procedures, process large quantities of data and carry out myriad routine activities.

Sharing their knowledge and experience with other people and helping them to resolve concrete problems is something they do willingly. Capable of expressing their thoughts and voicing their opinions clearly and matter-of-factly, they have little difficulty in convincing others that they are right. They cope well in situations of conflict and are open to constructive criticism from other people; it neither upsets them nor do they see it as a personal attack. At the same time, they are not easily dissuaded from their own views and opinions. When the need arises, they are able to discipline others and call their attention to shortcomings without feeling the need to tread delicately. They are excellent at managing money.

Potential weaknesses

Reading the feelings of others and perceiving their emotional needs is problematic for *inspectors*. Sparing in their praise, they also struggle when it comes to expressing love and affection. Their colleagues and those closest to them are often wearied by their driving urge to set everything in their sphere in order and then control it.

Assuming that they are always right, they tend to be premature in ruling out alternative solutions and other points of view. Looking at problems from a wider perspective and understanding opinions which differ from their own is also difficult for them and they will often dismiss other people's views in advance, without even trying to hear them out. When confronted by a problem, they have a tendency to blame others.

They cope badly with change and new situations. Their natural predilection for keeping strictly to guidelines, instructions and procedures can prove limiting in numerous circumstances, while their inclination to rely on previous experience and tried and tested solutions becomes an obstacle when they encounter new tasks requiring an approach which departs from the norm.

Personal development

Inspectors' personal development depends on the extent to which they make use of their natural potential and surmount the dangers inherent in their personality type. What follows are some practical indicators which, together, form a specific guide that we might call *The Inspector's Ten Commandments*.

Don't condemn others to relying on guesswork

Tell people how you feel and what you are going through. Give voice to your emotions. You will be helping your colleagues and your nearest and dearest immensely when you do. Whatever you say, it will usually be better than remaining silent.

Look at problems from a wider perspective

Try to look at problems from a wider perspective and different angles ... and through other people's eyes. Turn to others for their opinions, give various points of view consideration and keep different aspects of a matter in mind.

Appreciate the worth of creative ideas

Operating solely on the basis of dry facts and hard data brings a whole range of restrictions in its wake. Many a problem can only be solved by creative ideas, an innovative method – and even by intuition!

Leave some things to take their natural course

There is no way you can have everything under your personal control and no way you can manage to be in command of it all, either. Leave less important matters to take their natural course. Set less crucial decisions to one side. Stop putting all that effort into reforming other people. You will save a great deal of energy and avoid an equal amount of frustration.

Criticise less, praise more

Be more restrained in your criticism and more generous in your evaluation and praise of others. Show them some warmth and make the most of every occasion to say something nice to them. Then wait and see. The difference will come as a pleasant surprise!

Be more open to people

Being open to others is not synonymous with discarding your own convictions and viewpoints. Stop assuming that they have nothing of interest to offer. Before you reject someone else's ideas or opinions, give them some serious consideration and try to understand them.

Treat others kindly

People hate being seen as just a part of a system or a cog in a machine. They long for their emotions, feelings and enthusiasms to be perceived. So try to put yourself in their shoes and understand what they are going through, what fascinates them, what worries them and what they fear…

Start believing in a world which is more than just black and white

Things may be more complex than they seem to you. Your problems may not only be caused by others; they might also be caused, to some extent at least … by you! You might not always be in the right. Bring that thought to the forefront of your mind before you start accusing others or pointing out their mistakes and reproaching them.

Accept change

When you discard ideas which might bring about change or undermine the current order in advance, you are throwing away the opportunity for development and depriving yourself of countless valuable experiences. Change always brings a certain amount of risk with it, but it will usually be less than you expected.

Stop 'interrogating' people

When you talk to others, try to hold a conversation with them rather than bombarding them with questions – an approach which leaves some people with the impression that they are being interrogated.

Well-known figures

Below is a list of some well-known people who match the *inspector's* profile:

- **George Washington** (1732-1799); an American general and politician, the first president of the United States, considered to be the father of the American nation.
- **John D. Rockefeller** (1839-1937); an American entrepreneur and philanthropist, reportedly the richest man in history.
- **George H. W. Bush** (1924-2018); the 41st president of the United States and father of the 43rd president, George W. Bush.
- **Queen Elizabeth II** (Elizabeth Alexandra Mary, of the House of Windsor; 1926-2022); the Head of State of the United Kingdom and fifteen other realms of the Commonwealth of Nations.
- **Warren Edward Buffett** (born in 1930); an American stock exchange investor, he is one of the richest men in the world.
- **Malcolm McDowell** (Malcolm John Taylor; born in 1943); a British screen actor whose filmography includes *A Clockwork Orange*.
- **Sting** (Gordon Matthew Sumner; born 1951); an English musician, singer-songwriter, activist, actor and philanthropist who first became known as the lead singer, bassist and principal songwriter for the new wave rock band The Police.
- **Condoleezza Rice** (born in 1954); an American politician, she holds a doctorate in political sciences. During President George W. Bush's

presidency she served as the United States' 66th Secretary of State.

- **Gary Alan Sinise** (born in 1955); an American stage and screen actor whose filmography includes the *CSI: NY* TV series, he is also a director, producer and musician.
- **Jackie Joyner-Kersee** (born in 1962); a record-breaking, world-class American athlete, now retired, she won numerous medals and is ranked as one of the best female athletes of all time.
- **Evander Holyfield** (born in 1962); a retired American boxer. Considered one of the greatest heavyweights ever, he earned himself the nickname of 'the Real Deal'.
- **Queen Rania of Jordan** (also known as Rania Al-Abdullah; born Raina al Yassin in 1970); consort to King Abdullah II of Jordan, she is a renowned social activist. In 2011, *Forbes* magazine ranked her as one of the hundred most powerful women in the world.

The Logician (INTP)

The Personality in a Nutshell

Life motto: Above all else, seek to discover the truths about the world.

In brief, *logicians* …

are original, resourceful and creative. With a love for solving problems of a theoretical nature, they are analytical, quick-witted, enthusiastically disposed towards new concepts and have the ability to connect individual phenomena, educing general rules and theories from them. Logical, exact and inquiring, they are quick to spot incoherence and inconsistency.

   Logicians are independent, sceptical of existing solutions and authorities, tolerant and open to new challenges. When immersed in thought, they will sometimes lose touch with the outside world.

The *logician's* four natural inclinations:

- source of life energy: the interior world
- mode of assimilating information: intuition
- decision-making mode: the mind
- lifestyle: spontaneous

Similar personality types:

- the Strategist
- the Innovator
- the Director

Statistical data:

- *logicians* constitute between two and three per cent of the global community;
- men predominate among *logicians* (80 per cent)
- India is an example of a nation corresponding to the *logician's* profile[12]

The Four-Letter Code

In terms of Jungian personality typology, the universal four-letter code for the *logician* is INTP.

General character traits

Logicians are extraordinarily creative, unconventional and original people. Capable of connecting disparate facts and experiences and of building comprehensive and cohesive systems from them, they are unswerving in their quest for truth and exploration of the principles and rules governing the world.

---

[12] What this means is not that all the residents of India fall within this personality type, but that Indian society as a whole possesses a great many of the character traits typical of the *logician.*

Their lives are played out primarily within their unusually rich interior world. Often minimalist in their outward lives, they strive to simplify their existence and dislike owning too many things or having a plethora of obligations. Their needs are few; they have no fondness for flamboyance and their lifestyle is plain in the extreme, an attitude which allows them to focus to the full on the problems absorbing their thoughts.

Thinking

Logicians are characterised by their extremely high level of intellectual independence. They will frequently question orthodox views, challenge existing solutions and seek for inaccuracies, imprecisions and gaps in accepted theories. Mistrustful of recognised authorities in a given field, they are strongly attached to their own opinions. Nonetheless, they are capable of verifying their previous ideas in the light of new data and perceptions. Their minds are constantly engaged in a brainstorming process which is entirely their own, with their thoughts spinning non-stop in overdrive.

Studying

Logicians enjoy both solving problems of a logical kind and helping others to understand the principles and rules governing the world and human behaviour. Learning new things and experimenting are sources of immense pleasure to them and they have the ability to systemise knowledge, forming a logical whole and endowing it with a cohesive structure. By nature, they are logicians – hence the name for this personality type – and they are also inclined to be theoreticians. As a result, they are more interested in forging theoretical concepts than putting them into practice.

They cope well with change and are generally tolerant and flexible, with the exception of situations where someone undermines their convictions or behaves in a manner which affronts their principles. When that happens, they are quite capable not only of voicing their opposition, but also of taking up the fight in defence of their arguments. Undertakings with no rational grounds underpinning them are something they approach with reservation.

Pitfalls

On the whole, *logicians* find everyday, routine activities tiresome and dislike shopping for clothes, cosmetics and toiletries, paying bills and doing the housework, viewing such chores as thieves of their valuable time. As a result, they will neglect them, be it consciously or unconsciously.

Logical discrepancies, sloppy or imprecise statements and arguments which are big on verbosity, but low on content all irritate them immensely and they have tremendous difficulty in understanding people who fail to share their fervour for seeking the truths about the world. Intellectual laziness and incompetence get their hackles up, while they are simply flabbergasted by people who have no driving urge to develop, perceiving them, for instance, as dilettantes, even when they have many years of experience working in a given area.

Academic titles, status, position and popularity make no impression on them; what they value is competence, knowledge, experience and intelligence. They enjoy the company of honest, open and genuine people, who, regardless of their field, are knowledgeable about what they do.

As others see them

Other people see *logicians* as straightforward and honest, but as people who are, nonetheless, difficult to get close to. During an initial encounter, they can give the impression of being diffident and alienated. However, amongst their friends and acquaintances, they have a greater sense of certainty, particularly when they voice their own views or theories. They can gain a reputation for being unreliable, absent-minded and none too well organised on account of the fact that, when they are excited by new ideas, they will often forget prior arrangements and promises. In general, others find their mind-set difficult to understand and, to some people, they come across as both 'too clever by half' and unduly critical, while others are irritated by their tendency to split hairs and incessantly correct everyone and everything.

Seeing and solving problems

Logicians are nimble-minded, exceptionally quick-witted people who are completely at home in the world of abstract theories and enjoy occasional surges of inspiration and illumination. They love fresh challenges, are always happy to learn something new and their attitude towards hitherto unknown concepts is an enthusiastic one. The chance to experiment is more important to them than stability and a sense of security and they love innovative and unconventional approaches to problems. Endowed with an uncommon gift for identifying hypothetical possibilities and both formulating new theories and pouring cold water on old ones, they think in atypical, unconventional ways and will thus often arrive at solutions which no one else has even approached. Their thinking is global and what interests them are comprehensive, far-reaching solutions. They perceive disparate phenomena as part of a greater whole and identify the connections between them.

Logical arguments and decisions grounded in objectivity and rationality are what carry weight with them; they remain utterly unpersuaded by activities undertaken on the basis of subjective emotions and feelings. Capable of forming a precise definition of problems and focusing on the essential, they are quick to detect any and every inaccuracy and imprecision. Their pursuit of objective truth is more important to them than other people's well-being, as is treading the path of logic; hence their belief that operating on the basis of emotions, feelings, likes and dislikes is out of the question. When they have their nose to the scent in a quest, they are both dogged in the extreme and objective to a fault. They will seek solutions to problems regardless of whether it will be of any benefit to themselves and never give up on their search, even when they can see that a potential discovery will cost them dearly, for example, by overturning a viewpoint they have held thus far.

Communication

Logicians express themselves succinctly, precisely and as faultlessly as they possibly can. Indeed, when it comes to describing reality and defining problems, their exactitude outstrips that of all the other fifteen personality types. However, they are not in the least talkative by nature and mainly speak when they have something important to say. They tend to communicate rarely and are even capable of going for lengthy periods without uttering so much as a word. They are neither numbered among those people who talk simply to kill time or keep the atmosphere friendly, nor do they set much store by convention, politeness and courteous gestures. Celebratory parties and social gatherings are torture to them.

All of this means that, at times, they may well commit various kinds of gaffes or behave tactlessly, which can be mistaken for a dislike of people. They also find it challenging to listen to pronouncements which, in their opinion, are devoid of sense or contain erroneous information. In situations of that kind, they have a tendency to put people right, a habit which can sometimes cause tension in their relationships with others and lead to their being taken as someone who 'always knows best'.

In discussions they are invincible, since matching their logical and cohesive arguments is no simple matter. They are happiest when talking about problems of a theoretical nature which are currently bothering them. However, they may not always find themselves in the company of people who share their love of that type of searching conversation.

At times, they cut themselves off from others, avoiding all contact with them. Some people may erroneously assume them to be making a show of their distance and superiority, when what they are actually doing is fulfilling their natural need for the silence and solitariness that are essential to them if they are to collect their thoughts and 'recharge their batteries'.

In the face of stress

Logicians frequently become genuine experts in the fields they are involved in. Although they are normally self-assured and conscious of their own abilities, they are also well aware of their limitations, deficiencies and defects. Indeed, there are times when they quite simply feel overwhelmed by what they feel to be the sheer magnitude of their ignorance or are tormented by their fear of failing and of making mistakes.

In stressful situations, they lose their self-assurance and either begin to react to stimuli in ways which are out of all proportion or become exceptionally suspicious and mistrustful. They love spending their free time at home. Copious readers, they also enjoy logic games. Nonetheless, even when they are 'off-duty', their minds are always intensively at work, turning the problems which are currently engaging them over in their thoughts as they continue their unending search for truths and solutions.

Socially

The interior world of *logicians* is an intensely rich one, but they often give the impression of being removed from the world around them. Neither extending their group of friends and acquaintances nor developing their relationships with other people are among their priorities and, by the same token, others find it difficult to get to know them and penetrate their world.

Logicians dislike calling attention to themselves and feel uncomfortable when they find themselves at the centre of attention. They build new acquaintanceships slowly and cautiously, being reluctant to confide in others and rarely turning to them for help, since they have a fear of becoming dependent and losing their autonomy. Accepting criticism well themselves, they are also capable of voicing critical opinions addressed to others. Nonetheless, they do their best to avoid conflict, though not at any price.

As a rule, they have difficulty both in reading other people's emotions and feelings and in expressing their own. They are better able to convey their affections and show tenderness in writing than face to face. All of this, combined with their natural scepticism, critical assessment, mistrust and tendency to set people right means that they find building relationships with others a challenging affair. They are lost in situations which call for the expression of feelings or public displays of affection and find themselves on equally shaky ground in the face of tension and conflict. In such situations, failing to grasp the importance of people's injured emotions and hurt feelings, they will try appealing to logic in an effort to analyse the situation and establish the rational causes of the problem.

Amongst friends

Logicians are happy amongst those who share their interests or are experts in a particular field. They also enjoy being with people they view as authorities and with whom they can share their reflections. As they see it, relationships with other people should serve some purpose, such as the acquisition of knowledge or a search for truths about the world, for instance. Being uncertain of themselves in the area of emotions and feelings, they endeavour to use logic as their guide in their interpersonal communications, an approach which severely limits their field of view and means that they may sometimes hurt others by their behaviour, failing to perceive that they should show someone their gratitude or appreciation of their efforts, for instance. They simply have no grasp of how this can leave people feeling disappointed or disheartened.

As a rule, they have only a few friends or close acquaintances. Those relationships, however, are extremely deep and enduring. They most often strike up friendships with *strategists*, *innovators*, *practitioners* and other *logicians* who share their enthusiasms and interests, while *advocates*, *protectors* and *presenters* will most rarely figure among their friends.

As life partners

Logicians are neither predisposed towards establishing new friendships nor interested in being popular and liked by others. Nonetheless, a solitary life in no way seems to them to be ideal. As life partners, they are extraordinarily loyal, faithful and constant in their feelings and they take their responsibilities extremely seriously. With their minimalist approach to life, their own needs are usually modest. Everyday household duties are not something they excel at and they have a tendency to forget prior arrangements, deadlines and anniversaries.

Highly tolerant by nature, they offer their partner a great deal of freedom and expect the same themselves. They bring passion and enthusiasm to their relationships via the conduit of their inventiveness, imagination and rich interior lives. At times, however, they struggle to reconcile their ideas and visions with reality. The most critical problem they face stems from their inability to identify their partner's feelings and emotional needs. They may love them dearly and yet, at one and the same time, have absolutely no grasp whatsoever of their feelings, their emotions and what they are experiencing, a character trait which is often mistakenly perceived as a lack of interest. In difficult situations and moments of crisis, they may well start seeking the rational causes underlying the problems and endeavour to solve them logically, without noticing that their partner quite simply needs them to show some care, concern, warmth and love. They are often astonished to discover that someone should expect this of them, since they themselves have no such needs. At the same time, it is an issue which can give rise to problems within their relationships.

Logicians will sometimes accuse their partner of exaggerating or making exorbitant demands. When subjected to pressure, they might well withdraw from the relationship, recognising that the situation has outgrown them and that their partner does not accept them or has expectations which are too high. Experiences of this kind mean that they will sometimes choose the single life. The natural candidates for a *logician's* life partner are people of a personality type akin to their own; *strategists, innovators* or *directors*. Building mutual understanding and harmonious relations will be easier in a union of that kind. Nonetheless, experience has taught us that people are also capable of creating happy and successful relationships despite what would seem to be an evident typological incompatibility. Moreover, the differences between two partners can lend added dynamics to a relationship and engender personal development. Indeed, for many people, this is a prospect that appears more attractive than the vision of a harmonious relationship wherein concord and full, mutual understanding hold sway.

As parents

As parents, *logicians* are extremely loyal to their children and have a driving urge to bring them up to be independent adults who are guided by logic and are capable of forming rational and autonomous opinions. They respect their individualism, value their opinions and allow them to take part in making decisions concerning family life. As a rule, they do not impose limitations on their offspring, but allow them a great deal of freedom and space to develop.

Their flexibility, openness and tolerance may well trigger unlooked-for side effects, since their children sometimes have problems in distinguishing good and desirable behaviour from bad and reprehensible. They also run into trouble when it comes to meeting their offspring's emotional needs and it can happen that their children will resort to radical and undesirable behaviour in an attempt to call attention to themselves. Later in life, they appreciate their *logician* parents first and foremost for teaching them to be independent and for the respect they showed for their decisions and choices.

Work and career paths

What sets *logicians'* pulses racing is working on pioneering and innovative projects and they love stepping into areas which no one else has yet explored. Characterised by both their loyalty towards their employer and the high standards of their work, they are able to evaluate other people's skills and competence in a flash. In general, they are highly demanding of themselves and of others and any manifestation whatsoever of wastefulness, perfunctoriness and laziness irritates them enormously.

Views on workplace hierarchy

Logicians appreciate knowledge, experience, intelligence and open-mindedness in their superiors and expect nothing from them barring the fact that they create a space where those they supervise can work unhindered and then refrain from interfering, leaving them alone to get on with things.

They themselves dislike leading other people, checking up on them, disciplining them and issuing them with instructions. Even so, they have a tremendous influence on others and inspire them, since they are an inexhaustible source of new ideas and have no fear of taking risks.

Enthusiasms and stumbling blocks

Logicians have no liking at all for routine activities and cope badly in positions demanding their ready availability and compliance with rigid rules and bureaucratic procedures. They approach their duties and responsibilities very seriously, but may sometimes be neglectful when it comes to formalities and official requirements such as compiling reports, for instance.

Their preference is for solving complex problems of a theoretical nature and requiring logical thought, while their enthusiasm turns more towards doing the groundwork for projects than accomplishing them. Organisational and practical aspects are something they will readily leave to others.

As part of a team

Logicians are happiest working independently. They dislike being checked up on and supervised; their need is for autonomy and independence. Indeed, at times they can be obsessive as far as their privacy is concerned. They prize peace and quiet and are most content when they can work from home. However, they are capable of organising the workloads of a group if solving a vital problem demands it.

They fit into a team relatively well when it consists not of a formal, hierarchical structure, but of a loosely connected group of enthusiastic experts committed to the matter in hand. Their liking is for a tolerant environment which offers extensive freedom of action and the space to bring creative and innovative concepts to the light of day.

Professions

Knowledge of our own personality profile and natural preferences provides us with invaluable help in choosing the optimal path in our professional careers. Experience has shown that, while *logicians* are perfectly able to work and find fulfilment in a range of fields, their personality type naturally predisposes them to the following fields and professions:

- analyst
- archaeologist
- architect
- artistic director
- chemist
- computer programmer
- computer systems expert
- detective
- economist
- expert consultant and witness
- engineer
- film producer
- financial adviser
- historian
- IT specialist
- investment and stockbroking
- lawyer
- linguist
- mathematician
- musician
- philosopher
- photographer
- research and development specialist
- risk assessment expert
- scientist
- strategy specialist
- translator
- tertiary educator
- urban and rural planning
- writer

Potential strengths and weaknesses

Like any other personality type, *logicians* have their potential strengths and weaknesses and this potential can be cultivated in a variety of ways. *Logicians'* personal happiness and professional fulfilment depend on whether they make the most of the 'pluses' offered by their personality type and face up to its inherent dangers. Here, then is a SUMMARY of those 'pluses' and dangers:

Potential strengths

Logicians are extraordinarily intelligent, creative and inventive, with the ability to connect disparate facts and experiences and build comprehensive and cohesive systems from them. Unconventional and original, their attitude towards new concepts and ideas is an enthusiastic one. Their concentration skills are extraordinary and they are impossible to distract; dragging them away from a task they deem important is a struggle, since they are more than capable of turning their entire energy towards solving whatever problem is currently engaging them. They are characterised by their high level of intellectual independence and other people's opinions make no major impression on them. If a point of view seems to them to be logically lacking in cohesion and irrational, they will discard it without regard for whether or not a recognised authority stands behind it or the majority subscribe to it.

They have the ability to make excellent use of their experiences, successes and failures alike. By nature persevering, they will usually set themselves a high benchmark and, as a result, they frequently become genuine experts in the fields they are involved in. Perfectly at home in the world of abstract theories and complex concepts, they have the gifts of assimilating them and of logical, rational thinking, along with a natural talent for mathematics and the ability to formulate their thoughts precisely and succinctly. They are quick to spot any kind of incoherence, inconsistency or logical discrepancy; at the same time, their extraordinary precision and logicality go hand in hand with their tolerance, flexibility and open-mindedness. They accord other people freedom and independence, are able to make decisions quickly and have no problem handling criticism from others.

Potential weaknesses

Logicians are extremely logical, but their logic can be subjective and selective, since they have a tendency to focus on information which is connected to their current object of interest or constitutes a confirmation of their opinions and experience. At the same time, they might well discard arguments and findings which either go against their own experience or are not grounded in logic, and they are capable of simply ignoring people who live and perceive the world in a way different from their own. They frequently involve themselves solely in things which suit their inclinations and interest them, a tendency which can eventually limit their experiences and contact with others. Indeed, it might even lead to a form of self-isolation.

Logicians find voicing their own emotions challenging. They also struggle with perceiving the emotional needs of others and may well hurt them without the slightest awareness that they have done so. Sometimes unreliable, unpunctual, forgetful and absent-minded, they cope badly with everyday, routine activities. Implementing theoretical concepts in practice is also something they have little aptitude for. In stressful situations, they are likely to react to stimuli in ways which are out of all proportion and lose their sense of self-assurance. Deprived of the possibility of engaging in what fascinates them, they may begin to construct a negatively critical attitude towards the world around them. As it develops, it becomes manifest in the form of questioning the sincere intentions of others, correcting them to an abnormal extent and criticising anything and everything which goes against their own point of view.

Personal development

Logicians' personal development depends on the extent to which they make use of their natural potential and surmount the dangers inherent in their personality type. What follows are some practical tips which, together, form a specific guide that we might call *The Logician's Ten Commandments*.

Take an interest in people

Try putting yourself in their shoes. Give some thought to what they are going through, what fascinates them, what worries them and what they fear. Ask them how they feel, what they need and what their opinions are. Show them some warmth and be more generous in your praise. Then wait and see. The difference will come as a pleasant surprise!

Learn to manage your time and set priorities

Enthusiasm is your main driving force. Nonetheless, listing priorities, establishing time frames and planning out a job are not in the least the same thing as forging chains to shackle your creativity, fetter your activities and encumber you as you carry out the task. Perish the thought! They are tools and when you use them properly they will help you achieve the goals you are aiming for.

Allow people to make mistakes

Be more restrained in your criticism and correction of others. Continually setting people right and supplementing what they say makes an appalling impression. If the matter in hand is inconsequential, let people make mistakes and go beyond the facts. No one will suffer as a result – and just think of all the energy you'll save!

Say more

Share your thoughts and ideas with others. Express your emotions. Tell people how you feel and what you are going through. You will be helping your colleagues and your nearest and dearest immensely when you do. Whatever you say, it will usually be better than remaining silent.

Broaden your horizons

Test the water with things that go beyond the world of whatever you are currently interested in. Go somewhere you have never been before, talk to people you have never got to know before, take on tasks from fields you have never been involved in before. It will give you a host of valuable ideas and mean that you start seeing the world from a wider perspective.

Stop discarding other people's ideas and opinions

Just because other people's ideas and opinions conflict with you own, this does not automatically mean that they are wrong. Before you judge them as valueless, give them some serious consideration and try to understand them. The ability to listen could well revolutionise your relationship with others.

Remember important dates and anniversaries

Arrangements to meet people, the birthdays of those closest to you and family anniversaries may seem like rather trivial matters to you in comparison to whatever it is you are involved in. They matter a great deal to other people, though. So if you are incapable of remembering them, jot them down somewhere handy – and then remember to check those notes!

Stop isolating yourself

In all likelihood, you have never enjoyed gossip, chit-chat and social get-togethers. Nonetheless, nurture your contacts with your close friends and meet up with people who like discussing the topics that interest you. You could also try getting to know people online, via discussion groups, social media or sectoral fora, for instance.

Be more practical

Give some thought to the practical aspects of your theories and ideas. To make the very most of their potential, try persuading other people to come round to them and considering ways of turning them into reality. Why leave the fruits of your work to languish, neglected and unaccomplished to the full?

Focus on the positive

Instead of concentrating on what is missing, on mistakes, logical contradictions and questioning other people's good intentions, learn to identify the positive and fix your gaze on the bright side of life.

Well-known figures

Below is a list of some well-known people who match the *logician's* profile:

- **Blaise Pascal** (1623-1662); a French mathematician, physicist, philosopher and apologist.
- **Adam Smith** (1723-1790); a Scottish moral philosopher and economist whose works include *An Inquiry into the Nature and Causes of the Wealth of Nations*.

- **James Madison** (1751-1836); the 4th president of the United States and a signatory of the American Constitution.
- **Charles Darwin** (1809-1882); an English biologist, he formulated the theory of evolution.
- **William James** (1842-1910); an American philosopher, psychologist, psychotherapist and precursor of humanistic psychology and phenomenology.
- **Carl Gustav Jung** (1875-1961); a Swiss psychiatrist and psychologist, he founded analytical psychology.
- **Albert Einstein** (1879-1955); born into a Jewish family in Germany, he was one of the greatest physicists and logicians of all time. The creator of the theory of relativity and co-creator of the wave-particle theory of light, he was awarded a Nobel Prize "for his services to Theoretical Physics, especially for his discovery of the law of the photoelectric effect".
- **Dwight David Eisenhower** (1890-1969); an American general, he became the 34th president of the United States.
- **Gregory Peck** (1916-2003); an American stage and screen actor whose filmography includes *The Guns of Navarone*.
- **George Soros** (born in 1930); an American financier, currency speculator and philanthropist of Hungarian-Jewish extraction.
- **Bob Geldof** (Robert Frederick Zenon Geldof; born in 1951); an Irish singer-songwriter and social activist.
- **J. K. Rowling** (Joanne Murray; born in 1965); an English writer, the author of the Harry Potter books.

- **Tiger Woods** (Eldrick Tont Woods; born in 1975); an American professional golfer, considered to be one of the all-time greatest representatives of the sport.

The Mentor (INFJ)

The Personality in a Nutshell

Life motto: The world CAN be a better place!

In brief, *mentors* …

are creative and sensitive. With their gaze fixed firmly on the future, they spot opportunities and potential imperceptible to others. Idealists and visionaries, they are geared towards helping people and are conscientious, responsible and, at one and the same time, courteous, caring and friendly. They strive to understand the mechanisms governing the world and view problems from a wide perspective.

Superb listeners and observers, *mentors* are characterised by their extraordinary empathy, intuition and trust of people and are capable of reading the feelings and emotions of others. They find criticism and conflict difficult to bear and can come across as enigmatic.

The *mentor's* four natural inclinations:

- source of life energy: the interior world
- mode of assimilating information: intuition
- decision-making mode: the heart
- lifestyle: organised

Similar personality types:

- the Idealist
- the Counsellor
- the Enthusiast

Statistical data:

- *mentors* constitute one per cent of the global community and are the most rarely occurring of the sixteen personality types
- women predominate among *mentors* (80 per cent)
- Norway is an example of a nation corresponding to the *mentor's* profile [13]

The Four-Letter Code

In terms of Jungian personality typology, the universal four-letter code for the *mentor* is INFJ.

General character traits

Mentors may be the most rarely occurring of the sixteen personality types, but they have an enormous influence on the fates of other people and, indeed, of the world. They perceive things which are far from evident to others, seeing

---

[13] What this means is not that all the residents of Norway fall within this personality type, but that Norwegian society as a whole possesses a great many of the character traits typical of the *mentor*.

the connections between disparate events and identifying repeated patterns of behaviour. When working to solve problems, they analyse the situation from various angles and different perspectives. As a rule, they are capable of foreseeing the possible development of events and identifying the potential opportunities and dangers in a given set of circumstances.

They are also aware that another world exists, a world which can only be construed through intuition or faith. The spiritual dimension of life is frequently more important to them than the material one perceived via the senses.

Interior compass

By nature, *mentors* are idealists and they are usually characterised by their extremely high moral standards and ethical conduct. They will often ponder over how to make the most of their life's potential and they thirst both to improve themselves and to help other people find their place in the world, convinced that it is the natural duty of every human being to assist others and stand in the defence of the less powerful and those who are unable to look after their own interests. With their longing to meliorate the world, solve its problems and help people to develop, they believe that, if only everyone made a genuine effort to understand others, life would be easier and the world would be a much better place. When they involve themselves in something, they do so because they are aware that there is an issue to be solved and not for the sake of their careers or prospective honours.

Mentors may be visionaries, but they are also activists. Not content with concepts alone, they strive to breathe life into their ideas and have a sense that they are always 'on call', being ever at the ready to launch into action and take up the cudgels to defend those who are the victims of oppression. Their lives are guided by a clear aim: they have an extremely powerful conviction as to what is important and what needs to be done and there is little that can stop them from accomplishing their visions.

Mentors will often invoke a range of theories or concepts. Drawn to the world of the spirit, they have a liking for symbol and metaphor. At the same time, a host of widely accepted forms of behaviour and customs strike them as utterly devoid of sense and they struggle to come to terms with the fact that other people see them in a different light.

Perception

Mentors hunger for a better understanding of the world. They reflect on the meaning and sense of life and are absorbed by questions of a philosophical and/or religious nature. Intent observers, they endeavour to fit all the new information and data they acquire into their internal picture of the world. If that proves impossible, they will acknowledge that either that picture or their outlook might need rearranging or restructuring.

This internal process, invisible to the eyes of others, is something they engage in throughout their lives. Their minds are constantly at work in top gear and they are scrupulous in their analysis of new data. Today's world, where people are bombarded by an ever increasing volume of information, frequently sends *mentors* into overload. They try to cope with the sheer mass of the data coming their way by reducing it, ignoring things which are similar to something they have already assimilated.

As others see them

Other people see *mentors* as extremely warm, friendly and likeable, while their wisdom and creative approach to problems arouse widespread respect. On the other hand, they are highly intuitive and their personalities are complex, which makes them difficult to get to know and challenging to fathoming out. Indeed, they can give the impression of being both puzzling and mysterious; they have their own world and they guard it against others. The only people they will allow into it are those closest to them – but they can still come up with a number of surprises even for their nearest and dearest! Moreover, there are some aspects of their personalities which they themselves find baffling.

Given that they need solitude and calm in order to 'recharge their batteries', *mentors* will sometimes withdraw to the sidelines, though this is not to say that they keep people at a distance. On the contrary, they continue to show them warmth and take a genuine interest in them. They surround those closest to them with particular solicitude and will always make every effort to ensure that no one hurts or harms them.

Communication

In general, *mentors* are past masters of the spoken and written word. Capable of expressing their thoughts clearly, they communicate superbly with others. However, they are often averse to speaking in public, although they cope extremely well when forced to do so. They are also outstanding listeners and observers, not only decoding what other people say, but also reading their gestures and feelings. Being well aware of the immense power of words, they are usually able to keep the language they use under firm control and are equally as capable of remaining silent if they believe it to be for the best.

Mentors are unstinting in their praise and themselves enjoy the compliments of others. On the other hand, they find criticism hard to cope with, often taking it as a personal attack. Excessive bureaucracy and formalism irritate them immensely; however, they also dislike the kind of familiarity manifest in back-slapping, shoulder clapping and other forms of physical contact during a conversation.

Thinking

Mentors often reflect on the purpose of their life and on what they want to achieve in it, and they may well reassess their priorities and formulate them anew. They are often plagued by an inner sense of anxiety: with so many ideas, they will never succeed in bringing all of them to fruition and they frequently upbraid themselves for not making the very most of their capabilities and potential, or for not doing more for others.

With their ability to foresee future opportunities and dangers, the present serves them not as a goal, but as a springboard. In general, their eyes are fixed firmly on the future and they have no real perception of their previous achievements; indeed, they often remain unaware of just how much they have already accomplished. For *mentors*, the horizon is always teeming with fresh needs to be met and new tasks to be tackled.

Decisions

When confronted with the need to make a decision, *mentors* not only need time to weigh up the various possible solutions, but peace, quiet and, for preference, seclusion while they do so. Their ideas are often unconventional. They dislike conflict, but if they recognise that it will have positive results, they will not go out of their way to avoid it.

Order is something they prize greatly and they will struggle to function in surroundings where chaos holds sway. Before they set about doing something, they devote a good deal of energy and time to gathering the requisite information and establishing the best way of going about it. As a rule, they let their intuition be their guide and trust in their presentiments, a *modus operandi* which can sometimes lead to their neglecting other people's opinions or digging their heels in and sticking to their own view.

In the face of stress

Mentors are susceptible to stress. Often plagued by an inner tension, they frequently find it well nigh impossible to relax. This, in turn, can give rise to somatic problems such as high blood pressure. When they do succeed in tearing themselves away from their commitments, they prefer to relax in peace, in the company of their nearest and dearest and "far from the madding crowd".

Socially

Mentors have deep and complex personalities. At the same time, though, they are friendly and display enormous warmth towards others. They have no liking for convention or courteous gestures and derive no enjoyment from superficial relationships. Forging a friendship with people whose behaviour goes against their convictions or who try to give the impression of being something other than they are is beyond their capabilities.

They often have a talent for leadership, despite not being people of the leader-cum-showman ilk, since they neither seek the spotlight nor pursue recognition. Nonetheless, they are capable of exercising an extraordinary influence on other people. They are outstanding mentors ... hence the name for this personality type. Given their talent for spurring others to start looking at the world and their own situation in new ways, people find meeting them and talking to them to be a source of inspiration and a motivating force.

With their genuine interest in other people's problems, their ability to listen and their remarkable intuition, they make outstanding advisors and therapists. Their relationships with others are extremely direct and personal and they are not deceived by appearances, but have the gift of reading other people's real feelings and emotions, even when those people themselves are unconscious of them.

Amongst friends

Mentors seek natural, profound relationships. They value sincerity and authenticity and their commitment is absolute and limitless, on occasions even to the point where their critical faculties are suspended. Their ability to control their emotions and their need for solitude mean that strangers can sometimes make the mistake of perceiving them as distanced from their surroundings, whereas, in fact, they have an enormous liking for people and good interpersonal relationships matter to them greatly. They are faithful friends and, believing that true friendships make life better, they are ready to invest immense effort and energy in nurturing and improving their own.

Although they shun the pursuit of popularity, they are usually widely liked. People appreciate not only their friendly attitude, honesty and creative approach to their tasks, but also the fact that they help others to identify and make the most of their potential. They themselves are happiest amongst people who understand them and who accept and respect them for who they are.

Their circle tends to include representatives of well-nigh all the sixteen personality types. However, they most frequently strike up a friendship with *idealists*, *counsellors*, *protectors* and other *mentors* and, most rarely, with *animators*, *practitioners* and *administrators*. In general, their friendships are few, but their relationships with the people closest to them are profound and long-lasting.

As life partners

Mentors make highly devoted and caring partners. Their feelings run deep and they frequently see their relationship with their partner as something mystical and spiritual, yearning for that complete union of heart and mind which will allow them to share their most profound feelings, experiences, dreams and visions.

Demonstrative of their love themselves, they, too, enjoy gestures and expressions of affection and long for that perfect union, an attitude which means that they are not only devoted to their partner, but are also ready and willing to work at their relationships. However, when taken to extremes, it is an approach which can often prove wearing and frustrating for their partner, who may well fear that they are incapable of meeting those high expectations. It might also happen that *mentors* will seek their ideal outside their relationship.

The natural candidates for a *mentor's* life partner are people of a personality type akin to their own: *idealists*, *counsellors* or *enthusiasts*. Building mutual understanding and harmonious relations will be easier in a union of that kind. Nonetheless, experience has taught us that people are also capable of creating happy and successful relationships despite what would seem to be an evident typological incompatibility. Moreover, the differences between two partners can lend added dynamics to a relationship and engender personal development.

As parents

The role of parent comes as naturally to *mentors* as breathing and they take it extremely seriously. Loving and devoted, they are ready to give their children their all, demonstrating warmth and tenderness in abundance and, as a rule, enjoying close and profound relationships with them. They also take the time to explain to them how the world works, desiring to bring them up to be independent adults, capable of thinking and deciding for themselves, forming their own opinions and distinguishing good from bad. They go about this by allowing their offspring to take part in making a range of decisions, motivating them to learn and encouraging them to make the most of their talents and gifts. However, they also make high demands of them and are capable of severity.

Their offspring trust them immensely and will thus readily turn to them for help with their problems. They will sometimes resent the fact that they have to make much more of an effort than some of their peers; however, as adults, they are grateful to their *mentor* parents for demanding that of them and appreciate the way that they taught them to lead good lives and encouraged them to make the most of their talents and do something concrete with their enthusiasms.

Work and career paths

When they can see the sense of what they are doing, *mentors* have the ability to work hard and are ready to devote themselves to the task in hand. Whatever it may be, they will strive to accomplish it to the highest possible standard. Given their aversion to crowds and superficial interpersonal relationships, they are happiest working independently or in small groups.

As part of a team

Mentors dislike conflict, confrontation and antagonism, believing that harmonious collaboration and a friendly atmosphere are the best guarantees of success. They themselves bring that atmosphere to a team and they are often the people who will help others both to take a wider view of problems and to attain success.

When it comes to their superiors, they appreciate strong leaders who act in accordance with their ideals and, at one and the same time, support the people they supervise.

Aims

Mentors enjoy helping others to solve problems. To that end, they employ an approach which involves inducing them to ask the right questions and then seek the answers. The knowledge that they are being of some assistance gives them enormous satisfaction and, with their unshakeable belief that they can have an impact on the destiny of their country and, indeed of the world, they set themselves ambitious goals. While aims of that ilk might well strike other people as high-flown or simply unrealistic, *mentors* themselves take them extremely seriously.

Companies and institutions

Mentors fit in well in companies or institutions which are geared towards establishing equal opportunities, supporting the local community or helping people who are unable to cope with their problems. As such, they often find their niche in welfare and other social work, in counselling or consultancy and in education. They also make good writers and members of the clergy.

Often the minds behind all kinds of systemic solutions, including those related to the life of society, they are in their element in any position which demands creativity and provides them with independence of action.

Tasks

Mentors enjoy tasks which enable them to help other people and change the world for the better. On the other hand, they are at a loss when faced with the necessity of carrying out administrative work which requires meticulous attention to elaborate detail, the analysis of documents or the processing of data, and are equally as confounded when it comes to operating in situations involving a conflict of interests or performing a job which goes against their outlook on the world.

Professions

Knowledge of our own personality profile and natural preferences provides us with invaluable help in choosing the optimum path in our professional careers. Experience has shown that, while *mentors* are perfectly able to work and find fulfilment in a range of fields, their personality type naturally predisposes them to the following fields and professions:

- advisor
- the arts
- clergy
- consultant
- designer
- dietician
- editor
- educator
- filmmaker
- human resources
- journalist
- legal guardian
- librarian
- life coach
- mediator
- paramedic
- physician
- physiotherapist
- photographer
- project coordinator
- psychologist
- physiotherapist
- rehabilitation
- scientist
- social welfare
- sociologist
- teacher
- television producer
- therapist
- writer

Potential strengths and weaknesses

Like any other personality type, *mentors* have their potential strengths and weaknesses and this potential can be cultivated in a variety of ways. *Mentors'* personal happiness and professional fulfilment depend on whether they make the most of the 'pluses' offered by their personality type and face up to its inherent dangers. Here, then, is a SUMMARY of those 'pluses' and dangers:

Potential strengths

Mentors perceive things which are far from evident to others, seeing the connections between disparate events and repeated patterns of behaviour. When working to solve problems, they analyse the situation from various angles and different perspectives and have the ability to look ahead and identify future potential, possibilities and dangers. Their ideas are highly creative and unconventional and they have an excellent grasp of complex theories and abstract concepts.

They forge natural, sincere and profound interpersonal relationships, being genuinely interested in other people and their problems and sensitive to their feelings and needs. Characterised by their extraordinary intuition, empathy and natural warm-heartedness, they are splendid observers and listeners, capable of reading the feelings and emotions of others, inspiring them to discover and make the most of their potential and motivating them to take responsibility for their own lives.

Mentors strive for perfection and are able to penetrate beneath the surface of problems and identify their essence. When they see the sense of their work, they are capable of focusing on the task or matter in hand and are ready to make numerous sacrifices in devoting themselves to it. Conscientious and responsible, they treat any and every task they undertake seriously and are incapable of consciously working to anything less than their full ability. Indeed, given their desire to see everyone make the most of their potential and talents, they are extremely demanding of themselves and others alike. As past masters of the spoken and written word, they are able to express their thoughts clearly and comprehensibly.

Potential weaknesses

Mentors' idealism means that they often have trouble functioning in the real world and can be rather unfocused; for instance, when discussing a problem, they may well diverge from the matter in hand, drifting into considerations of a more general nature. They also struggle with everyday, routine activities and are inclined to forget details.

Their expectations of others can be unrealistic and may fail to make allowances for people's natural limitations, a tendency which often gives the impression that they are impossible to satisfy. As a rule, they assume that they are right, often not even offering an explanation of the basis for that conviction. They are also prone to dismissing other people's views in advance, without trying to hear them out. Their multilayered perception of reality often causes them to reflect on the rightness of the road they have chosen and the decisions they have made. They are frequently at a loss in situations requiring improvisation or rapid decisions.

Sharing their problems with others and accepting their help comes hard to them, as does coping in situations of conflict. They handle criticism very badly, often taking it as a personal attack and they respond poorly to stress, which drives them into a state of internal tension, frequently triggering somatic symptoms and depriving them of their faith in their own capabilities; indeed, at times, they will even turn to using substances.

Mentors are not only highly sensitive and easily hurt, but can also struggle to forgive, and may well go on nursing their injuries for a long time.

Personal development

Mentors' personal development depends on the extent to which they make use of their natural potential and surmount the dangers inherent in their personality type. What follows are some practical tips which, together, form a specific guide that we might call *The Mentor's Ten Commandments.*

Talk to people about your ideas

Not everyone will know how you came up with an idea, so why assume that it's obvious? Talking it over with your nearest and dearest or your colleagues not only does wonders for the atmosphere, but will also help you view it from a new perspective.

Stop fearing criticism

Quell your fear of expressing your own critical opinions and of accepting criticism from others. Criticism can be constructive. There is no law which says that it has to mean attacking people or undermining their worth.

Be more practical

You have a natural inclination to come up with idealistic notions which sometimes have little in common with real life. Give some thought to the practical aspects and to how they can actually be accomplished in this imperfect world we live in.

Stop dismissing other people's ideas and opinions

Listen carefully to what people have to say and try to understand their ideas before you dismiss them or announce that you have heard them before. Avoid assuming that no one else knows as much about a given matter as you do; this, in itself, is a mistake!

Stop being afraid of conflict

Conflicts do arise sometimes, even in our closest circles. They need not necessarily be destructive, though. In fact, they very often help us to uncover problems and solve them! So, when conflicts emerge, stop hiding your head in the sand and, instead, express your point of view and feelings about the situation openly.

Stop blaming others for your problems

Give some serious thought to where they spring from. Oversights and mistakes are not things that only happen to others. You, too, can be the root of a problem.

Stop conjuring up dark scenarios

Turn your focus away from threats and dangers. The fear they engender can become paralysing. Worry less and do more! Concentrate on life's brighter aspects and try to make the most of their potential.

Be more understanding

Show more patience towards other people's weaknesses and shortcomings. Remember that not everyone should be assigned the same tasks, because not everyone is skilled in the same fields. People's deficiencies are not manifestations of their ill-will, disinclination or laziness.

Take some time out

Try to get away from your responsibilities and duties once in a while and do something for the sheer pleasure, relaxation and fun of it. It will help you get a better perspective on things and you'll go back to your tasks with your mind and thinking refreshed.

Admit that you can make mistakes

None of us is infallible. Other people might well be absolutely right or partially right and you might be partially or absolutely wrong. Accept that fact and learn to admit your mistakes.

Well-known figures

Below is a list of some well-known people who match the *mentor's* profile:

- **Johann Wolfgang von Goethe** (1749-1832); the greatest German writer of the Classical period, whose poems, plays and prose works include *The ErlKing*, *Faust* and *The Sorrows of Young Werther* respectively, he was also a scholar and statesman.

- **Nathaniel Hawthorne** (1804-1864); one of America's greatest novelists and short story writers and a representative of Romanticism and transcendental philosophy, his works include *The Scarlet Letter*.

- **Emily Jane Brontë** (1818-1848); an English author and poet whose works include *Wuthering Heights*.

- **Fanny Crosby** (Frances Jane Crosby; 1820-1915); an American mission worker, poet, lyricist and composer who went blind shortly after birth, she was the author of more than eight thousand hymns and gospel songs and became one of the best-known women in the USA during her lifetime.

- **Mary Baker Eddy** (1821-1910); an American mystic, she was the founder of the Christian Science movement.

- **Mahatma Ghandi** (Mohandas Karamchand Gandhi; 1869-1948); one of the founders of the modern Indian state, he both supported and employed passive resistance as a tool for political struggle.

- **Nelson Mandela** (1918-2013); an activist in the cause of ending racial segregation in the Republic of South Africa, he went on to become the country's president and was awarded the Nobel Peace Prize.

- **Jimmy Carter** (James Earl Carter; born in 1924); the 39th president of the United States, an international activist in the cause of human rights and a holder of the Nobel Peace Prize.

- **Martin Luther King, Junior** (1929-1968); an American Baptist minister and activist in the cause of ending racial discrimination, he was awarded the Nobel Peace Prize.

- **Piers Anthony** (Piers Anthony Dillingham Jacob; born in 1934); an American science fiction and fantasy writer whose works include *Xanth*.

- **Michael Landon** (Eugene Maurice Orowitz; 1936-1991); an American screen actor, writer, director and producer whose filmography includes *Highway to Heaven*.

- **Billy Crystal** (William Edward Crystal; born in 1948); an American screen actor, director, writer and entertainer whose filmography includes *Analyze This*.

- **Mel Gibson** (Mel Columcille Gerard Gibson; born in 1956); an American screen actor whose roles include *Lethal Weapon*, he is also a director and producer with productions such as *The Passion of Christ* to his name.

- **Nicole Kidman** (born in 1967); an Australian-American screen actress and producer whose filmography includes *Cold Mountain*, she is also a singer and a UNICEF Goodwill Ambassador.

The Practitioner (ISTP)

The Personality in a Nutshell

Life motto: Actions speak louder than words.

In brief, *practitioners* …

are optimistic and spontaneous, with a positive approach to life. Reserved and independent, they hold true to their personal convictions and view external principles and norms with scepticism. They find abstract concepts and solutions for the future tiresome and would far rather roll up their sleeves and get to work on solving tangible and concrete problems.

Adapting well to new places and situations, they enjoy fresh challenges and risks and are capable of keeping a cool head in the face of threats and danger. Their general reticence and extreme reserve when it comes to expressing their opinions mean that other people may often find them impenetrable.

The *practitioner's* four natural inclinations:

- source of life energy: the interior world
- mode of assimilating information: via the senses
- decision-making mode: the mind
- lifestyle: spontaneous

Similar personality types:

- the Inspector
- the Animator
- the Administrator

Statistical data:

- *practitioners* constitute between six and nine per cent of the global community
- men predominate among *practitioners* (60 per cent)
- Singapore is an example of a nation corresponding to the *practitioner's* profile [14]

The Four-Letter Code

In terms of Jungian personality typology, the universal four-letter code for the *practitioner* is ISTP.

General character traits

Practitioners live for today. With their positive approach to life and the ability to enjoy the moment, it is rare for them

---

[14] What this means is not that all the residents of Singapore fall within this personality type, but that Singaporean society as a whole possesses a great many of the character traits typical of the *practitioner*.

to worry about the future. They exist in the here and now and, in general, dislike long-term plans, duties and obligations and are unlikely to devote overmuch time to preparation, preferring to act on impulse, rather than following a series of previously formulated steps. They are aesthetically tuned, but have no fondness for the flamboyant or bizarre, and their lifestyle is relatively simple.

Perception and learning

Practitioners spot details which escape the notice of others, but struggle when it comes to seeing the wider perspective, the long-term effects of their decisions and the connections between disparate facts and phenomena. As a rule, they view abstract theories and concepts with scepticism. With their natural 'feel' for things technical and their manual dexterity, they are practical to a fault. What appeals to them is the nitty-gritty of putting things into practice … hence the name for this personality type.

They are also more highly inclined towards risk-taking than any of the other fifteen personality types and generally number amongst those whose childhood was marked by their propensity to dismantle their toys or any device within their reach in order to find out how they were made. They often have fairly painful memories of lessons at school since they perceive dry, theoretical and monotonous tasks as tiresome in the extreme and, with their love of experiment and freedom to approach a task as they want, learn best and most readily by doing. The way things work fascinates them and, as a rule, they handle tools masterfully, carrying out all kinds of alterations, improvements and repairs with enormous skill. When solving a problem, they have the ability to zoom straight in on the equipment and materials they will need and then set to work without further ado. They excel at manual tasks and, even when doing something for the first time, may well give the impression of being experts.

Interior compass

Practitioners are flexible by nature and capable of adapting readily to new circumstances, although they are fiercely protective of their privacy and equally as firm about ensuring that no one else succeeds in organising their lives for them. They loathe being told what they should do or how they should live; indeed, on occasion, they will deliberately go so far as to behave contrary to expectations simply as a matter of principle. However, they accept criticism well and are also capable of carrying out critical appraisals of others.

Being independent in the extreme, they refuse to allow others to make decisions for them and harbour an intense dislike of being checked on and controlled. Freedom, independence and space are as necessary to them as oxygen and they are infuriated by any attempt to 'invade' their territory. At times, they can even be obsessive as far as their privacy is concerned.

In general, they are sceptical as regards widely recognised authorities and equally as dubious when it comes to norms and truths imposed from 'on high', preferring to live their lives in accordance with their own principles. On the whole, they do what they themselves believe to be right, without fretting over other people's opinions and evaluations and, being insusceptible to external pressure, are capable of standing by their convictions and predilections.

As a rule, they follow the principles of egalitarianism, believing that we are all equal and should all be treated in the same way. Titles, background and position make little impression on them, although they do respect people who have some kind of special experience or remarkable practical skill. By the same token, the respect and admiration of others gives them enormous satisfaction and they therefore like to have the sense that they are specialists in their field.

As others see them

Others view *practitioners* as self-assured, cold and highly puzzling. Even so, in matters requiring manual dexterity or technical know-how, they come across as experts and have a reputation for being resourceful, practical people who can always be counted on. Those around them are thus often surprised by their volatility – their enthusiasm wanes quickly and they often change their mind. Their short-term view of things and their lack of interest in problems which go beyond the here and now can sometimes irritate other people, who may well also be disconcerted by their mysteriousness, reticence and reluctance to share their thoughts and opinions.

In turn, *practitioners* themselves hold no truck with anyone who tries to instruct them or exert pressure on them. People who are capable of spending months discussing far-reaching plans without taking so much as a single practical step towards turning them into reality are a closed book to them. They also have enormous difficulty in assimilating the fact that, when they and others look at the same situation and have the same information at their disposal, they will come to diametrically different conclusions.

Communication

Practitioners' reticence means that people often perceive them as mysterious and impenetrable. They rarely consult others, but are independent in making their decisions, which sometimes comes as a surprise to their nearest and dearest or colleagues. The least communicative of all the sixteen personality types, they seldom have much to say and, when they do speak, they tend to be concise to the point of terseness. More often than not, though, their contribution to the conversation or discussion is highly pertinent and absolutely to the point.

Observation

Practitioners are splendid observers and unceasingly monitor their surroundings in search of new information. Quick to spot change, they evaluate any new data they acquire with an eye to either its potential impact on their own lives or the possibility of using it to solve the concrete problems they come up against. However, they also tend to discard information which is inconsistent with their experience, an approach which sometimes narrows their view and can even give rise to a growing vision of the world which is both alternative and wholly individual in nature.

Problem solving

When *practitioners* are solving a problem, they are capable of making a rapid assessment of the situation, taking all the measures and means available to them at that moment into consideration and making an on-the-spot decision which meets the occasion. They cope extremely well if a crisis develops and improvisation or rapid decisions are called for. By the same token, when tried and tested procedures or established rules fail and other people are at a loss as to what to do, *practitioners* follow their internal compass and keep a cool head, an ability which also serves them well when essential decisions need to be made in situations of increased risk or imminent danger, since they will act rationally and objectively, heedless of the emotional reactions going on around them.

Leisure

Knowing how to enjoy life and combine work and pleasure, *practitioners* have no trouble in finding time to relax, unwind and indulge in their hobbies. Their leisure pursuits often involve their manual dexterity and they also enjoy physical activities and simply having fun. They will happily meet up with people who share similar interests and views, thus deepening their knowledge and enabling them to acquire new information at one and the same time. Although they are relatively immune to stress, prolonged periods of tension can cause them to grow cynical and embittered and may also lead to their becoming increasingly self-isolated or reacting with inordinate vehemence.

Socially

Practitioners are highly reticent by nature, which makes them very unapproachable. However, the reason behind this is not the antipathy towards people which is sometimes suspected of them. On the contrary, they are tolerant, open to others and perfectly capable of forming healthy and friendly relationships.

On the other hand, they do hold to the assumption that conversations and get-togethers should serve some kind of purpose, such as collaborating to solve a problem. Spending time with other people is not something they consider to be an end in itself and, by the same token, they view integration meetings with the same intense dislike that they feel for social gatherings and celebrations. The world of conventions and courtesies leaves them utterly baffled and they are wholly incapable of making any kind of small talk, finding it astonishing that anyone has the time to talk about nothing. In general, gatherings with strangers hold as little charm for them as talking to people with completely different interests, an activity which strikes them as tiresome in the extreme.

Practitioners often run into problems as a result of their inability to express their feelings and emotions. In general, they assume that actions speak louder than words, which is why they prefer to convey their feelings and affections by doing something concrete. When the people closest to them or their friends or acquaintances need practical help, they can always be counted on.

Amongst friends

Practitioners value simplicity and independence in their relationships with others and will often consciously avoid the kind of contact which demands a more profound emotional engagement and involves expending a great deal of energy and time. They respect other people's privacy and independence, but set just as much store by their own, and take great pains to guard their own 'territory'. They are often visited by a powerful need for solitude, tranquillity and space, which is frequently misread by others as a display of distance or a lack of interest in their needs.

However, their friends are familiar with another side of their character and, in their midst, *practitioners* are not only happy to listen to them, but will frequently shower them with questions as well. Tolerant and flexible, they enjoy a reputation of being good company, and their ability to find their feet in all kinds of situations means that they are perceived as people who are always up and doing. Their ability to derive joy from life impresses others, as does their love of adventure and thrills.

Although they can listen to people with genuine interest, they themselves say little, expressing their own opinion rarely and exhibiting an extreme reluctance to open up to others. When pressed for their views, such replies as they do give may well be evasive or enigmatic. While they sometimes give the impression of being loners, the truth is that they need other people and feel isolated and superfluous without them. They forge closer relationships with people who share similar interests and views and will frequently have no more than a few friends and acquaintances, more often than not *inspectors*, *animators*, *logicians* and other *practitioners* and, most seldom, *counsellors*, *mentors* and *enthusiasts*.

As life partners

Practitioners afford their partners a great deal of the freedom that they themselves need, since they find any attempt to limit them intolerable. They bring spontaneity and enthusiasm to their relationships, habitually focusing on the present moment and devoting little time to cogitating over what the future might hold. This is not to say that they are incapable of staying in one relationship for a lifetime, though. It simply means that their view of things is not a long-term one – for *practitioners*, every day is a fresh page. Nonetheless, given that this is their usual mode of thought, the notion of taking a vow which binds them "until death do us part" might well fill them with apprehension.

Reticent by nature, it is rare for them to voice their views, opinions and feelings. The greatest challenge they face in their relationships is the other side of that same coin; in other words, their inability to identify their partner's feelings and emotional needs, which is often mistakenly perceived as a lack of interest. They may love them dearly and yet, at one and the same time, have absolutely no grasp whatsoever of their emotions and what they are feeling and experiencing. By the same token, they can simply fail to understand that their partner needs compliments and affection. Given that they themselves have no such emotional requirements, the fact that others do can come as a shock to them and leave them confounded, since they have no idea whatsoever as to how to meet them.

When a crisis looms in their relationship, *practitioners* will normally strive to save it. However, if no results are forthcoming from their efforts, they may throw in the towel, resigning themselves to the fact that the situation has got beyond their control or concluding that their partner's demands are excessive. On the whole, they have no major problems with ending toxic and destructive relationships.

The natural candidates for a *practitioner's* life partner are people of a personality type akin to their own: *inspectors*, *animators* or *administrators*. Building mutual understanding and harmonious relations will be easier in a union of that kind. Nonetheless, experience has taught us that people are also capable of creating happy and successful relationships despite what would seem to be an evident typological incompatibility. Moreover, the differences between two partners can lend added dynamics to a relationship and engender personal development. Indeed, for many people, this is a prospect that appears more attractive than the vision of a harmonious relationship wherein concord and full, mutual understanding hold sway.

As parents

Practitioners make flexible and tolerant parents who allow their children considerable freedom and the space to develop without excessive supervision. Nonetheless, they are capable of applying discipline and doling out punishments when the situation requires it. However, they feel no obligation to instil them with their own values, explain the world to them or tell them how to live, an attitude which can sometimes mean that their offspring have little knowledge of the rules that make the world go round.

Practitioners have difficulty in engaging with their children emotionally and with taking the time to talk to them and share fun and games with them. Indeed, it may well be that they are, *de facto*, more of an absence than a presence in their lives. In effect, the relationship between *practitioner* parents and their offspring is often coloured by a certain emotional distance and can run into serious trouble if the other parent also struggles to meet this aspect of their children's needs. On the other hand, they excel when it comes to providing their children with a variety of appealing activities and, in general, they are unstinting with their money and outstanding organisers of all kinds of expeditions and trips. For the *practitioners*, these are occasions when they can get to know their offspring better and, for the children, they are the most treasured moments of their childhood and will remain engraved in their memory throughout their lives.

Work and career paths

Practitioners' enthusiasms are their key to success. When they are engaged in something they love, they can move mountains. As people of action, they like to be up and doing. Change is meat and drink to them and they quickly tire of tasks which demand lengthy concentration or planning and require them to focus on the future. To a *practitioner*, the ideal undertaking is one with a short time span.

Companies and institutions

Bureaucratised institutions with rigid structures and precisely defined procedures are a torment to *practitioners:* planning, reporting and accounting for what they do are activities from another planet as far as they are concerned. Viewing routine as a form of torture, they much prefer variety and have impressive multi-tasking skills, although they normally find starting something far easier than following it through to the end.

They fit in well in companies which give their employees freedom in carrying out their tasks rather than imposing restrictions on them, and they are at their happiest when solving concrete, tangible and practical problems. Risk and experiments hold no fear for them, although they would rather work in areas which they are thoroughly familiar with. As time goes by, they will frequently become genuine experts in the fields which interest them.

As part of a team

Practitioners are perfectly capable of collaborating closely with other people. However, in their case, this will not normally lead to their forging emotional ties with the group.

As a rule, they will be the ones who bring objectivity and realistic evaluations to the work and display the ability to analyse facts coolly and without emotional engagement.

Views on workplace hierarchy

In general, given that *practitioners* are quite capable of self-motivation and thus have no need of close supervision, they appreciate superiors who provide their staff with freedom of action. When they hold a managerial position, they are quick to discern their organisation's problems and identify the weak links. Realists by nature, they are not subject to illusion and their perception of the world around them is almost never coloured by rose-tinted glasses. Trying to persuade others and themselves that "things can only get better" and that "it will all come out in the wash" is alien to them. By the same token, they suffer no qualms when it comes to ridding the organisation of poor employees without further ado.

With their dislike of consultation and their aversion to turning to others for their opinions, they hold no brief for collegial and democratic management styles, much preferring to make their decisions independently. One frequent outcome of this approach is that they fail to delegate sufficiently and wind up overburdened as a result.

Unafraid of taking risks, making bold decisions and playing for high stakes, they will sometimes hazard everything on one throw. With no fear of difficult decisions, they are capable of acting without needing comprehensive data and neither emotion nor sentiment influence what they do. Accusations are sometimes levelled at them for failing to take the human cost into account and, indeed, their primary interest is normally the objective good of the organisation rather than the staff's feelings.

Professions

Knowledge of our own personality profile and natural preferences provides us with invaluable help in choosing the optimal path in our professional careers. Experience has shown that, while *practitioners* are perfectly able to work and find fulfilment in a range of fields, their personality type naturally predisposes them to the following fields and professions:

- anti-terrorism
- the armed forces
- aviator
- carpentry, joinery and cabinet-making
- computer programmer
- computer systems analyst
- the construction industry
- crisis management
- detective
- driver
- economist
- electrician
- electronics
- engineer
- entrepreneur
- farmer
- firefighter
- IT specialist
- jeweller
- lawyer
- lifeguard
- locksmith
- pharmacist
- mechanic
- metalworker

- musician
- police officer
- security and protection
- sportswoman/sportsman
- technician

Potential strengths and weaknesses

Like any other personality type, *practitioners* have their potential strengths and weaknesses and this potential can be cultivated in a variety of ways. *Practitioners*' personal happiness and professional fulfilment depend on whether they make the most of the 'pluses' offered by their personality type and face up to its inherent dangers. Here, then, is a SUMMARY of those 'pluses' and dangers:

Potential strengths

Practitioners are spontaneous, flexible and tolerant. As excellent listeners and observers, they spot details which escape the notice of others, using the information they acquire to build an internal database unique to themselves and then applying it to solving concrete problems. Practical by nature, they have inbuilt manual and technical skills. They are self-assured, enthusiastic and optimism is their middle name. Their approach to life is positive ... *practitioners* have the ability to enjoy every moment. Change holds no fear for them and they would always rather be up and doing. When those close to them need their practical assistance, they will spare neither time nor energy in providing it.

No matter what, *practitioners* will stand firm by their convictions, remaining insusceptible to external pressure. They can handle criticism and have no trouble in expressing it themselves or calling other people's attention to shortcomings. Capable of making decisions on the basis of partial data and acting under conditions of increased risk, they cope extremely well in situations of threat and danger, crises and rapidly shifting circumstances. When others are overcome by emotion, *practitioners* keep a cool head, making objective and rational decisions. They are unafraid of bold moves and risk, a character trait which also means that they are capable of ending toxic and destructive relationships.

Potential weaknesses

The inability to express their feelings is one of the greatest weaknesses which *practitioners* face, along with their insensitivity to the emotional needs of others, an aspect of their natures which can mean that they cause hurt without even being aware of it. Their reticence may also be a source of problems, as may the fact that they have little grasp of how to suit their mode of communication to the moment. Their loathing of any kind of supervision or oversight can lead to their becoming uniquely obsessive as regards their privacy and even to their self-isolation.

Coping with long-term tasks and strategic planning comes hard to *practitioners*, since they have difficulty in seeing the wider perspective, the long-term effects of their decisions and the connections between disparate facts and phenomena, to say nothing of assimilating complex, abstract theories. Given that they are quick to grow bored, they also find focusing on one thing for an extended period an uphill struggle and are easily distracted. As such, they tend to find starting something far easier than following it through to the end.

Inclined to dismiss anything that conflicts with their own experience, they surround themselves with people who share their interests and views, a *modus operandi* which can lead to their developing their own alternative vision of the world. Despite their openness to new knowledge and experiment in the fields which interest them, they themselves rarely step beyond the areas that they are already familiar with.

WHY ARE WE SO DIFFERENT?

Personal development

Practitioners' personal development depends on the extent to which they make use of their natural potential and surmount the dangers inherent in their personality type. What follows are some practical tips which, together, form a specific guide that we might call *The Practitioner's Ten Commandments*.

Think ahead

You are capable of solving problems of the immediate and practical kind. However, the most crucial issues most often demand a global approach and long-term action. If you want to tackle them, you need to broaden your outlook and expand your consideration of time spans.

Give theory its due

Every time you discard something which has no immediate practical application, you call down a whole range of limitations on yourself. True, not every theory can be put to use in solving concrete problems, but they can all still extend our viewpoint and help us to understand the world. Also, never forget that they often inspire practical undertakings in the future as well!

Broaden your horizons

Test the water with things that go beyond the world of whatever you are currently interested in. Talk to people with views and interests other than your own. Undertake tasks you have never touched before. It will give you a host of valuable ideas and mean that you start seeing the world from a wider perspective.

Finish what you start

You launch into new things enthusiastically, but have problems with finishing what you have already begun, a *modus operandi* which usually produces mediocre results. Try sorting out what is most important to you and deciding how you want to accomplish it. Then knuckle down and turn your back firmly on all those tempting distractions!

Stop dismissing other people's ideas and opinions

Just because other people's ideas and opinions conflict with your own, this does not automatically mean that they are wrong. Before you judge them as valueless, give them some serious consideration and try to understand them.

Say more

Share your thoughts and ideas with others. Express your emotions. Tell people how you feel and what you are going through. You will be helping your colleagues and your nearest and dearest immensely when you do. Whatever you say, it will usually be better than remaining silent.

Treat others kindly

People have no desire to be seen as nothing more than tools serving to accomplish a goal. They long for their emotions, feelings and enthusiasms to be perceived. Mix with people, communicate with them, try to put yourself in their shoes and understand what they are going through, what fascinates them, what worries them and what they fear. Then wait and see. The difference will come as a pleasant surprise!

Stop dismissing universal principles

You make your way through life guided by your own interior compass and believing that happiness is not dependent on universal rules. Society is, though! Give some thought to what would happen if everyone ignored the principles underlying community life and began to live solely in accordance with their own, personal rules.

Ask others for help

When you experience difficulties or troubles, share that fact with people you trust. Stop hesitating when you have a problem – ask others for their help!

Keep your impulsiveness reigned in

Before you make a decision or commit yourself to something, devote a little time to gathering some relevant information, analysing it and evaluating the situation coolly and objectively. When you take that approach, you will most likely find yourself with less to do and, more to the point, you will end up doing it better.

Well-known figures

Below is a list of some well-known people who match the *practitioner's* profile:

- **Leonardo da Vinci** (Leonardo di ser Piero da Vinci; 1452-1519); an Italian Renaissance painter, architect, philosopher, musician, poet, inventor, mathematician, mechanic, anatomist and geologist, to name but some of his skills, he is probably the most widely talented person in history and is generally acknowledged as the archetypal 'Renaissance man'.
- **Michelangelo** (Michelangelo di Lodovico Buonarroti Simon; 1475-1564); a painter, sculptor, architect and poet, he was one of the greatest artists of the Italian Renaissance.
- **Charles Bronson** (Charles Dennis Buchinsky; 1921-2003); an American screen actor of Lipka Tatar and Lithuanian-American origins, his filmography includes *The Dirty Dozen*.
- **Alan Bartlett Shepard** (1923-1998); the first American astronaut.

- **Clint Eastwood** (born in 1930); an American screen actor, director, producer, film composer whose filmography includes *Dirty Harry*. He has won numerous prestigious awards and is also a politician.

- **Woody Allen** (Allan Stewart Konigsberg; born in 1935); an American screenwriter, director, actor, musician, producer, film composer and comedian whose filmography includes *The Purple Rose of Cairo*, he has won numerous prestigious awards.

- **Bruce Lee** (Lee Jun Fan (1940-1973); an American screen actor of Chinese extraction whose filmography includes *Enter the Dragon*, he was also a master of the martial arts.

- **Frank Zappa** (1940-1993); an American musician, bandleader, songwriter, composer, recording engineer, record producer, and film director, he fronted The Mothers of Invention rock group.

- **Michael Douglas** (born in 1944); an American screen actor, director and producer whose filmography includes *Wall Street*.

- **John Malkovich** (born in 1953); an American screen actor of Croatian descent whose filmography includes *In the Line of Fire*, he is also a producer, director and fashion designer.

- **Rowan Atkinson** (born in 1955); a British stage and screen actor, comedian and screenwriter whose filmography includes the *Mr Bean* television series and feature films.

- **Meg Ryan** (Margaret Mary Emily Anne Hyra; born in 1961); an American screen actress and producer, best-known for her roles in romantic comedies such as *When Harry Met Sally*.

- **Tom Cruise** (Thomas Cruise Mapother IV; born in 1962); an American screen actor and producer whose filmography includes the *Mission Impossible* movies.

The Presenter (ESFP)

THE ID16™© PERSONALITY TYPOLOGY

The Personality in a Nutshell

Life motto: Now is the perfect moment!

In brief, *presenters* …

are optimistic, energetic and outgoing, with the ability to enjoy life and have fun to the full. Practical, flexible and spontaneous at one and the same time, they enjoy change and new experiences, coping badly with solitude, stagnation and routine.

With their liking for being at the centre of attention, they are natural-born actors and their speaking abilities arouse the interest and enthusiasm of their listeners. Focused as they are on the present moment, they will sometimes lose sight of their long-term aims and can also have problems with foreseeing the consequences of their actions.

The *presenter's* four natural inclinations:

- source of life energy: the exterior world
- mode of assimilating information: via the senses
- decision-making mode: the heart
- lifestyle: spontaneous

Similar personality types:

- the Advocate
- the Artist
- the Protector

Statistical data:

- *presenters* constitute between eight and thirteen per cent of the global community
- women predominate among *presenters* (60 per cent)
- Brazil is an example of a nation corresponding to the *presenter's* profile[15]

The Four-Letter Code

In terms of Jungian personality typology, the universal four-letter code for the *presenter* is ESFP.

General character traits

Presenters are extraordinarily optimistic and spontaneous, with an ability to enjoy every moment and a driving urge to make the most of life. When they do something, they commit themselves to it with every ounce of their energy.

---

[15] What this means is not that all the residents of Brazil fall within this personality type, but that Brazilian society as a whole possesses a great many of the character traits typical of the *presenter*.

They love change, new experiences and surprises, and will always gravitate towards the action, wherever it might be.

As others see them

Presenters like people and know how to gain genuine pleasure from any and every get-together and conversation. Concern for others and their love of shared fun lie at the heart of their interpersonal relationships, while their optimism, openness and ability to enjoy life arouse other people's admiration and quite often cause them to start taking a more positive view of the world.

Usually brimming with energy, they are the life and soul of any gathering – wherever they appear, their behaviour makes them the focus of attention and other people will always have a wonderful time and forget their problems in their company. Indeed, they will sometimes have the impression that they are taking part in some kind of performance, since *presenters* are not only natural-born actors, but also have a superb sense of humour. Capable of commenting on reality and talking about their own myriad adventures and vicissitudes in a strikingly colourful way, they are perfectly capable of holding forth for hours when they have an audience, introducing a diverse range of subplots and a host of digressions along the way. Even when their listeners are well aware of their tendency to heighten and embroider the facts, they still hear them out with bated breath ... and will often also be struck with envy for their fascinating lives and the ability to take delight in every day.

Presenters themselves gain an enormous sense of satisfaction from the fact that they can infuse others with optimism and help them to have fun or inspire them to act. If they are involved in a gathering, they will frequently take on the role of compère or master of ceremonies and are absolutely in their element when introducing the programme and presenting the people taking part ... hence the name for this personality type.

With the sincere interest, acceptance and liking they feel for others, the majority of their relationships are excellent. However, some people are irritated by their carefree, nonchalant style and by the fact that they bend their efforts to focus attention on themselves and continually expect recognition and acceptance. Others accuse them of being superficial, irresponsible and incapable of reflecting more profoundly on life.

As the reverse side of that coin, people who take life too seriously set *presenters'* teeth on edge and they are infuriated by passivity, pessimism, faint enthusiasm and apathy, while any incidence of giving efficiency and profit priority over human happiness acts on them like a red rag to a bull. They also have difficulty in understanding loners who live in a world of their own and are engrossed in abstract theories or philosophical delvings. Indeed, they themselves find long-term solitude extremely hard to bear: no *presenter* has it in them to become a hermit!

Amongst others

Presenters are a bottomless well of fresh news, up-to-the-minute information and the latest jokes – so much so that many another person wonders where and how on earth they manage to get hold of it all. In general, they also know how other people are doing and what they are up to. However, this is not in the least because they have a leaning towards gossip; what it springs from is their genuine interest in people, their ability to put themselves in their shoes and the fact that they are both excellent listeners and skilled observers of human behaviour. In short, they make outstanding confidants and confidantes and other people sense this and are thus happy to share their experiences with them. Talking to a *presenter* leaves people heartened and inspired, helped by the awareness that someone has listened to them attentively, understood what they have been going through and given voice to what they themselves are feeling.

As a rule, they will make the most of any and every chance to get together with people and have a good time with them. They almost never give a family celebration or social gathering a miss and tend to seize every opportunity for making merry, be it a birthday, a name day, an anniversary or any and every other kind of 'high day and holiday', and are just as delighted to organise such events themselves, including lavish parties to mark more significant occasions. Even when they are snowed under with work, they manage to find the time to drop in on their friends. By the same token, unexpected visits will also always give them joy.

As *presenters* see it, the here and now matters more than the future and people are more important than work, duties and obligations. Relinquishing their pleasures and the opportunity to enjoy themselves thus comes very hard to them. Indeed, they love entertainment and having fun so much that it will sometimes become an end in itself for them and, in their pursuit of pleasure, new experiences and experiment, they may well shed all boundaries and inhibitions. In fact, their inclination to take risks can sometimes lead not only to their exposing themselves to danger, but even to ruining their health or to their descent into addiction.

Attitudes

Presenters set tremendous store by both their own freedom and independence and that of others. As such, they are highly sensitive to any manifestation of constraint in that respect. Exhibiting zero tolerance when it comes to attempts to exercise excessive control over people, standardise them, pigeonhole them or treat them like cogs in a machine, they themselves respect other people's individualism and believe that every person has their own, unique value and is irreplaceable.

By nature wholly uninterested in abstract theories and concepts which cannot be transferred directly into life as it is being lived in the present, they would rather move through a world of concrete data and tangible facts. Deliberating on hypothetical possibilities and potential opportunities, hazards or threats is a form of torture to them and it is rare indeed for them to spend time envisioning long-term plans for the future.

This aversion to planning means that they would rather wait and see what each day brings and respond there and then, depending on how things develop. They live life in the immediate present, endeavouring to make the most of what today offers and rarely indulging in memories of the past or cogitating about the future. For instance, given their focus on the present moment, the notion of 'putting something away for a rainy day' or 'saving for retirement' is alien to their mindset: if *presenters* have some spare funds, they would rather put them to use here and now. In their book, time spent worrying over what tomorrow may bring is time wasted. Better to relish the moment and deal with problems as and when they occur and, since they are highly flexible and endowed with superb improvisational skills, they are well equipped to do so, coping well in rapidly shifting circumstances which demand immediate reaction to fresh factors and lightning-fast adaptation to new situations.

Perception and thinking

Presenters have a developed aesthetic sense and spatial imagination, along with a natural artistic talent. With their finger on the pulse as far as 'trending now … what's in and what's out' is concerned, they are often interested in the fashion scene. Their homes are distinctive for their style and they have the ability to furnish and decorate them in a way which endows the space with a warm cosiness. They display greater culinary skills than most, an aspect of their nature which goes hand in hand with their love of good food.

Learning most readily through observation, experimentation and experience, *presenters* are pragmatic by nature, with an interest in what they can touch, experience or taste. They enjoy practical tasks and are happy to help other people solve concrete, tangible problems, sparing neither time nor energy in their efforts. When they run into a complex issue or complicated situation, they will do everything within their power to simplify things. At the same time, however, they have a tendency to trivialise matters and the solutions they proffer can thus be inadequate and makeshift in that they avert the problem or get rid of it temporarily, but fail to root it out once and for all.

Presenters dislike situations which are difficult, ambivalent or anything less than limpidly transparent. Their image of the world is usually black and white, so any contact with the fuzziness of a reality where white is not entirely white and black is not wholly black causes them an immense sense of unease. Their reaction is often to retreat into simplification, whereby they will whitewash the 'white' to bleached perfection or densify the 'black' to the darkest of depths.

Decisions

When *presenters* have to make a decision, they will consider its impact on other people and frequently both consult their friends and acquaintances and reach for the opinions of those around them. They are generally guided by common sense and, distrusting intuition and presentiments, they base their thinking on facts and hard data. On the whole, being capable of assessing a situation and the existing possibilities rapidly, they are not inclined to spend overmuch time on analysing all the pros and cons, but tend to avail themselves of their lightning-fast ability to select what they deem to be the best and most sensible solution. This means that they normally make decisions fairly quickly.

Presenters fare best when it comes to current and immediate issues relating to concrete and tangible problems. On the other hand, they face the greatest difficulty when confronted with the need to make decisions which require them to foresee long-term consequences, turn their thoughts to the future and take into consideration factors which have not yet occurred, such as potential threats or hazards that may crop up at a more distant moment.

Enthusiasms

Presenters are attracted by anything fresh and original, be it new friends and acquaintances, new ideas, new products, new experiences, new fashions – the list is endless! They are usually familiar with the latest trends, innovations and novelties and will often be the first in their circle to know about newly opened restaurants, clubs or pubs, upcoming events and concerts and the latest products and offers on the market.

They revel in the fact that every day may bring something new and every moment might have a surprise in store. This, of course, means that they suffer when life turns monotonous and boring, offering them nothing but routine and stagnation. Nonetheless, they are capable of finding something exciting in every situation and normally make an effort to introduce some element of fun and appeal into any job they are doing in order to be able to extract some kind of pleasure from it.

Communication

Talking to other people gives *presenters* enormous pleasure and they are unrestrained when it comes to adding their voice to a group. Natural-born speakers, compères and presenters, their presence introduces a warm, friendly atmosphere and they are more than capable of keeping their audience entertained. They have no fear of appearing in public and their affinity for the spotlight is inbuilt. When they lead a presentation or announce a public appearance, they make full use of their acting abilities, gift for improvisation and sense of humour.

They have the ability to fire their listeners with enthusiasm, influence the way they see the world and spur them into action. Called upon to explain a task, goal or initiative, they do so in a way which is both utterly natural and uncommonly appealing. Their usual style is extremely clear, precise, down-to-earth and direct. On the other hand, they dislike expressing their thoughts in writing and most definitely favour verbal communication and person-to-person contact.

With their superb interpersonal skills and gift of empathy, they are able both to 'read' people and spot their hidden motives and problems. However, voicing critical opinions and calling other people's attention to inappropriate behaviour, for instance, is something they find tough to deal with. In turn, they themselves can scarcely bear criticism levelled at them by others; they struggle to apply it constructively and often perceive it as an act of spitefulness or as an attack on them or an attempt to undermine their values. When that happens, they are capable of reacting strongly in their own defence and may well end up saying things they will later regret.

In the face of stress

Tasks requiring lengthy concentration, deep reflection, working independently or long-term, strategic planning will usually trigger tension and a sense of anxiety in *presenters*. Under the influence of lasting stress, they may well start constructing black scenarios in their thoughts or seek relief from the tension by turning to sensual pleasures or substances. Fortunately, though, they do also have the ability to relax more constructively, pursuing various sporting activities or organising parties, picnics and family outings in order to spend time with their friends, acquaintances and nearest and dearest. If one thing is certain, it is the fact that they will never number amongst those whose idea of a perfect break is immersing themselves in a good book or solving brain-teasers!

Socially

Presenters are extremely outgoing and highly approachable. They treat everyone as if they were old friends and people who are meeting them for the first time will often have the impression that they have known them for ages. 'Direct', 'uncomplicated' and 'flexible to the max' are all descriptions which fit *presenters* like a glove!

People are a highly important aspect of their lives. Caring for others gives them tremendous joy and, when a helping hand is held out to them, they are equally as capable of availing themselves of it. With an eye always firmly fixed on a pleasant atmosphere and warm interpersonal relations, they find situations of conflict almost impossible to bear and will do anything to prevent them from arising. By the same token, their efforts to avoid disagreeable conversations often trigger their inclination to sweep a problem under the carpet or pretend that it is non-existent.

Amongst friends

In the main, *presenters* are extremely open, outgoing and ready to strike up new acquaintanceships. With their ability to 'read' people on the spot, they will often know exactly who they are dealing with after no more than a few minutes of conversation with someone. Warm, friendly relationships with others are one of the most important things in their lives and, with their genuine desire for people's happiness, they are unstinting with their time, energy and money when it comes to helping them or, quite simply, to whiling away the time pleasantly in their company. They find solitude hard to bear, but it is their good fortune to be surrounded by people most of the time, since their optimism, sense of humour, warmth, empathy and sincerity act like a magnet to others. People quite simply enjoy their company and are happy to share their experiences and problems with them; and the trust and sympathy of others is a source of happiness and satisfaction to *presenters* themselves.

Other people's opinions count for a great deal with *presenters* and they are open to the influence of their surroundings. However, although they are able to adapt to the current situation and take the needs of others into consideration, they will not allow themselves to be used. In general, their friends and acquaintances are legion, but the majority of these relationships are fairly superficial in nature. They are given to devoting most of their attention to new relationships and neglecting those which have existed for some time. They tend to have no more than a handful of close friends, who are most often *advocates*, *artists*, *enthusiasts* or other *presenters* and, most rarely, *strategists*, *directors* and *logicians*.

As life partners

As a partner for life, *presenters* bring warmth, energy and optimism to the relationship. For the person by their side, boredom is simply not an option, since they make it their personal business to ensure that something is always going on and provide their partner with all kinds of attractions. Within the microcosm of their family, the *presenter* usually takes on the office of 'foreign minister', assuming responsibility for its contact with the wider world and acting as its representative there. As a rule, they set great store by birthdays, anniversaries and every other kind of family celebration, and not only love organising get-togethers of all sorts but will also gleefully step into the role of master of ceremonies if given half a chance. They spare neither time nor money on arranging such events, an attitude perceived by some as a sign of extravagance. Indeed, given that their partners will often see other, more pressing needs, while *presenters* themselves can think of almost nothing which takes priority over enjoying a celebration with family and friends, this tendency can sometimes lead to tension within their relationship.

The fact is that *presenters* are, by nature, extremely generous; they neither calculate nor are they niggardly in the least. Their love is unconditional; they give of themselves unstintingly and expect nothing in return. Their feelings are deep, fervent and sensual and their partner's happiness is their dearest wish. They do all they can to meet their needs, showing them enormous warmth and unrestrainedly offering them tender words and affectionate gestures. They, too, need warmth, closeness and acceptance. Given that they are profoundly affected by any kind of cutting remark or unflattering comment, they are easily hurt and they tend not only to treat criticism of their actions as a personal attack, but also to respond with a counter-attack.

However, discussing tough and unpleasant issues is anathema to *presenters* and they will try to avoid conflicts and arguments at any price. They also face problems coping with long-term obligations and, since their nature is to live for today rather than turn their thoughts to the future, swearing constancy "until death do us part" will normally demand enormous commitment on their part. At the same time, their need for new experiences, their inclination to experiment, their leaning towards risk-taking and their love of sensual pleasures can pose a threat to the stability of their relationships

The natural candidates for a *presenter's* life partner are people of a personality type akin to their own: *advocates, artists* or *protectors*. Building mutual understanding and harmonious relations will be easier in a union of that kind. Nonetheless, experience has taught us that people are also capable of creating happy and successful relationships despite what would seem to be an evident typological incompatibility. Moreover, the differences between two partners can lend added dynamics to a relationship and engender personal development. Indeed, for many people, this is a prospect that appears more attractive than the vision of a harmonious relationship wherein concord and full, mutual understanding hold sway.

As parents

Presenters make extremely caring parents who show their children great warmth and have the ability to see the world through their eyes, a skill which means that they know what will bring them the most joy. They provide a host of attractions, arranging happy surprises and celebrating their successes with enormous pride, which is tremendously encouraging and motivating. They love spending time with their offspring, having fun with them and talking to them. In general, hubbub and commotion leaves them completely unperturbed; when the children are enjoying themselves, their *presenter* parents are happy. Practical parenting tasks come easily to them and parental responsibilities hold no fears for them. They encourage their offspring to be themselves, live out their own dreams and make the most of their own strengths.

As a rule, they are not overly demanding and struggle to put discipline into practice, especially since they themselves are often not entirely convinced as to its point. As a result, their children sometimes have problems in distinguishing good and desirable behaviour from that which is bad and reprehensible. *Presenter*s usually prefer partnership parenting and, in the main, they are tolerant, uncomplicated and understanding. However, they can sometimes be strict and impatient, since their approach frequently lacks cohesion and consistency. If the other parent is unable to operate in a more organised fashion, their children might lack a sense of security and stability, as well as clear rules telling them how the world is run.

As adults, their children usually recall their *presenter* parents as warm, caring and sincere. They have fond memories of the countless unforgettable attractions they provided and of the way that they offered them a great deal of freedom, encouraged them to fulfil their dreams and gave them unconditional support during tough moments.

Work and career paths

Motion, variety and change are meat and drink to *presenters*, who are attracted to work which offers possibilities for being creative, experimenting and solving concrete, tangible and practical problems.

Companies and institutions

Presenters are happiest working for organisations with a non-linear structure, where the staff are given considerable freedom of action and a say in decisions affecting them. They enjoy being wherever things are going on and find bureaucracy, hierarchies, routine, repetitive tasks and rigid procedures unbearable, while writing up accounts of their activities, preparing reports and compiling data are tasks which they consider tiresome in the extreme. They also have no liking for working individually. However, they excel when it comes to work demanding interpersonal skills, inventiveness, flexibility and the ability to improvise. They fit in well in institutions geared towards the good of society and bringing about tangible and positive changes in the life of the local community or the country or on a global scale.

Tasks

Presenters will throw themselves wholeheartedly into accomplishing tasks they believe in. They like knowing that their activities have a positive impact on other people's lives and help them to solve their problems, and they are usually greatly concerned to ensure that their colleagues, clients and those under their care are satisfied.

In general, they dislike work of a conceptual nature and are at a particular loss when they are unable either to refer to similar experiences from the past or count on pointers from someone else. Concentrating and focusing on tasks requiring long-term commitment is also something they often find challenging, especially when the results of their work are a distant prospect or the aim of the job is less than crystal clear. They are easily distracted and, in the battle for their attention, it is usually the newest and most powerful stimulus which will emerge victorious. Once a new, more exciting project appears on the horizon, they will struggle to continue with what they have already begun. They are happiest when engaged on short-term jobs and are capable multitaskers.

As part of a team

When working as part of a team, *presenters* are uncomplicated and flexible members who value a healthy and friendly atmosphere and take care to ensure that no one feels passed over or excluded. It is absolutely normal for them to forge strong bonds with their colleagues and just as rare for them to give a social gathering or integration event a miss.

Given that they themselves make every effort to avoid conflicts and disputes, they find people who set out on the path to confrontation, fight to win power and authority and are capable of hurting their colleagues wholly incomprehensible. However, their own readiness to do all they can to meet the needs of others and make their jobs easier means that they are skilled at building compromises and what very often happens is that they naturally emerge as the group's representative, acting as its spokesperson and presenting its position to a wider audience.

Views on workplace hierarchy

Presenters prefer superiors who see those they are in charge of as people and not as tools serving to accomplish a goal. They like their bosses to be flexible, open to innovative solutions and ready to point their subordinates in the general direction they should take, while affording them freedom in accomplishing their tasks and respecting their individual style of working.

When they themselves take on the responsibility of leading others, they adopt a similar approach, valuing their relationships with those in their charge and never failing to put people before results and achievements. However, when they hold a management position, their overly lenient attitude and inability to discipline the weaker members of their team frequently poses a problem.

Professions

Knowledge of our own personality profile and natural preferences provides us with invaluable help in choosing the optimal path in our professional careers. Experience has shown that, while *presenters* are perfectly able to work and find fulfilment in a range of fields, their personality type naturally predisposes them to the following fields and professions:

- acting
- advisor
- carer
- consultant
- entrepreneur
- events organiser
- fashion designer
- florist
- human resources
- insurance agent
- interior designer
- leisure and recreation centres
- lifeguard
- musician
- paramedic
- life coach
- photographer
- psychologist
- physician
- public relations

- radio or television presenter
- receptionist
- sales representative
- social welfare
- sports trainer
- stylist
- teacher
- therapist
- travel agent
- visual artist
- vet

Potential strengths and weaknesses

Like any other personality type, *presenters* have their potential strengths and weaknesses and this potential can be cultivated in a variety of ways. *Presenters*' personal happiness and professional fulfilment depend on whether they make the most of the 'pluses' offered by their personality type and face up to its inherent dangers. Here, then, is a SUMMARY of those 'pluses' and dangers:

Potential strengths

Presenters are enthusiastic, spontaneous and flexible. Capable of reacting rapidly to shifting circumstances and adapting to new conditions, they are practical and learn fast. With their love of experiment and fearless attitude towards risk, they cope well with change and, being optimistic by nature, they are not disheartened by obstacles and difficulties. They also have the ability to enjoy every day and make the most of every moment. Their enthusiasm and optimism is infectious and tends to have a positive impact on others and, when they work as part of a group, they are able both to integrate the team and build comprises. Their interest in other people and concern for their happiness and well-being is genuine, as is their respect for their freedom and individuality. They are always ready to lend a helping hand and, at one and the same time, have no trouble in either accepting assistance from others or in making the most of their experience and advice.

Excellent observers of the world around them and of human emotions and feelings, they are just as skilled at rapidly 'reading' other people. With their outgoing, open nature, they are easy to get to know and, in general, they are sought-after companions. Their optimism and sense of humour draws others to them, while their warm, sincere interest encourages people to confide in them. Their inherent acting skills go hand in hand with a developed artistic and aesthetic sense, and they are natural-born speakers, compères and presenters, endowed with the ability to arouse the interest and enthusiasm of their listeners. Remarkably generous and ready to meet the needs of others, they love not only helping them, but also giving them gifts, offering them a variety of attractions, preparing surprises for them and finding ways for them to while away the time pleasantly – all of which is helped by their ability to adapt to whatever the circumstances may currently be.

Potential weaknesses

Presenters face an uphill struggle when it comes to extending their thoughts beyond the here and now, carrying out jobs which demand that they envisage what may happen in the future or sacrifice current pleasures for the sake of distant benefits. Tasks which require lengthy focus and concentration or require them to work alone are a source of misery to them, particularly when the outcome of their efforts will only become visible with time. They also view the world of abstract concepts and complex theories as unmapped and impenetrable territory and are inclined both to ignore anything which cannot be turned into practical action and to over-simplify, or quite often, even to trivialise problems. To *presenters*, the ideal solution will always be one

310

which is straightforward, fast and requires nothing much in the way of penetrating reflection. While this approach enables them to get rid of a problem that has arisen – and thus turn their energies to more pleasant pursuits – it rarely affords them an understanding of the underlying causes. By the same token, their focus on fun, pleasure and entertainment means that they sometimes fail to discern life's more profound dimensions.

Understanding diverse standpoints and looking at a situation or issue through the eyes of others can also be problematic for *presenters*, and they often fear opinions and points of view which diverge significantly from their own. They find criticism levelled at them by other people extremely hard to take, treating it as either an attack or a manifestation of spitefulness and, in general, they are incapable of putting it to constructive use. This works both ways, since they themselves find it equally difficult to express a critical opinion. When faced with problems, unpleasant situations or conflict, *presenters* tend to turn tail and run. As a rule, they do no better when it comes to routine tasks and repetitive activities and, in general, managing finances is not one of their strengths either.

Personal development

Presenters' personal development depends on the extent to which they make use of their natural potential and surmount the dangers inherent in their personality type. What follows are some practical tips which, together, form a specific guide that we might call *The Presenter's Ten Commandments*.

Keep your focus fixed

Determine your priorities and make a serious effort to finish what you undertake. Keep your eyes firmly fixed on the most crucial tasks and stop letting yourself be distracted by less important matters. Do that and you will find yourself avoiding frustration and achieving more.

Finish what you start

You launch into new things enthusiastically, but have problems with finishing what you have already begun – a *modus operandi* which usually produces mediocre results. Try sorting out what is most important to you and deciding how you want to accomplish it. Then knuckle down – and stick to the plan!

Stop being afraid of conflict

When you find yourself in a situation of conflict, stop hiding your head in the sand and, instead, voice your point of view and feelings openly. Conflict very often helps us to expose problems and solve them.

Keep your impulsiveness reigned in

Before you make a decision or commit yourself to something, devote a little time to gathering some relevant information, analysing it and evaluating the situation coolly and objectively. When you take that approach, you will most likely find yourself with less to do and, more to the point, you will end up doing it better.

Ask

Stop assuming that, if other people are silent, it means that they are indifferent or hostile. If you really want to know what they think, ask them.

Stop fearing criticism

Quell your fear of expressing your own critical opinions and of accepting criticism from others. Criticism can be constructive. There is no law which says that it has to mean attacking people or undermining their values.

Set yourself free from other people's opinions

You accept others, don't you? So start accepting yourself and stop evaluating yourself on the basis of what other people have to say about you. They could be wrong. They could even be lying. When it comes to making decisions about your life, who could possibly be more competent than you?

Avoid provisional solutions

When faced with difficulties, you have a tendency to act fast and go for solutions which are either provisional or simply defer the problem. Try looking at the wider picture and the long-term perspective instead. Devote some time to it and make it your aim not only to get rid of the issue itself, but also to solve it once and for all.

Stop fearing ideas and opinions which are different from yours

Before you reject them, give them some consideration and try to understand them. Being open to the viewpoints of others is not synonymous with discarding your own.

Start believing in a world which is more than just black and white

Try to look at problems in a wider context and from various angles. Things may be more complex than they seem to you. Your problems may not only be caused by others; they might also be caused by you! Remember, you may not always be in the right!

Well-known figures

Below is a list of some well-known people who match the *presenter's* profile:

- **Pablo Picasso** (1881-1973); a Spanish painter, sculptor, print artist and theatre designer, he pioneered the Cubist movement and is considered to be one of the most outstanding visual artists of the twentieth century.

- **Leonard Bernstein** (1918-1990); an American composer, pianist and conductor.

- **Gene Hackman** (born in 1930); an American screen actor, director and producer whose filmography includes *Crimson Tide*, he has won numerous prestigious awards.

- **Elvis Presley** (1935-1977); an American singer and screen actor, he was a precursor of rock and roll and an icon of twentieth-century popular culture.

- **Al Pacino** (Alfred James Pacino; born in 1940); an American theatre and screen actor, filmmaker and screenwriter of Italian descent, his filmography includes *The Devil's Advocate*.

- **Joe Pesci** (Joseph Franco Pesci; born in 1943); an American screen actor whose filmography includes *Goodfellas*.

- **John Goodman** (born in 1952); an American film actor whose filmography includes *Blues Brothers*.

- **Branscombe Richmond** (born in 1955); an American screen actor whose filmography includes the *Renegade* TV series.

- **Linda Fiorentino** (born in 1958); an American screen actress whose filmography includes *Men in Black*.

- **Kevin Spacey** (Kevin Spacey Fowler; born in 1959); an American theatre and screen actor whose movies include *K-PAX*, he is also a director and producer.

- **Woody Harrelson** (born in 1961); an American screen actor whose filmography includes *Welcome to Sarajevo*.

- **Steve Irwin** (1962-2006); an Australian naturalist, television presenter and environmental activist.
- **Dean Cain** (Dean George Tanaka; born in 1966); an American film actor, producer, screenwriter and director whose filmography includes *Firetrap*.
- **Julie Bowen** (Julie Bowen Luetkemeyer; born in 1970); an American screen actress whose filmography includes *Venus and Mars*.
- **Josh Hartnett** (born in 1978); an American screen actor whose filmography includes *Black Hawk Down*.

The Protector (ISFJ)

The Personality in a Nutshell

Life motto: Your happiness matters to me.

In brief, *protectors* …

are sincere, warm-hearted, unassuming, trustworthy and extraordinarily loyal. With their ability to perceive people's needs and their desire to help them, they will always put others first. Practical, well-organised and gifted with both an eye and a memory for detail, they are responsible, hard-working, patient, persevering and capable of seeing things through to the end.

Protectors set great store by tranquillity, stability and friendly relations with others and are skilled at building bridges between people. By the same token, they find conflict and criticism difficult to bear. Given their powerful sense of duty and their constant readiness to come to the aid of others, they can end up being used by people.

The *protector's* four natural inclinations:

- source of life energy: the interior world
- mode of assimilating information: via the senses
- decision-making mode: the heart
- lifestyle: organised

Similar personality types:

- the Artist
- the Advocate
- the Presenter

Statistical data:

- *protectors* constitute between eight and twelve per cent of the global population
- women predominate among *protectors* (70 per cent)
- Sweden is an example of a nation corresponding to the *protector's* profile [16]

The Four-Letter Code

In terms of Jungian personality typology, the universal four-letter code for the *protector* is ISFJ.

General character traits

Protectors like people! With their interest in the experiences and problems of others and their awareness of their feelings,

---

[16] What this means is not that all the residents of Sweden fall within this personality type, but that Swedish society as a whole possesses a great many of the character traits typical of the *protector*.

they are more open to them than any of the other introverted personality types and will spend their entire life scanning their surroundings in search of those who need help.

As others see them

Other people perceive *protectors* as sincere, kind and always ready to offer a helping hand. They have a reputation for being extremely friendly, tranquil and unassuming. Given their propensity for putting other people first, their inherent need to help them and their ability both to perceive their positive potential and to elicit the best in them, they are widely popular.

Their attitude to others

A powerful force impels *protectors* to act: their sympathy for those in need, for the poor, for the suffering and for the wronged, and they are ever ready to take them under their wing, offering them practical and emotional support and surrounding them with protection ... hence the name for this personality type. With their desire to defend others against hardship, adverse decisions and afflictions, they will spare neither time nor effort in helping them to solve their problems, yet their support is always extremely discreet and tactful; imposing themselves and pursuing recognition is simply not the way they operate.

Organisational modes

Protectors keep themselves to themselves and are sparing with words. Hard-working, responsible and well-organised, they have a head for detail and bear in mind the kind of minutiae that escape the notice of others. This is a character trait which also applies to their interpersonal relationships; even after years have gone by, they will have a precise recall of exactly what someone said or of a specific gesture or facial expression.

They have a genuine faith in other people and are able to spot the best in them. Prizing harmonious collaboration, an open, warm and friendly atmosphere, security and stability, they are driven by their sense of good and strive for concord and unity. Unforeseen situations and sudden change upset them; they are happiest when everything happens according to plan. In general, they have a fondness for tradition and, preferring tried and tested modes of action which have survived the test of time, they approach new solutions with a degree of mistrust. Nonetheless, if they can see that employing them will produce evident benefits, then they are inclined to accept them.

Wastefulness goes against the grain with *protectors*. Thrifty by nature, they give due consideration to the uncertainties of the future and thus tend to put money aside 'for a rainy day'.

Thinking

Protectors build their own unique 'internal database', storing information concerning events affecting themselves and others. They are able to connect new facts with previous experiences and have a clear picture of what the world and relationships between people should be like. It is this which forms their reference point; their activities are geared towards turning their vision into reality. By the same token, being practitioners by nature, they will rarely concern themselves with abstract theories.

Encounters with opinions which differ from their own are something of a problem for them, causing them an enormous sense of unease and disrupting their interior calm, leading to a response which will usually be an attempt either to reconcile the disparate views or, at the very least, to reduce the divide between them.

Communication

Protectors are excellent listeners and are perceived by others as wonderful conversationalists, even when they actually say very little. They are happiest in intimate surroundings and prefer their conversations to be *tête-à-tête*, since talking to just one person allows them to give all their attention to whatever is being discussed. On the whole, though, they will struggle to establish any kind of meaningful connection with people who are chaotic, who go through life in a permanent state of absent-mindedness, who are incapable of punctuality or who are simply unreliable.

Criticising others openly is difficult for them, as is expressing their disapproval of something publicly. Indeed, some people resent them for making unfavourable remarks behind people's backs rather than directly to the person concerned.

Given their sense of the continuity of processes, their orderliness and the fact that they like to follow the proper sequence when they do things, *protectors* prefer to have time to think and ready themselves when faced with taking part in a discussion or giving a presentation. The outcome will usually be a speech or talk which is composed and cool-headed, but powerful enough to move the listeners.

Decisions

Protectors steer well clear of risk and of the unknown and unfamiliar. With their dislike of haste, they approach decisions carefully, step by step, needing time in order to give calm consideration to the various options available to them and often making notes and carrying out a written analysis of those possibilities while turning things over in their minds. They also give thought both to the way a given decision will affect other people and to how they will perceive it. The final result of these deliberations will be based on hard facts and previous experience.

In general, *protectors* have a very highly developed sense of duty and responsibility. Seldom will they refuse when asked to help or do someone a favour, a character trait which means that they are often used by others and frequently find themselves overburdened. However, even in situations of that kind, they rarely resort to complaints or accusations, not wishing to jeopardise their relationships with others by speaking out.

Aesthetics

Protectors possess an excellent spatial imagination and the ability to arrange their surroundings in a way which is both functional and yet still reveals their sensitivity to beauty. As a result, their homes and workstations are distinctive not only for their orderliness and the highly practical way in which they are organised, but also for the tastefulness of their décor, to say nothing of their immense cosiness … people are always happy to spend time in a space created by a *protector*.

They set great store by other people's anniversaries and birthdays, showing their liking through kind gestures and happy surprises. With their skill for identifying what fills others with enthusiasm, what they enjoy and what they need, even the smallest of the gifts given by a *protector* will always be a source of enormous joy, being not only tasteful, but also highly thoughtful and wholly suited to the recipient.

Leisure

Protectors are incapable of relaxing unless they know that there are no uncompleted tasks awaiting them; and so, given their propensity for taking on myriad responsibilities, it is hardly surprising that they have very little in the way of what they would deem to be free time! This state of affairs is further exacerbated by the fact that their concept of 'free time' diverges markedly from the norm; to a *protector*, it equates with 'time to help my nearest and dearest' and 'time to help my friends and acquaintances'. It is rare, indeed, to see them doing something simply for their own pleasure.

Socially

The ties which bind *protectors* to others are highly particular and personal in nature, since they see them not only as colleagues, superiors, subordinates, clients or people in their care, but also as individuals who have their own world, their own enthusiasms, their own feelings and their own emotions. What lies at the heart of their relationships is the notion of service and their longing to feel useful.

They also have a need for confirmation that they have done a good job and that their opinions are shared by others. Although they are genuinely embarrassed by praise, they find sheer indifference on the part of others very hard to bear and are equally as disheartened by open criticism. In stressful situations, they will start conjuring up a range of black scenarios, imagining all sorts of misfortunes which might be lying in wait for them, losing faith in their own abilities and seeing the future through gloom-tinted glasses.

Only too happy to come to the aid of others, they will often give no sign that they are grappling with problems of their own, preferring not to burden other people with their troubles. They tend not to express their dissatisfaction or discontent outwardly, and are inclined to bottle up their emotions. However, having kept them firmly suppressed for a long time, they might then give way to an uncontrolled explosion, much to the astonishment of those around them.

Amongst friends

Protectors are genuinely interested in the lives and problems of their friends. In their case, one thing which will never serve as an instrument for self-advertising, for instance, or as a tool for building their career, is friendship. Its bonds are a crucial aspect of their world and will normally endure throughout their lives, since they take them as seriously as any of their other responsibilities.

Their friends appreciate them because they are not focused on themselves, their interest is both genuine and wholehearted and they can always be counted on. They also value them for their ability to perceive the needs and problems of others.

A positive attitude towards others and the ability to identify something of worth in everyone are both common character traits among *protectors* and mean that they are happy in the company of people representing all sixteen of the personality types. However, they most frequently strike up a friendship with *artists*, *advocates*, *mentors* and other *protectors* and, most rarely, with *innovators*, *logicians* and *directors*.

After periods of intensive activity or a lengthy time spent with a group of people, they need solitude and tranquillity in order to gather their thoughts and 'recharge their batteries'. However, in no way at all is this a manifestation of antipathy towards others.

As life partners

The axis of the *protector's* world is their family. In general, they set great store by traditional values and are both highly devoted to those closest to them and solicitous of their welfare, security and well-being. They also strive for good and healthy relationships and are capable of investing enormous energy in that cause. Their feelings run very deep, even though this intensity may not always be perceived via 'the naked ear', since they tend to express it not through words, but via concrete actions and warm gestures of affection. They themselves attach enormous value to any and every manifestation of fondness, feeling and gratitude from their partner. Highly faithful and uncommonly loyal, they take their responsibilities extremely seriously and their relationships tend to last a lifetime.

Their relationship with their partner is their highest priority and, even when it has soured beyond mending or is harmful or toxic, they face a struggle in trying to break free of it and, if their partner leaves them, they have equal difficulty in coming to terms with that. In either situation, they tend to blame themselves, seeking to identify their own mistakes and shortcomings. Given that their unselfishness and focus on others is part of their nature, they are often used and, more to the point, will generally accept that state of affairs. They cope badly in situations of conflict and will do anything they can to avoid touching on thorny subjects, preferring to remain silent about problems, either bearing them patiently or pretending that they do not exist.

The natural candidates for a *protector's* life partner are people of a personality type akin to their own: *artists*, *advocates* and *presenters*. Building mutual understanding and harmonious relations will be easier in a union of that kind. Nonetheless, experience has taught us that people are also capable of creating happy and successful relationships despite what would seem to be an evident typological incompatibility. Moreover, the differences between two partners can lend added dynamics to a relationship and engender personal development.

As parents

Protectors make highly responsible parents, tending to the needs of their children and taking their parental responsibilities extremely seriously. Desiring to bring their offspring up to be independent and responsible adults, they believe in the necessity of teaching them to behave appropriately from the earliest years; as a result, their parenting style is not only devoted, but also decisive. In general, they run their homes along lucid principles, thanks to which their children both know how they should behave and enjoy a sense of security. However, *protectors* themselves sometimes have problems with enforcing those selfsame rules and taking the requisite disciplinary action – before they punish a child for behaving badly, they first need to convince themselves that doing so will be for the best.

Their offspring often take advantage of their *protector* parent's devotion, operating on the assumption that they will do anything for them. When their adult children face problems, they are inclined to seek the fault in their own parenting errors. In general, though, they are following a false trail, since they do an excellent job, providing a secure childhood and a wonderful home filled with warmth. As adults, their children appreciate them for their devotion, care and for instilling them with healthy principles and a sense of responsibility.

Work and career paths

Protectors are extremely persevering and ready both to devote themselves to what they are doing and to give up their own pleasures in favour of the task in hand. They are happiest in jobs which are rooted in helping others or supporting those who are unable to cope themselves and they enjoy tasks that allow them to solve human problems. When they work in a business, they love advising and assisting people to select the product or service which best suits their requirements and, if they work for a social institution, they will always be dedicated in giving their care to those in need of help.

Environment

In general terms, the awareness of belonging to a larger group or community that they can identify with is important to *protectors* and they also prefer companies or institutions which establish structures designed to help ease tensions amongst the staff. When they are working on a task, they require moments of solitude and calm in order to think through what they have to do and prepare for it away from the daily hustle and bustle. However, if they can see the necessity for team work, they will willingly get involved, although they will feel more at ease in a small group of no more than a few people. They bring a warm and pleasant atmosphere to the team, are always supportive of the other members and are often instrumental in helping the group achieve a consensus.

When it comes to approach, they prefer regular, well-prepared meetings where the time, date and agenda are all established in advance. Surprises, improvisation and unexpected discussions of problems, where they have no opportunity to think things over first, are anathema to them.

Tasks

Capable of seeing things through to the end, *protectors* derive tremendous satisfaction from a job well done. With their highly meticulous natures and ability to focus on detail, they see nothing tedious in routine activities and their reliability, friendly attitude and willingness to extend a helping hand to others all make them sought-after employees. They like clearly defined tasks and much prefer to work on things they are familiar with and which allow them to draw on their experience. When confronted by something new, they need more time to take it on board than many other people do. However, once they have thoroughly familiarised themselves with it, they will accomplish it to a greater exactitude than most.

Protectors make uncommonly loyal staff members and, with their own ability to give their all in pursuit of accomplishing their employer's aims, they find those who consciously neglect their duties absolutely incomprehensible.

Preferences

Instructions, rules and regulations are meat and drink to *protectors*, who like to know what they have to do and how they should do it and are fully capable of adapting themselves completely to existing guidelines and prescripts. At a loss in situations where they have to come up with something new or move into the unknown, they cope just as badly when circumstances deprive them of the chance to refer to concrete instructions or call on previous experience and either demand that they improvise or force them into making a rapid decision. Organisational changes, new procedures and transformations also knock them off their feet; they prefer a stable environment where things all stay very much the same.

Views on workplace hierarchy

Protectors appreciate well-organised superiors who are capable of spotting the devotion and dedication of those they supervise and who provide them with the support they need. They favour clear guidelines, concrete aims and comprehensible rules which apply to all the staff.

Although they like to have an influence on the course of affairs and the decision-making process, they make unwilling leaders. They would rather work behind the lines, supporting the 'high command', a *modus operandi* which enables them to avoid the necessity of disciplining people, calling their attention to shortcomings or solving conflicts, and also absolves them of responsibility for implementing unpopular decisions.

Those *protectors* who do become leaders introduce extremely exacting standards and are rigorous about maintaining a high level of efficacy and efficiency, demonstrating zero tolerance for wastefulness. They set out clear, concrete aims for the people they supervise and then provide the support they need in order to achieve them. On the other hand, when forced to hold an 'unpleasant conversation' with one of their personnel, the *protector* will often end up far more exhausted and stressed than the staff member concerned. Given that they feel ill-at-ease when telling someone to do something, issuing instructions is another problem area for them, as is the very delegation of duties itself; indeed, they themselves will often carry out tasks which should, by rights, be handed off to their staff. This, in turn, produces an undesirable outcome, with the *protector* becoming overworked and fatigued, while their staff are deprived of the opportunity to learn, develop and improve their skills.

Professions

Knowledge of our own personality profile and natural preferences provides us with invaluable help in choosing the optimal path in our professional careers. Experience has shown that, while *protectors* are perfectly able to work and find fulfilment in a range of fields, their personality type naturally predisposes them to the following fields and professions:

- acting
- administrator
- advisor
- bookkeeper
- clergy
- the construction industry
- designer
- education officer
- entrepreneur
- estate agent
- farmer
- gardener
- human resources
- interior designer
- insurance agent
- librarian
- manager
- medical technician
- musician
- office manager
- paramedic
- personal trainer
- physician

- physiotherapist
- psychologist
- sales assistant
- sports trainer
- social welfare
- teacher
- therapist
- vet

Potential strengths and weaknesses

Like any other personality type, *protectors* have their potential strengths and weaknesses and this potential can be cultivated in a variety of ways. *Protectors'* personal happiness and professional fulfilment depend on whether they make the most of the 'pluses' offered by their personality type and face up to its inherent dangers. Here, then, is a SUMMARY of those 'pluses' and dangers:

Potential strengths

Protectors are uncommonly loyal and take their responsibilities extremely seriously. Hard-working, persevering and patient, they are always ready to commit themselves to the full, sparing neither time nor energy in fulfilling their tasks and seeing things through to the end, undiscouraged by obstacles and setbacks. They are open to others, genuinely interested in them and capable of perceiving their feelings, enthusiasms and emotions. Their attitude is friendly and they are discreet, loyal and geared towards the needs of other people, putting them first and giving no real thought to themselves.

Other people feel good in their company, since they are excellent listeners and offer practical and emotional support to those in need of help or caught in the midst of a crisis. Consensus is one of their watchwords; they create a healthy, constructive atmosphere and will always strive to build bridges between people and assist them in reaching a compromise.

Their spatial imagination is as superb as is their sense of practicality. Orderliness comes as naturally to them as breathing, they see nothing tedious about carrying out routine activities and have no difficulty in following complex procedures. Given their natural talent for organisation, their head for detail and their ability to keep in mind the kind of minutiae that escape the notice of others, they make excellent resource managers.

Potential weaknesses

Being oriented towards serving others and rather lacking in assertiveness, *protectors* are sometimes neglectful of their own needs and backward in defending their own interests. Indeed, they often find themselves incapable of articulating their expectations or voicing their opinions, particularly when they veer towards the critical, and are equally as unable to end toxic and damaging relationships. Their tendency to remain silent on thorny subjects and avoid difficult conversations, even when they are essential, renders them vulnerable to deceit, manipulation and being used by others. They struggle just as much with expressing their feelings, which run deep and intense; indeed, their constant suppression of negative emotions will sometimes lead to uncontrolled and destructive explosions.

They find it difficult to cope in fields of activity which are completely new to them and, being rather inflexible, they quickly find themselves completely at sea in situations demanding swift decisions or improvisation and tend to be knocked off their feet by crises. They also have a problem with delegating duties and responsibilities, as well as tendency to do too much for others and help them whether they like it or not.

When it comes to viewing reality, *protectors* frequently struggle to look at the bigger picture. Understanding other people's views when they conflict with their own also comes hard to them; indeed, simply encountering those opinions can cause them deep discomfort. Inclined to perceive their own ideas as exclusively 'right', they are prone to negating anything which goes against their convictions and discarding it prematurely. They have no real mechanisms for handling criticism either, and frequently take unfavourable opinions of their outlook or activities as a personal defeat and a sign that they have disappointed people.

Personal development

Protectors' personal development depends on the extent to which they make use of their natural potential and surmount the dangers inherent in their personality type. What follows are some practical tips which, together, form a specific guide that we might call *The Protector's Ten Commandments*.

Stop fearing other people's ideas and opinions

Being open to the viewpoints of others is not synonymous with discarding your own. Stop fearing ideas and opinions which are different from yours. Before you reject them, give them some consideration and try to understand them.

Look at problems from a wider perspective

Try to look at problems in a wider context, from various angles ... and through other people's eyes. Reach for their opinions, give thought to various points of view. Take all the different sides of the matter into consideration.

Learn to say 'no'

When you disagree with something, why be afraid to speak out? When you are simply unable to take yet another task onto your shoulders, then just say so. Learn to say 'no', particularly when you feel that someone is abusing your help or trying to land you with everything!

Stop being afraid of new experiences

Try something new every week or every month. Go somewhere you have never been before, talk to people you have never got to know before, undertake tasks you have never done before. It will give you a host of valuable ideas and mean that you start seeing the world from a wider perspective.

Stop being afraid of conflict

Conflicts do arise sometimes, even in our closest circles. They need not necessarily be destructive, though. In fact, they very often help us to uncover problems and solve them! So, when they emerge, stop hiding your head in the sand and, instead, express your point of view and feelings about the situation openly.

Leave some things to take their natural course

There is no way you can have everything under your personal control. There is no way you can manage to be in command of every single thing. Leave those less important matters to take their natural course. You will save energy and avoid frustration.

Stop doing everything for others

You may thirst to help people, but if you do everything for them, they will never learn anything new for themselves and you will be perpetually overburdened. When you give others a helping hand, let them take responsibility for their own lives, make their own mistakes and draw their own conclusions from them for the future.

Accept help from others

You operate in the belief that you should be helping other people and that others usually seek support from you. Well, when you have a problem, turn the tables on that assumption! Stop hesitating, ask others for their help and then grasp the hand they offer!

Stop fearing criticism

Quell your fear of expressing your own critical opinions and of accepting criticism from others. Criticism can be constructive. There is no law which says that it has to mean attacking people or undermining their worth.

Be kinder to yourself

Try to help yourself with the same solicitude that you give to the happiness and well-being of others. Be more understanding of yourself. Try to get away from your responsibilities and duties once in a while and do something for the sheer pleasure, relaxation and fun of it.

Well-known figures

Below is a list of some well-known people who match the *protector's* profile:

- **Alfred, Lord Tennyson** (1809-1892); one of England's most popular poets, whose works include *The Lady of Shallot* and *Idylls of the King*, the most famous nineteenth-century adaptation of the legend of King Arthur and the Knights of the Round Table. He served as Poet Laureate for more than forty years.
- **Charles Dickens** (1812-1870); an English author regarded as the greatest literary colossus of the Victorian era. His novels, such as *Oliver Twist*, contained a powerful vein of social criticism and moral critique. He was also a prolific writer of short stories, the editor of a weekly journal and a vigorous campaigner for social reform.

- **Louisa May Alcott** (1832-1888); an American writer and pioneer of women's literature, she served as a volunteer nurse during the Civil War.

- **Teresa of Calcutta, MC** (Agnes Gonxha Bojaxhiu; 1910-1997); an Albanian-born, Roman Catholic nun and missionary more commonly known as Mother Teresa, she founded the Missionaries of Charity and spent most of her life engaged in humanitarian work in India. A holder of the Nobel Peace Prize, she was beatified in 2003.

- **William Shatner** (born in 1931); a Canadian screen actor whose filmography includes the *Star Trek* TV series and films, he is also a director, producer, writer, singer and comedian.

- **Connie Sellecca** (born in 1955); an American screen actress whose filmography includes *The Wild Stallion*.

- **Diana, Princess of Wales** (*née* Lady Diana Francis Spencer; 1961-1997); the first wife of Charles, Prince of Wales and the mother of his two sons, she was deeply involved in charitable activities.

- **Michael Jordan** (born in 1963); a retired American basketball player, he is considered the greatest of all time in the discipline and is now an entrepreneur.

- **Kiefer Sutherland** (born in 1966); a British-born, Canadian screen actor whose filmography includes *A Few Good Men*, he is also a producer and director.

- **Rose McGowan** (born in 1973); an American screen actress whose filmography includes the *Charmed* TV series.

- **Tori Spelling** (Victoria Davey Spelling; born in 1973); an American screen actress whose filmography includes the *Beverly Hills, 90210* TV series, she is also an author.

- **Sarah Polley** (born in 1979); a Canadian screen actress whose filmography includes *The Secret Life of*

Words, she is also a director, a screenwriter and a social and political activist.

The Strategist (INTJ)

THE ID16™© PERSONALITY TYPOLOGY

The Personality in a Nutshell

Life motto: I can certainly improve this.

In brief, *strategists* ...

are independent and outstandingly individualistic, with an immense seam of inner energy. Creative, inventive and resourceful, others perceive them as competent, self-assured and, at one and the same time, distant and enigmatic. No matter what they turn their attention to, they will always look at the bigger picture and they have a driving urge to improve the world around them and set it in order.

Well-organised, responsible, critical and demanding, they are difficult to knock off balance – and just as hard to please to the full. Reading the emotions and feelings of others is something they find very problematic.

The *strategist's* four natural inclinations:

- source of life energy: the interior world
- mode of assimilating information: intuition
- decision-making mode: the mind
- lifestyle: organised

Similar personality types:

- the Logician
- the Director
- the Innovator

Statistical data:

- *strategists* constitute between one and two per cent of the global community
- men predominate among *strategists* (80 per cent)
- Finland is an example of a nation corresponding to the *strategist's* profile[17]

The Four-Letter Code

In terms of Jungian personality typology, the universal four-letter code for the *strategist* is INTJ.

General character traits

Strategists are independent, intelligent and creative people with a rich interior life; theirs is a world teeming with reflections, concepts and ideas. Their focus is on the future and they dislike looking back. When they analyse a problem, they delve beneath the surface and have the ability to

---

[17] What this means is not that all the residents of Finland fall within this personality type, but that Finnish society as a whole possesses a great many of the character traits typical of the *strategist*.

identify aspects of the issue which are imperceptible to others. They are generally perceived as 'deep' and highly knowledgeable and they themselves value knowledge and competence in others.

Perception and thinking

Shrewd and clear-headed, *strategists* never cease to monitor the world around them in search of fresh concepts and, once a new idea has taken root in their minds, their thoughts will immediately turn to putting it to practical use. Their ability to connect disparate facts and data and uncover the relationships between them means that their general overview of things always hits the nail square on the head. They are quick to spot shifts in their surroundings and changing circumstances and, no matter what the situation, they are aware of the various possible scenarios for its development and capable of foreseeing potential problems and dangers. All of this makes them first-class strategists ... hence the name for this personality type. As the new data acquired through their constant surveying of their surroundings flows in, they are also able to put it to use in verifying the strategies they have already shaped.

Being exceptionally logical and rational, they are very good at analysing events coolly and evaluating them objectively and impartially. Their intuition is their guide and they have great faith in it. They present their opinions and viewpoints as something patently obvious and usually assume in advance that they are right – an assumption which, indeed, often proves to be correct! Given their love of solving complex problems of a theoretical nature, they find repetitive and routine activities tedious in the extreme.

Studying

Being of an enquiring disposition, when a concept interests a *strategist*, they will make every effort to explore and comprehend it thoroughly. In general, they have a wide range of interests in their youth and, over the course of time, will systemise their knowledge, constructing an internal map of the world which is entirely their own and enables them to comprehend reality and the phenomena that occur in it. The hunger to understand it and a thirst for knowledge are encoded in their character and they drive their own learning process, posing questions and then seeking the answers to them, analysing the cause-and-effect relationships between disparate phenomena and reflecting on the general rules governing human behaviour.

Rational arguments are what carry weight with them and they exhibit zero tolerance when it comes to logical inconsistency or incoherence in a concept, internal contradictions in a system and overlapping areas of authority, not to mention inefficiency, in an organisation. Despite their extensive knowledge and acumen, they move through the world well aware of the gaps in their wisdom and, when they are unfamiliar with something, they choose to admit it and will never pretend to an expertise that they do not possess. They are also capable of learning from their own mistakes and drawing conclusions from them for the future.

Organisational modes

Strategists have a predilection for order and tolerate neither wastefulness nor chaos. Perfectionists by nature, they are quite capable of working incessantly to improve on and perfect whatever they are involved in. They are also pragmatic in the extreme and, when they spot a new task on the horizon, they are equally as able to abandon their efforts to 'fix' something which is already functioning well in order to give themselves over to the next challenge.

When they undertake something, they will always strive for perfection in accomplishing it and are wholly incapable of consciously working to less than their full potential. Seeing something through to the end gives them a sense of satisfaction, and also of liberation, since it enables them to focus to the full on tackling the next thorny task or knotty problem.

Decisions

On the whole, when they need to make a decision, *strategists* prefer to have time to consider the various options and weigh up their possible consequences. Circumstances which demand that they act quickly or force them to improvise agitate them immensely.

They are highly independent, so much so that, at times, they can even give the impression of being 'incompatible' with those around them. Other people's opinions and behaviour have almost no impact whatsoever on the way they conduct themselves and their decisions will frequently come as a shock to those around them, since they follow neither prevailing views nor generally predominant trends – *strategists'* own thoughts and the conclusions they reach count for more with them than anything that others might think.

Their sense of self-assurance is stronger than in any of the other fifteen personality types. Indeed, so unwavering is it that it is often mistakenly taken as a manifestation of arrogance, condescension or disdain for other people.

Problem solving

With their ability to view a problem in its entirety and look at the bigger picture, *strategists* analyse an issue from various angles and perspectives. They are also able to discard unimportant information and concentrate on the essential data, subjecting it to logical and objective scrutiny.

Their thoughts are focused on the future; they take various possible scenarios into consideration and are capable of foreseeing the long-term consequences of both undertaking different courses of action and not undertaking them. Other people often have a struggle to keep up with them, since they are frequently absorbed in solving problems which have yet to occur! They will also sometimes set to and accomplish ideas which are so far-fetched and, at first glance, so downright 'weird' that others find themselves wondering how on earth they ever came up with such a thing. At the same time, they are extremely flexible and have no difficulty in taking changing situations into consideration or bearing new premises or circumstances in mind and then verifying their earlier views and ideas in the new light this throws on them.

Communication

Strategists' minds are flooded with concepts, ideas and images which are all but incomprehensible to anybody other than themselves and would be unintelligible to anyone else in their original, 'naked' form. However, they do also have the ability to meet the needs of the outside world by finding a way to elucidate their thoughts and present them as organised, cohesive and consistent systems. Effective and highly convincing when they are proving that they are right, they sometimes tend to 'massage' the facts slightly in order to fit them to the system in question. They are able both to employ clear images and simple examples when explaining complex theories and to transform a general concept into a ready-to-use, long-term strategy.

Enthusiasms

Strategists long to improve reality, fix the world and help people, all of which they set out to do not only by proffering ready-made solutions to a problem, but also by asking the kind of questions which prompt people to think and inspire them to act and change their attitude or way of looking at things. When they are convinced that a task is worth doing, they will give themselves over to it entirely. With their own propensity for sacrificing their leisure time in whatever cause they are engaged in, neither sparing their energy nor watching the clock, they tend to be astonished by the fact that not everyone shares their fervour. On the other hand, they will struggle mightily to commit themselves fully to something which has failed to convince them of its merits.

In general, they see the world as matter which can be formed and moulded in line with various concepts and notions and the possibility of giving substance to ideas and transforming reality gives them enormous satisfaction. Often the minds behind all kinds of effective, systemic solutions and plans of action, once they have developed a system and succeeded in implementing it, they will happily entrust others with looking after it while they themselves launch into new challenges.

In the face of stress

Two traits which are a source of problems for *strategists* are their inability to relax and their lack of effective tools for coping with stress. The outcome of this is that, under intense pressure, they may well start behaving in ways which are completely alien to them, becoming distracted, focusing excessively on details, get bogged down in trivia and mindlessly repeating various actions, such as tidying up things which are not out of place or cleaning something that is already pristine. In their efforts to relieve their tension, they might also try turning to substances.

Socially

Strategists rarely show their emotions and are rather sparing in their praise, giving others the impression that they are reticent and severe, whereas, in reality, they are sensitive and caring, especially when it comes to their nearest and dearest. Their apparent conservatism is also no more than external, since they are actually very open to anything and everything new and spend their entire lives actively seeking out fresh ideas and concepts.

Nonetheless, interpersonal relations present them with quite a challenge: they are at a loss when they have to read other people's emotions and feelings and they fail to spot the significance of small gestures. Coquetry and coyness leave them cold, as does any other kind of flirtation, and they expect others to behave rationally and sensibly and to express their thoughts directly. When they are engaged in a conversation, they have no particular need for physical contact of the back-slapping, shoulder-clapping or nudging kind. By the same token, communication at a distance, via media such as e-mails, for instance, suits them very well.

Strategists dislike repeating themselves. They are not interested in convincing other people that they are right and make no attempt to understand anyone who rejects their views from the outset. Given their tendency to assume that what they are talking about should be patently obvious to everyone, they not only sometimes fail to explain their point in a way which gets the idea across to their listeners, but also tend to blame them for any eventual misunderstanding of the mental 'shortcuts' that they themselves find limpidly clear. On the other hand, their excellent intuition and readiness to 'mend' their relationships with people are a definite strength.

Amongst friends

Strategists' self-assurance, knowledge and intelligence usually arouse respect, although they are frequently seen as people who keep others at a distance and are difficult to approach and get to know. Many a person is irritated by the fact that they always 'know best', while some people, fearing their penetrating minds, tend to presume that they can see right through others and feel ill-at-ease in their presence as a result.

However, in reality, they make highly tolerant, discreet and faithful friends and those who know them well value their friendship, freely acknowledge their inventiveness, resourcefulness and knowledge and are aware of the fact that they are simply not nearly as stern and serious as they sometimes appear. In the company of people they are close to, they are quite capable of letting go and having a good time and, with their deep-rooted sense of humour, their jokes and comments are often not merely amusing, but also extremely quick-witted. They have a particular liking for get-togethers which give them the chance to learn something new and they value conversations with people who know more than they do or who are experts in their field. They also enjoy discussing their ideas and indulging in a shared analysis of all kinds of theories with their friends.

Harmonious relationships with others matter a great deal to *strategists*. Nonetheless, there are times when they need some distance and are impelled to step back, withdraw and spend some time in solitude. This is not in the least a manifestation of antipathy towards others, but a natural part of their make-up, a way of protecting their inner world. On the other hand, purely social gatherings, along with idle chit-chat, gossip and courteous gestures, bore them to tears. They most often make friends with *logicians*, *directors*, *inspectors* and other *strategists* and, most rarely, with *presenters*, *artists* and *advocates*.

As life partners

Strategists are highly independent and make it their business to assure their partner of the independence they themselves prize. They take their responsibilities towards their nearest and dearest extremely seriously and their relationships are generally healthy, stable and enduring. However, on occasion, their constant quest for new ideas and thirst to improve their understanding of the world can lead them to radically redefine their views and so, with time, their understanding of their previous commitments to other people might change as well.

They live out their lives first and foremost within their interior landscapes and are endowed with powerful imaginations, so much so that, at times, they will struggle to reconcile their idealistic visions with the imperfect real world. Their own emotional needs are modest and they have difficulty in perceiving those of other people. It is not in their nature to be demonstrative or shower their partner with compliments; they show their devotion through concrete action and find themselves lost without a compass in situations which require them to read other people's feelings or voice their own. Their partner might therefore well develop a sense of deficiency. However, *strategists* perpetually strive to improve reality and themselves alike and, since they also adopt this approach in their life partnerships, they are certainly capable of achieving a great deal.

On the whole, their relations with others are good for the simple reason that they generally refuse to continue with any that have turned sour. Once they become convinced that a relationship needs ending, they are capable of doing just that ... and the same applies in their life partnerships. This is not to say that splitting up is a painless experience for them, no matter how it may seem to others.

The natural candidates for a *strategist's* life partner are people of a personality type akin to their own: *logicians*, *directors* or *innovators*. Building mutual understanding and harmonious relations will be easier in a union of that kind. Nonetheless, experience has taught us that people are also capable of creating happy and successful relationships despite what would seem to be an evident typological incompatibility. Moreover, the differences between two partners can lend added dynamics to a relationship and engender personal development. Indeed, for many people, this is a prospect that appears more attractive than the vision of a harmonious relationship wherein concord and full, mutual understanding hold sway.

As parents

Strategists make highly devoted and responsible parents who take their role extremely seriously. They help their children to understand the world, teach them the skills of independent decision-making and critical thinking and will usually give great attention to their education, since they are intent on developing their potential and bringing them up to be intelligent and self-sufficient. However, they may not give enough weight to their offspring's emotional needs and, as a result, might fail to demonstrate a sufficient amount of love, warmth and affection. They thus need to cultivate their receptiveness in this respect in order to avoid the possibility of a growing emotional distance between them and their children.

When they succeed in avoiding those mistakes, they are wonderful parents to their children and great authority figures. They are also instrumental in their development, encouraging them to explore the world, acquire knowledge and face up to challenges. As a result, their offspring usually grow up to become responsible, creative and independent adults with no fear of taking up the gauntlets that life throws down at their feet.

Work and career paths

Strategists love breathing life into theoretical concepts and have a predilection for systemising and organising the world in a constant endeavour to set it right. They are excellent candidates for the sciences and the world of scholarship, make splendid engineers and inventors, and they are in their element in any position which demands clear-sightedness, intelligence and independence.

As part of a team

Strategists enjoy working alone on tasks which provide them with autonomy and impose no restraints on their freedom of action. Over-zealous supervision from their superiors is a source of irritation to them, since they value their privacy and dislike being disturbed and interrupted. Nonetheless, they are always happy to work with other talented people, although they feel most comfortable in a loose-knit group with no rigid hierarchy.

They remain focused on the goal, even when others lose sight of it, and they never miss a deadline or fail to discharge their duties. What other staff members can find irritating about them is their extreme independence, their perfectionism, their impatience, the fervour they bring to their tasks, their self-assurance and their conviction that they are always right.

Companies and institutions

Strategists will be restless and unhappy in companies where compliance with the accepted regulations or detailed procedures takes precedence over creative ideas and concrete achievements. They appreciate competent superiors who provide their staff with support and give them freedom in accomplishing their tasks.

Views on workplace hierarchy

Strategists have natural leadership skills, but are happy to stay behind the scenes, providing the 'front line' with support. On the other hand, if the situation demands it, they will have no hesitation about stepping to the fore and, even though they feel no urge to seek authority, they will very often hold managerial positions, since they excel when it comes to anything requiring organisational and strategic planning abilities.

As bosses, they keep a firm eye on the effectiveness and efficiency of the organisation or department for which they are responsible. Highly demanding on the whole, they will sometimes give the impression of being people who are difficult to satisfy to the full.

As a rule, they will throw their staff in at the deep end, though they will always assist them when it comes to identifying future challenges and shifting circumstances. Disorder, wastefulness, passiveness and lack of commitment are anathema to them and they are wholly capable of coldly eliminating anything which proves to be impractical or ineffective; *strategists* look at things objectively, with no concern for sentimental or emotional considerations. As such, they feel no attachment to particular solutions and are ready to discard them the moment they fail to perform as required. Who introduced them and how long they have been in place is of no great significance to them.

Professions

Knowledge of our own personality profile and natural preferences provides us with invaluable help in choosing the optimal path in our professional careers. Experience has shown that, while *strategists* are perfectly able to work and find fulfilment in a range of fields, their personality type naturally predisposes them to the following fields and professions:

- administrator
- architect
- computer programmer
- computer systems analyst
- designer
- economist
- editor
- engineer
- executive director
- financial analyst
- investment and stockbroking
- IT specialist
- IT systems designer
- judge
- lawyer
- manager
- photographer
- physician

- politician
- project coordinator
- property / infrastructure developer
- psychologist
- research and development director
- risk assessment expert
- scholar
- scientist
- strategic planning expert
- teacher
- technician
- tertiary educator
- urban and rural planning
- writer

Potential strengths and weaknesses

Like any other personality type, *strategists* have their potential strengths and weaknesses and this potential can be cultivated in a variety of ways. *Strategists'* personal happiness and professional fulfilment depend on whether they make the most of the 'pluses' offered by their personality type and face up to its inherent dangers. Here, then, is a SUMMARY of those 'pluses' and dangers:

Potential strengths

Strategists have penetrating minds and spotting things which remain hidden to others is a piece of cake to them. Quick to identify cause-and-effect relationships and repetitive patterns in human behaviour, they are outstanding analysts and strategists, with the ability to look at problems from a wide perspective and find optimal solutions. When a difficult situation arises, they are also able to predict various scenarios for its development. They are highly independent and impervious to criticism, but perfectly capable of changing their opinion when they see the possibility of improving something or identify a better solution. With a tenacious approach to their work, they devote enormous energy to anything that matters to them, an attitude which means that they usually attain their goals.

Inventors by nature, they have the intelligence and ability to comprehend complex theories, a logical mindset, and a persistence which enable them to discover new solutions or put existing ones to use in fresh and creative ways. Endowed with a healthy sense of their own worth, they cope well in situations of conflict and are capable of evaluating issues with a cool eye, objectively and without emotion. They take their responsibilities extremely seriously and are always ready both to learn something new and to work to improve themselves and their relations with other people. However, should the need arise, they are fully capable of freeing themselves from destructive or toxic relationships.

Potential weaknesses

Reading the feelings of others and perceiving their emotional needs is problematic for *strategists*, as is expressing their own. They are often viewed as withdrawn, impervious and given to keeping people at a distance. Their attitude not only creates tension in their contact with others, but frequently hurts them, while they themselves remain oblivious to the fact that they have caused someone pain. By the same token, in situations of conflict, they endeavour to solve the problem by applying logical arguments and appealing to common sense, whilst underrating the importance of other people's feelings and emotions. As a result, they often fail to understand that many an issue can be resolved by offering spiritual support, encouragement and comfort – a sphere in which *strategists* tread gingerly at best. When all these problems accumulate, they can lead to the point where, feeling like outsiders, they will retreat into self-imposed isolation, blaming other people for problems which are actually of their own making.

Their constant striving to improve anything and everything is something that frequently proves wearisome to the other members of their household and their colleagues alike, as do both their self-assurance and their conviction that they are always right. Problems are also triggered by their high, often unrealistic, expectations of others. They have a low threshold of tolerance for other people's weaknesses and review their achievements with a critical eye. In the world seen from their standpoint, there are shortcomings, defects and errors wherever they look. They probe for inconsistencies in other people's reasoning and for gaps in their argumentation, and on many an occasion this will lead them to discard their opinions and suggestions prematurely. Another potential source of problems for *strategists* is their natural leaning towards workaholism and an inability to relax.

Personal development

Strategists' personal development depends on the extent to which they make use of their natural potential and surmount the dangers inherent in their personality type. What follows are some practical tips which, together, form a specific guide that we might call *The Strategist's Ten Commandments*.

Praise others

Continually reproaching other people for their mistakes is simply not going to help them. Be more restrained in your criticism and more generous in your evaluation and praise of others. Show them some warmth and make the most of every occasion to say something nice to them. Then wait and see. The difference will come as a pleasant surprise!

Leave some things to take their natural course

There is no way you can have everything under your personal control. There is no way you can manage to be in command of every single thing. Leave those less important matters to run their natural course. You will save energy and avoid frustration.

Try to grasp the fact that not everything needs improving

There are some things which are quite good enough as they are. There are others where attempting improvement is a futile endeavour. The same applies to people, so be more understanding of them – and stop trying to 'fix' absolutely everything and everyone.

Stop discarding other people's ideas and opinions

Before you judge them as valueless, give them some serious consideration and try to understand them. Avoid assuming that no one else knows as much about a given matter as you do; this, in itself, is a mistake!

Look for the positive

Stop seeking out errors, shortcomings and weaknesses wherever you look. Stop focusing exclusively on flaws and defects. Do what the song says and "accentuate the positive" in life as well. Probe for the pluses in various situations and turn the spotlight of your gaze on what other people have done well instead.

Allow others to be right

Take an important fact on board – other people can be partially right. They can even be entirely right! Learn to acknowledge that you might be wrong and that someone else might not be. A word of warning though: when you set out on that path, your nearest and dearest, friends and colleagues may well be astonished to the point of shock!

Accept help from other people

Stop hesitating before you ask others to help you when you have a problem. Just do it, before the situation becomes really serious.

Take some time out

Try to get away from your responsibilities and duties once in a while and do something for the sheer pleasure, relaxation and fun of it. You will find that you resume your tasks with your mind and thinking refreshed when you do.

Stop isolating yourself

In all likelihood, you are never going to develop a taste for social get-togethers, gossip, idle chit-chat and the courteous exchange of pleasantries. Nonetheless, your life will be richer if you nurture your contact with those closest to you and make the effort to meet up with people who share your enthusiasms and interests.

Smile

You might not be aware of this, but, as a *strategist*, you frequently present a grimly serious visage. Learn to control your facial expressions. Get rid of that formidably ominous countenance. It scares people. Smile more, instead. It might be a trifle, but it can produce amazing results.

Well-known figures

Below is a list of some well-known people who match the *strategist's* profile:

- **Sir Isaac Newton** (1643-1727); an English physicist, astronomer, mathematician and philosopher, he formulated the laws of motion and universal gravitation.

- **Thomas Jefferson** (1743-1826); the 3rd president of the United States.

- **Jane Austen** (1775-1817); an English author whose works include *Pride and Prejudice*.

- **Karl Marx** (1818-1883); a German philosopher, thinker and revolutionary activist whose works include *The Communist Manifesto* and *Capital. A Critique of Political Economy (Das Kapital)*, he was one of the co-founders of the International Workingmen's Association, also known as the First International.

- **Susan B. Anthony** (Susan Brownell Anthony; 1820-1906); an American activist who campaigned for social equality, the abolition of slavery and women's rights, she was the co-founder of the National Woman Suffrage Association.

- **Friedrich Nietzsche** (1844-1900); a German classical philologist, philosopher and writer, he formulated concepts such as that of the *Übermensch* (Superhuman). His works included *Ecce Homo*.

- **Lise Meitner** (1878-1968); an Austrian nuclear physicist who was one of the first in the field to articulate the theory of splitting the nucleus of an atom.

- **Niels Bohr** (1885-1962); a Danish physicist, he created the first, simplified, quantum model of the structure of an atom and was awarded the Nobel Prize in Physics.

- **C. S. Lewis** (Clive Staples Lewis; 1898-1965); a British novelist, poet, essayist, literary critic, academic, mediaevalist and broadcaster whose works include *The Chronicles of Narnia*.

- **Alan Greenspan** (born in 1926); an American economist, he served as the Chairman of the Federal Reserve of the United States for almost a decade and is considered an authority in the fields of economy and monetary policy.
- **Colin Powell** (1937-2021); an American general and politician.
- **Arnold Schwarzenegger** (born in 1947); an American bodybuilder and actor of Austrian origins, he served two terms of office as the governor of California.
- **Dan Aykroyd** (born in 1952); a Canadian-American film actor, whose filmography includes *Blues Brothers*.
- **Lance Armstrong** (born in 1971); an American Olympic-class road racing cyclist.

Additional information

The four natural inclinations

1. THE DOMINANT SOURCE OF LIFE
   ENERGY

   a. THE EXTERIOR WORLD
      People who draw their energy from
      outside. They need activity and contact
      with others and find being alone for any
      length of time hard to bear.

   b. THE INTERIOR WORLD
      People who draw their energy from their
      inner world. They need quiet and solitude
      and feel drained when they spend any
      length of time in a group.

2. THE DOMINANT MODE OF ASSIMILATING INFORMATION

a. VIA THE SENSES
People who rely on the five senses and are persuaded by facts and evidence. They have a liking for methods and practices which are tried and tested and prefer concrete tasks and are realists who trust in experience.

b. VIA INTUITION
People who rely on the sixth sense and are driven by what they 'feel in their bones'. They have a liking for innovative solutions and problems of a theoretical nature and are characterised by a creative approach to their tasks and the ability to predict.

3. THE DOMINANT DECISION-MAKING MODE

a. THE MIND
People who are guided by logic and objective principles. They are critical and direct in expressing their opinions.

b. THE HEART
People who are guided by their feelings and values. They long for harmony and mutual understanding with others.

4. THE DOMINANT LIFESTYLE

a. ORGANISED
People who are conscientious and

organised. They value order and like to operate according to plan.

b.   SPONTANEOUS
People who are spontaneous and value freedom of action. They live for the moment and have no trouble finding their feet in new situations.

The approximate percentage of each personality type in the world population

Personality Type:	Proportion:
• The Administrator (ESTJ):	10-13%
• The Advocate (ESFJ):	10-13%
• The Animator (ESTP):	6-10%
• The Artist (ISFP):	6-9%
• The Counsellor (ENFJ):	3-5 %
• The Director (ENTJ):	2-5%
• The Enthusiast (ENFP):	5-8%
• The Idealist (INFP):	1-4%
• The Innovator (ENTP):	3-5%
• The Inspector (ISTJ):	6-10%
• The Logician (INTP):	2-3%
• The Mentor (INFJ):	ca. 1%
• The Practitioner (ISTP):	6-9%
• The Presenter (ESFP):	8-13%
• The Protector (ISFJ):	8-12%
• The Strategist (INTJ):	1-2%

The approximate percentage of women and men of each personality type in the world population

Personality Type:	Women / Men:
• The Administrator (ESTJ):	40% / 60%
• The Advocate (ESFJ):	70% / 30%
• The Animator (ESTP):	40% / 60%
• The Artist (ISFP):	60% / 40%
• The Counsellor (ENFJ):	80% / 20%
• The Director (ENTJ):	30% / 70%
• The Enthusiast (ENFP):	60% / 40%
• The Idealist (INFP):	60% / 40%
• The Innovator (ENTP):	30% / 70%
• The Inspector (ISTJ):	40% / 60%
• The Logician (INTP):	20% / 80%
• The Mentor (INFJ):	80% / 20%
• The Practitioner (ISTP):	40% / 60%
• The Presenter (ESFP):	60% / 40%
• The Protector (ISFJ):	70% / 30%
• The Strategist (INTJ):	20% / 80%

Bibliography

- Arraj, Tyra & Arraj, James: *Tracking the Elusive Human, Volume 1: A Practical Guide to C.G. Jung's Psychological Types, W.H. Sheldon's Body and Temperament Types and Their Integration*, Inner Growth Books, 1988
- Arraj, James: *Tracking the Elusive Human, Volume 2: An Advanced Guide to the Typological Worlds of C. G. Jung, W.H. Sheldon, Their Integration, and the Biochemical Typology of the Future*, Inner Growth Books, 1990
- Berens, Linda V.; Cooper, Sue A.; Ernst, Linda K.; Martin, Charles R.; Myers, Steve; Nardi, Dario; Pearman, Roger R.; Segal, Marci; Smith, Melissa: *A Quick Guide to the 16 Personality Types in Organizations: Understanding Personality Differences in the Workplace*, Telos Publications, 2002
- Geier, John G. & Downey, E. Dorothy: *Energetics of Personality*, Aristos Publishing House, 1989
- Hunsaker, Phillip L. & Alessandra, J. Anthony: *The Art of Managing People*, Simon and Schuster, 1986

- Jung, Carl Gustav: *Psychological Types (The Collected Works of C. G. Jung, Vol. 6)*, Princeton University Press, 1976
- Kise, Jane A. G.; Stark, David & Krebs Hirsch, Sandra: *LifeKeys: Discover Who You Are*, Bethany House, 2005
- Kroeger, Otto & Thuesen, Janet: *Type Talk or How to Determine Your Personality Type and Change Your Life*, Delacorte Press, 1988
- Lawrence, Gordon: *People Types and Tiger Stripes*, Center for Applications of Psychological Type, 1993
- Lawrence, Gordon: *Looking at Type and Learning Styles*, Center for Applications of Psychological Type, 1997
- Maddi, Salvatore R.: *Personality Theories: A Comparative Analysis*, Waveland, 2001
- Martin, Charles R.: *Looking at Type: The Fundamentals Using Psychological Type To Understand and Appreciate Ourselves and Others*, Center for Applications of Psychological Type, 2001
- Meier C.A.: Personality: *The Individuation Process in the Light of C. G. Jung's Typology*, Daimon Verlag, 2007
- Pearman, Roger R. & Albritton, Sarah: *I'm Not Crazy, I'm Just Not You: The Real Meaning of the Sixteen Personality Types*, Davies-Black Publishing, 1997
- Segal, Marci: Creativity and Personality Type: *Tools for Understanding and Inspiring the Many Voices of Creativity*, Telos Publications, 2001
- Sharp, Daryl: Personality Type: *Jung's Model of Typology*, Inner City Books, 1987
- Spoto, Angelo: *Jung's Typology in Perspective*, Chiron Publications, 1995
- Tannen, Deborah: *You Just Don't Understand*, William Morrow and Company, 1990
- Thomas, Jay C. & Segal, Daniel L.: *Comprehensive Handbook of Personality and Psychopathology, Personality and Everyday Functioning*, Wiley, 2005

- Thomson, Lenore: *Personality Type: An Owner's Manual*, Shambhala, 1998
- Tieger, Paul D. & Barron-Tieger Barbara: *Just Your Type: Create the Relationship You've Always Wanted Using the Secrets of Personality Type*, Little, Brown and Company, 2000
- Von Franz, Marie-Louise & Hillman, James: *Lectures on Jung's Typology*, Continuum International Publishing Group, 1971

About the Author

Jaroslaw Jankowski holds a Master of Education degree from Nicolaus Copernicus University in Toruń, Poland and an MBA from the Brennan School of Business at the Dominican University in River Forest, Illinois, USA. The research and development director of an international NGO and an entrepreneur, he is also involved in voluntary work. He is not only committed to promoting knowledge about personality types, but is also the creator of ID16™©, an independent personality typology based on the theory developed by Carl Gustav Jung.